The Jossey-Bass Nonprofit & Public Management Series also includes:

How Foundations Work

How Foundations Work

What Grantseekers Need to Know About the Many Faces of Foundations

Dennis P. McIlnay

Jossey-Bass Publishers • San Francisco

Credits appear on page 204

Substantial discounts on bulk quantities of Jossey-Bass books are available to
corporations, professional associations, and other organizations. For details and
discount information, contact the special sales department at Jossey-Bass Inc.,
Publishers: (415) 433–1740; Fax (415) 605-2665.

For sales outside the United States, please contact your local
Simon & Schuster International Office.

Jossey-Bass Web address: www.josseybass.com

 Manufactured in the United States of America on Lyons Falls Turin Book.
This paper is acid-free and 100 percent totally chlorine-free.

Library of Congress Cataloging-in-Publication Data

McIlnay, Dennis P., 1948–
    How foundations work : what grantseekers need to know about the many
faces of foundations / Dennis P. McIlnay. — 1st ed.
        p. cm. — (Jossey-Bass nonprofit and public management series)
    Includes bibliographical references and index.
    ISBN 0–7879–4011–9
    1. Endowments—United States.   2. Research grants—United States.
3. Fundraising—United States.   I. Title.   II. Series.
HV41.9.U5M35   1998
361.7'632'0973—dc21   98-9762
                                                                              CIP

FIRST EDITION
HB Printing 10 9 8 7 6 5 4 3 2 1

**The Jossey-Bass
Nonprofit and Public Management Series**

Contents

To my wife, Kathy, and to
Brittani and Christopher Raybuck

Preface

Judges. Editors. Citizens. Activists. Entrepreneurs. Partners. These roles, or *faces* as I call them, are six metaphorical identities of foundations and they represent a new way to understand foundations' complex and often contradictory nature. As I develop the metaphors in this book, I suggest that foundations have unique values, languages, rituals, customs, and behaviors: a personality, in other words, that distinguishes them from other types of organizations. In more than a thousand books, studies, and articles on foundations that I have examined, none takes a metaphorical approach to analyzing them. The idea that organizations have personalities has been called *culture* or *saga,* a collective understanding by the members of organizations of their nonstructural and nonrational dimensions, their expressive aspects, their social ideals (thou shalt; thou shalt not), and the stories that convey them (Clark, 1984, pp. 36–37; Louis, 1992, p. 512).

Foundations are mysterious, and they are poorly understood even by the people in nonprofit organizations that receive grants from them. They play an important role in society but remain remarkably unknown and unstudied. Few books on foundations are analytical. Most are descriptive and anecdotal, relying on "war stories" but little or no research. Many others are quantitative, reciting numbers, types, assets, and grants; from this information we do gain some understanding of foundations' basic characteristics, but we still do not grasp their more substantive features and we know next to nothing about what goes on *inside* them.

The world of foundations has become increasingly complex, but our thinking about them rarely matches this complexity, and many people prefer to pretend such intricacy does not exist. Some grantseekers understand foundations so poorly that they are blind to reality, their views ranging from the ignorant to the simplistic.

Others readily accept the apocryphal myths about foundations passed from one generation of practitioners to the next. For example, a common perception is that foundations are risk takers that make grants to cutting-edge organizations unlikely to receive aid from conventional sources such as corporations or the government. But this is more fiction than fact; most foundations steadfastly avoid risky people and organizations. The first purpose of this book, therefore, is to help nonprofit managers and fund-raisers improve their understanding of foundations and increase their ability to get grants from them.

Useful research for managers of nonprofits often takes the form of synthesis, the large-scale integration of information with the goal of cumulating knowledge on one subject. Synthesis assembles disparate information, thereby facilitating its access and application. As a work of integration, this book can help connect scholars and practitioners. The two tend to live in different worlds, increasingly alienated from each other, but this is unwise; it puts the work of researchers at risk of becoming irrelevant in the real world. Nor can reflective practitioners separate themselves from scholars, whose work may provide them with new images of organizations and ideas about managing them (Schon, 1983, pp. 308, 309, 323).

Nothing is as practical as a good theory, as the saying goes, and the metaphors in this book represent a new theory that can be used for the very practical purpose of understanding foundations. I wrote the book because of my love of foundations and because they are so important but so poorly understood. I wanted to try to integrate the diverse and seemingly discrete information on foundations and bring order to it. I also wanted to trace the origins of their culture and to use their organizational personalities as the basis for a new theory that would explain their unfamiliar nature through the familiar images of judges, editors, citizens, activists, entrepreneurs, and partners. The book focuses on independent (rather than corporate, community, or operating) foundations because they are the largest and wealthiest type, comprising nearly 90 percent of the nation's thirty-eight thousand foundations, holding 86 percent of all foundation assets, and making almost 80 percent of all foundation grants.

Audience of the Book

The book is designed primarily for managers and fund-raisers in the nation's one million nonprofit organizations. These people include presidents, executive directors, vice presidents for development, deans, directors of development, directors of foundation and corporate relations, annual fund directors, major gift officers, campaign directors, grants officers, program managers, and department chairs. The book should appeal to practitioners because it contains little-known insights on foundations disclosed *by foundation people themselves.* The recommendations herein should help practitioners rise above the pedestrian information in the how-to-get-grants literature. I believe the best way to become a better raiser of funds from foundations is to try to *understand* them, especially their values, grantmaking philosophies, and the principles (which they so seldom discuss publicly) that they follow in grantmaking decisions.

The book will also be of interest to the trustees and staff of foundations and to philanthropists and their advisors who are considering establishing foundations. Students and professors in graduate programs and research centers on philanthropy and the management of nonprofit organizations will benefit from the book, people from academic departments such as anthropology, economics, management, organizational behavior, political science, public administration, or sociology. Trustees of nonprofits, legislators and public officials concerned with foundations, and the media will also be interested in the book.

The People of Foundations

In suggesting that metaphor can help people understand foundations better, the book advocates traditional learning at the feet of the masters, in this case the people who created the idea of foundations, such as Henry Ford, John D. Rockefeller, and Andrew Carnegie, and those who have led foundations in this century. The book relies on primary source material from the people who know foundations best: their founders, trustees, and staff members. These and others I allow to speak for themselves by choosing their most representative or insightful statements from the thousands they have made.

Many of the people quoted have held multiple positions in foundations and other organizations, and, where this overlap occurs, I have classified them according to my best assessment of their most prominent posts. This is unavoidably arbitrary because some careers defy such categorization; Paul Ylvisaker, for example, served as an advisor to donors of foundations, a trustee of foundations, a researcher on foundations, a professor, and dean of the graduate school of education at Harvard University. Despite this overlap, the people in the book represent nine main groups:

- *Donors* are philanthropists, such as Henry Ford, Andrew Carnegie, John D. Rockefeller, and Julius Rosenwald, many of whom wrote books, monographs, or articles in which they discussed their philosophies of philanthropy.

- *Advisors to donors* worked hand in hand with philanthropists to help establish foundations. Examples are Frederick Gates, counselor to John D. Rockefeller, and Samuel S. Marquis, executive assistant to Henry Ford. Many advisors were lawyers or bankers, and their first-hand accounts of the early days of some of the nation's most prominent foundations are interesting and instructive.

- *Trustees* are members of the governing boards of foundations, usually recommended by the nominating committees of such boards and elected by the full boards. Some trustees have written extensively on topics such as the governance of foundations, the interaction of foundations and the federal government, and the mission of foundations as members of the nonprofit sector.

- *Staff members* are the executive directors, financial managers, and program officers of foundations, the people who act as their administrators day by day and carry out the policies established by their donors and trustees. Examples are Frederick P. Keppel, first president of the Carnegie Corporation; Henry Pritchett, an early president of the Carnegie Foundation for the Advancement of Teaching; and Susan Berresford, president of the Ford Foundation. Some staff members of foundations have written on grant-making and the management of foundations.

- *Grantseekers and grantees* are members of what is called the "donee group" comprising the nation's one million nonprofit organizations. Grantseekers are people or organizations who apply for foundation grants; grantees are those who have received them.

Some have written about foundations, usually about how to get their grants.

- *Government officials* are members of Congress and officers of federal agencies that oversee foundations, especially the Internal Revenue Service (IRS). For example, Representative Wright Patman and Representative J. J. Pickle headed committees that investigated or sponsored legislation on foundations; Marcus Owens is director of the Exempt Organizations Division of the IRS.
- *Researchers* include scholars affiliated with colleges or universities as well as unaffiliated researchers who study foundations. Examples are Waldemar Nielsen, Teresa Odendahl, and Richard Magat.
- *Officers of associations or organizations in philanthropy* represent the interests of foundations or other nonprofits before Congress or federal agencies, such as Dorothy S. Ridings, president of the Council on Foundations; Sara Engelhardt, president of the Foundation Center; and Robert Bothwell, executive director of the National Committee for Responsive Philanthropy.
- *Journalists* include editors and reporters in the mass media as well as in publications on foundations or philanthropy. Examples are Holly Hall, a reporter for the *Chronicle of Philanthropy*, and Jody Curtis, editor of *Foundation News and Commentary*.

Order of the Book

The book has eight chapters. Six of them discuss the metaphors of foundations; Chapter One serves as the introduction and Chapter Eight as the conclusion. At the end of each metaphor chapter are two sections, one discussing the implications of the findings of the chapter for grantseekers and the other making recommendations to foundations.

Chapter One describes the forces that created today's environment in foundations, one as turbulent as at virtually any time in their hundred–year history. The chapter discusses what it is like to be a foundation now, especially the difficulty of responding to unprecedented demands on their limited resources from almost every corner of society. In response to the pressures, many foundations are reassessing their missions, program interests, and relations with Congress, the IRS, and grantseekers. The chapter also discusses nonprofits' poor understanding of foundations and the difficulty of creating partnerships with them under such circumstances. Furthermore, it presents the advantages of metaphor as a tool for studying organizations and a means of portraying the multiple personalities of foundations.

Chapter Two discusses the process and difficulty of grantmaking by examining the principle of rationality in grantmaking, arguments for the purposefulness of grantmaking, the subjectivity of grantmaking, the isolation of grantmakers, the attributes of good grantmakers, and the problems of arrogance and impersonality associated with grantmaking. The decision-making theory of Herbert Simon, James March, and Michael Cohen is applied to foundations, and the grantmaking philosophies of several early philanthropists and foundations are reviewed as a basis for modern grantmaking doctrines. Principles and criteria of grantmaking are discussed to show how foundations judge the realism of grant proposals and the competence of people to be involved in grant projects.

Chapter Three examines how foundations resemble editors when they evaluate the writing in grant proposals as an indication of the quality of grantseekers. The chapter presents definitions of grant proposals and their elements dating to the Middle Ages and reviews the facts and folklore on proposals according to philanthropists, foundation officers, fund-raisers, and researchers. With tongue in cheek, Chapter Three identifies a language of proposal writers that I call *Proposalese*, explaining its most prominent characteristics and tracing its lineage.

Chapter Four discusses the idea that foundations, like citizens in a democracy, have legislated and voluntary responsibilities to their fellow citizens—grantseekers, other foundations, the federal government, and the American people. This chapter presents the traditional arguments on both sides of the issue of public accountability, namely the privacy of foundations versus the interest of the public, and traces the history of the relationship of foundations and Congress and the development of laws designed to improve the public accountability of foundations. The chapter also documents the record of foundations in performing legislated and voluntary public accountability practices before and after the Tax Reform Act of 1969, the most important law governing the accountability of foundations.

Chapter Five examines the perception that foundations are a major supporter of social movements to form or change public policy. The chapter argues that they generally are not, as most foundations are mainly involved in nonpolitically subsidizing conventional organizations. The chapter also discusses the political ideologies of foundations and presents the traditional arguments for and against public policy grantmaking as well as the record of liberal and conservative grantmaking by foundations, the history of foundation support of social movements, and the record of foundation grants to women and minorities.

Chapter Six examines the belief that foundations are risk takers, suppliers of venture capital to people or organizations too risky to receive grants from orthodox donors such as corporations or the government. The chapter argues that they usually are not, that they tend to avoid risky people, projects, and organizations. The metaphor of foundations as entrepreneurs considers two principles that I call *discontinuity* and *continuity*, the two sides of the issue of whether foundations should provide short-term or long-term support. The chapter also discusses the opinions of foundations and grantseekers on the potential of grantees for self-sufficiency, the advantages and disadvantages of short-term and long-term grants, and the record of the incorporation of grant projects into the budgets of grantees after grants have ended.

Chapter Seven examines the perception that the relationship between foundations and nonprofits is a partnership in the solution of problems, arguing that the relationship is strained because both parties violate each other's trust, and explains their interdependence and the necessity of trust between them if their relationship is to be open, candid, and in the highest traditions of philanthropy. The chapter also discusses why achieving partnership is difficult and documents violations of trust by foundations and grantseekers.

Chapter Eight is a synthesis of the findings of the book with predictions about the behavior of foundations in the future.

Acknowledgments

It is said that every book has many authors, and the many people who have influenced my work have thus contributed to this book. Foremost among them are Bill Toombs, professor emeritus of higher education administration at The Pennsylvania State University, and Marty Finkelstein, professor of higher education administration at Seton Hall University, who long ago encouraged my research on foundations. I would like to acknowledge my colleagues in the business administration department of Saint Francis College: Bruce Bradley, Bruce Elwell, Margaret Garcia, Jim Logue, Ed Monborne, Dorothy Pisarski, Tom Swope, Tom Thomas, and my gifted office mate Mahabub Islam. I would also like to thank the many undergraduate and graduate students at the college whose interest in the book has been gratifying. I would like to thank Kathleen Owens, vice president for academic affairs, who arranged a one-semester sabbatical that helped me finish the book; Kathy Gilmour, director of public relations, who reviewed an early chapter; Joe Melusky, professor of political science, who helped with information on the responsibilities of citizens; and the staff of Pasquerilla Library, especially Peggy Hanlon, interlibrary loan librarian, who located many of the volumes represented in the book. Many other people at Saint Francis often asked about the book, especially Dick Crawford, Bob Crusciel, Sister Mary Ann Dillon, Dan Fredericks, Tom Maher, Mike McKale, Marie Melusky, John Murphy, Father Christian Oravec, Ray Ponchione, Gerry Rooney, Pete Skoner, Kevin Southard, and Tim Whisler. Most of all at Saint Francis, I would like to thank Randy Frye, chair of the business administration department and director of the master of business administration program, for his unfailing encouragement in all aspects of my work. He is the best boss imaginable.

I owe a special debt of gratitude to Roxane Hogue, secretary of the business administration department and master of business administration program, for supervising a team of students who helped to catalog many of the works represented in the book and managed a database of thousands of references on foundations. These students were Pam Hodge, Wendy Hodge, Kim Hoover, Jim Magee, Tim Miller, and Mindi Nagy. Two Saint Francis students, Jason Henahan and Laura Hodge, performed service beyond the call of duty by typing a multitude of information into the database. These two research assistants consistently demonstrated a degree of diligence, enthusiasm, and professionalism which belied their young age, and I owe them a particular debt of thanks. I would also like to thank Alan Shrader, editor at Jossey-Bass, who showed immediate enthusiasm for the idea of analyzing foundations using metaphors; Rachel Livsey, associate editor, who guided the book from the review process through production and printing; and Susan Williams, assistant editor, who provided advice on the style and structure of several early chapters. Thanks also to Jonathan Peck of Dovetail Publishing Services, who managed production of the book, and to Rick Reser for his graceful copyediting.

Lastly, I am grateful to my parents, Paul and Katherine McIlnay; my brother, Tom, his wife, Vicky, and their children, Erin, Ryan, and Megan; and my sister, Patty McIlnay, and her husband, Joe Mosso. I am also grateful to my wife's parents, Andy and Pat Randall, her sisters, Andrea Randall and Lisa Yohman, and her husband, Mark. I would like to acknowledge Lisa's late husband, Nathan McCullough, and my friends, especially Jeanne and Fred Ade, Joanne and Paul Ade, Monica and Frank Bizousky, Chuck Dees, Travis Elden, Richard Endres, Anne and Jim Gallagher, Ann Heverly, Jeanne Heverly, Mary Jo Jubelirer, Bob McGregor, Colleen and Dave Montrella, Maggy and Bob Moore, Jim Moran, Jack Potteiger, Jim Sheetz, Don Stefanelli, and Hunter Swope. I would also like to acknowledge our friend, Pat Raybuck, and her two children, Brittani and Christopher, who mean so much to my wife and me. Most of all, I am grateful to my wife, Kathy, who has been my partner through twenty-five years of the thick and thin of personal and professional life. She has enriched my life in more ways than I can say.

Hollidaysburg, Pennsylvania　　　　　　　　　　　　Dennis P. McIlnay
February 1998

The Author

Dennis P. McIlnay is professor of management at Saint Francis College in Loretto, Pennsylvania, where he teaches management and organizational behavior to undergraduate students and students in the college's master of business administration program. He holds an Ed.D. in higher education administration from Seton Hall University (1987), an M.Ed. in higher education administration from The Pennsylvania State University (1982), and a B.A. in English from Saint Vincent College (1970). Before becoming a professor, he held administrative positions at Seton Hall University, Mount Aloysius College, and Westmoreland Community College as an admissions officer, director of public relations and publications, director of continuing education, institutional researcher, grants officer, dean of college relations, and director of university advancement. He also served as president of a management consulting firm.

McIlnay was inducted into the United States Army in 1970 and was awarded the Army Commendation Medal. He received the national silver medal for fund-raising improvement in 1985 at Seton Hall University from the Council for the Advancement and Support of Education. At Saint Francis College, he was elected secretary-treasurer of the faculty senate and chair of the faculty salary and benefits committee. He received the Salute to Teaching Award from the Pennsylvania Academy for the Profession of Teaching in 1990 and the Outstanding Educator Award from the students of Saint Francis College in the same year. His publications include a previous book on foundations entitled *Foundations and Higher Education: Dollars, Donors, and Scholars* (1991) as well as articles on foundations in *Nonprofit and Voluntary Sector Quarterly, Foundation News and Commentary, Philanthropy Matters,* and *Currents.* He is a member of the editorial board of *Foundation News and Commentary,* received a research grant from the Lilly Endowment and the Indiana University Center on Philanthropy for a study of the public accountability of foundations, and has presented conference papers on foundations, philanthropy, and the management of nonprofit organizations. He is a member of the Association for Research on Nonprofit Organizations and Voluntary Action, the International Society for Third-Sector Research, and the National Committee for Responsive Philanthropy. When he is not writing or teaching, Dr. McIlnay enjoys bass fishing in the Juniata River near his home in central Pennsylvania.

Isn't it queer: there are only two or three human stories, and they go on repeating themselves as fiercely as if they had never happened before; like the larks in this country, that have been singing the same five notes over for thousands of years.

—WILLA CATHER, *O PIONEERS!* (1913, P. 119)

. . . since words stand for things, those words are most pleasing that give us fresh knowledge. Now strange words leave us in the dark; and current words (with the things they stand for) we know already. Accordingly, it is metaphor that is in the highest degree instructive and pleasing.

—ARISTOTLE, *RHETORIC* (1932, P. 206)

How Foundations Work

Chapter One

Foundations at the Crossroads

> *There can be no doubt either, among those familiar with the facts, that the wholesale college giving and the consequent wholesale college begging of the last twenty years have gone far to transform the American college president into a soliciting agent. . . . Today the typical board of trustees is not seeking a scholarly president; it is seeking a president who can get money. . . . Many a college president spends his best years in the hopeless endeavor to grasp . . . a reward that has been dangled before his eyes, with the kindest intentions, by one of the endowed foundations.*
>
> HENRY S. PRITCHETT, *ANNUAL REPORT OF THE CARNEGIE CORPORATION* (1922, PP. 17–18)

As foundations approach the end of the Twentieth Century, their environment is nearly as confounding as ever in their hundred-year history. They face unprecedented competition for their grants because of extraordinary growth in the number of nonprofit organizations and the diversity of problems confronting the nation. They are pressured for better accountability from the federal government in the wake of scandals at Covenant House, the National Association for the Advancement of Colored People, and the Foundation for New Era Philanthropy, and their founders and trustees demand better management and a stronger return on philanthropic investment. Congress and the national administration are reducing or eliminating aid for many health, social, cultural, and educational programs, causing thousands of nonprofits to turn to foundations for support.

In response, foundations are reassessing their missions. Jody Curtis (1996), executive editor of *Foundation News and Commentary,* the magazine of the Council on Foundations, has called this period the "Re" Decade because the use of "re" words such as reexamination and redefinition has become common as foundations struggle to reevaluate missions and reinvent strategies. But the current reassessment of mission is not the first; many large foundations have intermittently reevaluated their philosophy, priorities, and framework of operations. Earl Cheit and Theodore Lobman, who studied the relationship of foundations and higher education for the Commission on Private Philanthropy and Public Needs, a research group created by foundations in 1973, discovered that many foundations reexamine their purposes and program interests. Perhaps they do so in response to Landrum Bolling, former chair of the Council on Foundations and past president of the Lilly Endowment, whose message to members of the council in 1977–78 was entitled "A Time for Reassessment" (Cheit and Lobman, 1979, p. 4).

The present reexamination, however, may be the most widespread in the history of foundations. The Institute for Educational Affairs, an interest group created by conservative foundations in 1977, sponsored its first "Philanthropy Roundtable" in 1986 to urge foundations to reflect on their programs and priorities with greater scrutiny. Leslie Lenkowsky, then president of the institute, explains that one of its main purposes is to prompt foundations to evaluate the effectiveness of their support. They should "think more about how they can achieve their objectives," he says, as well as "look more closely at what the groups they support really are accomplishing" (Desruisseaux, 1987a, pp. A72–A75). The Pew Charitable Trusts did this, deciding in 1989 to undergo a major reorganization of leadership and grantmaking priorities and to commit to more collaboration with other foundations and better accessibility to grantseekers and the general public. This was significant for a foundation that until 1979 did virtually all its grantmaking anonymously. Rebecca W. Rimel, president of Pew, said the reorganization was "very dramatic" and explained that it evolved from an assessment of operations undertaken because the former mission and structure could not accommodate the demands pressing on the foundation (McMillen, 1990a, p. A27).

At 1995 meetings of the Institute for Educational Affairs and the National Network of Grantmakers, a recently formed association of liberal grantmakers, both liberal and conservative foundations expressed concerns about the stagnancy, secrecy, and arrogance of foundations, bland or irrelevant giving, lack of public accountability, and grantmaking philosophies that avoid risk. Also that year, the Indiana University Center on Philanthropy sponsored a gathering of nonprofit leaders. They concluded that nonprofits have lost the sympathy of many Americans and that the most important challenge facing them is to reaffirm the tradition of civic engagement in the nation (Arenson, 1995; Curtis, 1996).

Author and trustee John Nason, one of the most respected members of the foundation community, says that foundations, like all organizations, can become complacent, so periodic renewal of purpose is essential to their health. Appointing a new chief executive often occasions this. Some boards have even decided to devote a meeting each year to discussing mission. But many forego reevaluation; they prefer vague missions that do not restrict them from dispensing funds more or less according to their whims. One such trustee said, "I like being a foundation trustee. It gives me an opportunity to make all my friends happy" (Nason, 1989, pp. 23–24). Better would be to heed the advice of John D. Rockefeller III (1971), who upon retiring from the board of the Rockefeller Foundation after forty years said that foundations cannot overemphasize the need for a constant critical review of programs and a willingness to reexamine established assumptions.

Numerous others have commented on the need for reassessment and ways to achieve it (see, for example, Lenkowsky, 1989; Bailey, 1995). Regardless of how it is accomplished, though, reassessment has serious implications for nonprofits. Some have forged historic partnerships with foundations to strengthen entire sectors such as higher education; others are just beginning to try to establish such alliances. But though the relationship between the two is important to the development of the charitable sector, many people in nonprofits have a very poor understanding of foundations. This can blind them to the realities confronting foundations and impede their ability to create partnerships with them.

Even as foundations exist in an increasingly turbulent environment, many nonprofits cling to perceptions that are simplistic, outdated, and often incorrect. For example, they commonly believe that foundations are risk takers, but this is at best only partially true and at worst untrue. To embrace such impressions oversimplifies the foundations' true situation; nonprofits that do so fail to grasp all the realities facing them. A new way of seeing foundations is therefore needed, one that enables people to discard their myths and understand the complex culture of foundations.

Metaphor: A New Way of Seeing Foundations

Metaphor, a way of describing one phenomenon in terms of another, can help us see the many faces of foundations. Metaphor allows articulation on subjects for which there is no specific language, allowing expression of ideas that might otherwise be inexpressible. For example, using the metaphor of foundations as citizens might help us see how the responsibilities of foundations resemble those of citizens. In other words, foundations may be figuratively portrayed by describing what they literally are not.

Metaphors create purposeful falsehoods and seem simultaneously intelligible and unintelligible, true and untrue. This paradox invites us to think about matters in new and often enlightening ways. Metaphors ask us to see A as B even when the two are so dissimilar that it would ordinarily be a mistake to describe one as the other. But they invite us to find the similarity in dissimilarity, the evident in the hidden, the heretofore unseen connections between such things as foundations and citizens. They have what Donald Schon (1983) called a generative ability, in that they can generate new images or new perspectives. Metaphors lack readily apparent meaning, so we have to establish their significance for ourselves, helping us create ownership of the insight. The message of a metaphor is thus immediate and personal, one reason that good metaphors strike such interesting and powerful chords. Metaphor is most instructive when there is an element of tension, conflict, or opposition between the topic (in this case foundations) and the vehicle (citizens), so that the reader is surprised, even charmed, at the juxtaposition of the two ideas, exclaiming, as it were, "True enough! And I never thought of it" (Aristotle, 1932, pp. 206, 212; cited in Morgan, 1993, pp. 277, 290, 291).

Metaphors are especially useful in studying organizations because they help us to escape the confinement of our perceptions and assumptions about them. Using them can therefore help managers, who face the challenge of finding new ways to perceive and manage organizations. Viewing organizations as machines, for example, would focus us on the efficiency of their structures and processes, as in the principles of mechanical engineering, the basis of Frederick Winslow Taylor's scientific management. Viewing organizations as organisms, as in systems theory, we would note that they behave like biological systems: they import external resources, transform them into products or services, and export the products or services to the external environment, completing the cycle of interdependence between the organization and its environment. Both these views are valid; using both creates complementary and competing insights with inherent strengths and weaknesses, presenting alternative perceptions of organizations and different approaches to managing them (Morgan, 1993).

The metaphors in this book represent some new ideas on foundations, but by no means are they exhaustive. Foundations are many things at once, and no metaphor or set of metaphors can capture all their dimensions. The metaphors of foundations as judges, editors, citizens, activists, entrepreneurs, and partners do, however, offer new portraits of the many faces of foundations.

Misconceptions About Foundations: A Brief History

Myths and misconceptions about foundations have persisted almost from their beginning in this century. Within a few years of the establishment of three of the nation's earliest and most prominent foundations, the Carnegie Corporation (1911) and the Rockefeller (1913) and Ford (1936) Foundations, Carnegie secretary Robert M. Lester (1935) said that the most amazing thing about foundations was that so few people, even the informed, understood them. In his 1936 classic, *Wealth and Culture*, Eduard Lindeman admitted that after eight years of investigation he and his associates could find only one book on foundations: Carnegie president

Frederick P. Keppel's *The Foundation* (1930). Lindeman concluded that no substantial body of literature on foundations had yet been produced. Other researchers then and now agree (see, for example, Hollis, 1938; Kiger, 1954; Macdonald, 1956; Magat, 1989. Magat noted that most early foundation literature consisted of personal essays or sympathetic accounts by founders, trustees, or staff members).

Attempts have since been made to compile useful data about foundations. In 1956, for example, the Foundation Library Center (later renamed the Foundation Center) was founded through a $300,000 grant from the Carnegie Corporation; it later attracted support from the Ford, Kellogg, Rockefeller, and Russell Sage Foundations. Its first president was F. Emerson Andrews, an original staff member of the Russell Sage Foundation who had himself noted the lack of information on foundations. The center maintains such data at its headquarters in New York City and at two hundred other libraries throughout the country.

Still, even the government has had trouble learning about foundations. A 1952 Congressional investigating committee sent letters to a hundred executives in education, business, labor, religion, and government who were considered well informed, asking them what they knew about foundations. About 30 percent of them did not reply; of the rest, about two-fifths said they knew so little that they declined to express an opinion. At committee hearings, however, a few hostile witnesses accused foundations of "interlock," defined as a diabolical conspiracy to collaborate in order to subvert (Special Committee to Investigate Tax-Exempt Foundations and Comparable Organizations, 1954, p. 25). This criticism, exacerbated by foundations' reticence and sometimes outright secrecy, caused many of them to be labeled as "separate islands," disinclined to communicate with grantseekers, Congress, the public, and even each other (Joseph, 1986a, p. 54).

Inaccessibility, secrecy, and uncooperativeness have long characterized the behavior of foundations. Few have employed communications staff; even fewer have conducted communication programs. Some have never stated their grantmaking priorities publicly, and most have never issued newsletters, guidelines for grantseekers, or annual or biennial reports. Only about eleven hundred of the nation's approximately thirty-eight thousand foundations publish annual reports. Some do not return telephone calls or answer mail from applicants; others refuse to meet with grantseekers even to explain that their projects are not of interest. A few have unlisted telephone numbers, post office boxes for addresses, or addresses that are those of law firms or bank trust departments.

Few foundations communicate even with each other; historically, few new ones have contacted older foundations to take advantage of their experience. Robert M. Lester (1935) reported that in the 1920s and 1930s only three new foundations had communicated with any of the Carnegie foundations for advice on governance, management, or grantmaking. Other experts have further documented this kind of reluctance (Hutchins, 1956; Field, 1954).

Congressional investigations in the 1960s culminated in the Tax Reform Act of 1969, the most important law affecting foundations (see Chapter Four for more on its provisions). During the investigations, witnesses testified that many foundations were intellectually inert, lacking the most basic facts about themselves, reluctant to open their records to historians, unwilling to cooperate with each other, and unable to respond to criticism in a responsible rather than a polemical way (Nielsen, 1985; Reeves, 1970). The Tax Reform Act of 1969 subjected foundations to taxation for the first time in American history (4 percent on net investment income, reduced to 2 percent in 1978) and required them to advertise their name, address, and telephone number in a newspaper of general circulation.

In the 1970s, the lack of information on foundations became so pronounced that a whole grantsmanship industry sprang up to provide information to grantseekers that foundations could not or would not furnish. Available facts on foundations then consisted mostly of routine descriptions of grants in a handful of foundation annual reports, plus anecdotal and sometimes contradictory observations by grantseekers or foundation trustees and managers (Cheit and Lobman, 1979). Almost nothing was known about the executive directors and program officers of foundations until Arnold Zurcher and Jane Dustan wrote *The Foundation Administrator* in 1972, but Orville Brim (1973) said that the foundation community still had virtually no collective information on its management policies and practices.

Collaboration between foundations remains rare today, according to many observers (see Kitzi, 1997). However, the study of foundations and nonprofits has increased with the establishment of organizations such as Independent Sector, the Aspen Institute's Nonprofit Sector Research Fund, the Association for Research on Nonprofit Organizations and Voluntary Action, and some thirty research centers in colleges and universities, including at Indiana University, New York University, Case Western Reserve, and the University of San Francisco. The oldest such institute was founded at Yale in 1977 out of concern that although the United States relied heavily on the voluntary sector to conduct most of its social, cultural, and educational programs, nonprofits were poorly understood, lacking not only a body of research but a connective theory of their governance and functions (Brewster, 1989). "When we started, it was almost a deserted beach," said John Simon, one of the founders of the Yale Program on Nonprofit Organizations, and most academics were pathetically uninformed about foundations, nonprofits, and the importance of philanthropy in American life (Bailey, 1988, p. v). Many others have echoed the need for more information on foundations, among them Boulding, 1973; Boris, 1985; and Odendahl, 1990.

Considering the sums of money involved and the significance of their work, foundations have been oddly neglected in the research on nonprofit organizations. Major gaps in knowledge remain on many matters: relations with grantseekers, investment strategies and performance, access to foundations and their public accountability, relations with Congress and the Internal Revenue Service, ethical problems, staff selection and training, governance, public policy formation and advocacy, board-staff relations, innovation and risk taking, regulation, and grantmaking philosophies.

Research has increased in the past decade, although the field still suffers from years of neglect and the absence of stipends, focal points, and forums for presenting findings and identifying questions for further study. Progress is being made, however. Modern research on foundations originated in the late 1960s and has continued ever since (see, as examples, Commission on Foundations and Private Philanthropy, 1970; Commission on Private Philanthropy and Public Needs, 1975; Odendahl, 1987). Book publishers are involved: Jossey-Bass, Inc., Transaction Books, and Sage Publications recently created new series on philanthropy and nonprofits, and the Foundation Center issued a bibliography that listed some four hundred publishers of works on nonprofits.

Two new journals on the subject are being published: *Nonprofit and Voluntary Sector Quarterly* and *Nonprofit Management and Leadership*. Other new periodicals include the *Chronicle of Philanthropy, NonProfit Times, Journal of Volunteer Administration, Journal of Contemporary Issues in Fund Raising*, and *Voluntas: The International Journal of Voluntary and Nonprofit Organizations*.

The publications of other disciplines have occasionally shown interest in philanthropy and nonprofits; see Magat, 1990. Publication of the annual *Research in Progress* by the Indiana University Center on Philanthropy has heightened awareness of research on nonprofits, as has the Foundation Center's *Literature of the Nonprofit Sector* (1989), which contains nearly five thousand entries.

Foundation and nonprofit archives have also made more information accessible. Most prominent among these are the Rockefeller Archive Center and the Ford Foundation Archive, as well as the Western Reserve Historical Society, the Chicago Historical Society, the Minnesota Historical Society, and the Bancroft Library at the University of California at Berkeley.

Philanthropy as an academic study has gained momentum, but many important questions remain unanswered; whether the field becomes established depends partly on whether it can overcome decades of prejudice and neglect. A problem with much of the research on foundations and other nonprofits is that it is too theoretical to deal directly with real problems. Pablo Eisenberg, president of the Center for Community Change, says (1991b) that an enormous amount of research does not reflect much understanding of the issues facing nonprofits and that many researchers lack practical experience with organizations and their problems. Clearly aware of these shortcomings, the Ford Foundation and the Kellogg Foundation gave $250,000 to the Association for Research on Nonprofit Organizations and Voluntary Action (ARNOVA) in 1995 to encourage researchers to collaborate more closely with practitioners in nonprofits to ensure that their research is useful (Greene, 1995). Also, to facilitate cooperation with practitioners in nonprofits, ARNOVA has established a formal relationship with the National Society of Fund Raising Executives and its sixteen thousand members (Winkler and Mason, 1996).

Who Is Hurt by Failing to Understand Foundations?

The poor understanding of foundations has a particularly negative effect on college presidents, professors, the general public, and fund-raisers. Because their duty is to get money for their organizations, fund-raisers seemingly should have a better insight into foundations than most others. Ironically, however, many have only seat-of-the-pants knowledge of what they do, especially as it applies to foundations. Several experts have commented on this state of affairs, including Arnaud C. Marts (1966, p. 11), the dean of American fund-raisers, who complained that most fund-raisers knew very little about philanthropy and were unable to trace the origin of American philanthropy or relate charitable giving to its larger historical context. Patricia Read, former vice president for research at the Foundation Center, described this phenomenon as "one of the biggest, constant challenges we face" (Desruisseaux, 1986b, p. 38), and Thomas Broce, who has had experience on both sides of the table as a fund-raising consultant, former president of Phillips University, and president of the Kerr Foundation, said that "most laymen (including most fund raisers) actually know very little about (foundations)" (1979, p. 103).

Similarly, many college presidents lack experience in the development functions of annual and capital fund-raising, alumni relations, major gifts, and corporate and foundation grants. According to James Fisher (1980), former president of Towson University and the Council for the Advancement and Support of Education, the leading organization of development professionals in higher education, most new college presidents are like he was in 1969: "fresh, anxious, confident—and inexperienced" (p. viii), especially in the functions of institutional advancement.

Many professors also understand foundations poorly and disdain fund-raising, often treating the campus development staff with poorly concealed contempt. Fund-raising brings commercial values to higher education, and although long evident in colleges and universities, such values are still thought by some academics to infect academe with the corrupting profit motive. Some professors think that grantsmanship, which helps finance the research of many who attack it, debases scholarship. Although many professors know very little about fund-raising, they are quick to criticize the values and performance of fund-raisers and quite willing to base their judgments on opinion and hearsay to an extent intolerable in their own disciplines (Payton, 1984).

Among the general public, some people have heard of the Ford Foundation or the Rockefeller Foundation, but most know next to nothing about the goals or operations of foundations in general. Most seem not to care one way or the other, and because foundations manage to elude publicity better than most other nonprofits, people have little to help them form an educated opinion. Perhaps the most remarkable feature of foundations is their inconspicuousness, especially in an age when seemingly every organization gets its Warholian fifteen minutes of fame. Foundations receive very little media attention, even to announce their grants or programs, and hardly any critical media focus, despite some recent stories about abuses in the nonprofit community. I am not aware of a major story on foundations in the mass media, either print or broadcast, although a 1993 *Philadelphia Inquirer* seven-part series on the nonprofit sector did devote one part to foundations. This lack of coverage is disturbing given the wealth and power of foundations in our democracy; it makes it difficult for people to inform themselves on the subject even if they want to.

Sara Engelhardt, director of the Foundation Center and a former staff member of the Carnegie Corporation, admits that the public "doesn't know what a foundation is" and is not about to "wander into our libraries" to try to find out" (Kirkman, 1995, p. 22). The best hope for reversing this situation probably lies with television magazine programs that attract large audiences, but neither the commercial networks nor the Public Broadcasting Service have shown interest. *Foundation News and Commentary* is the only publication devoted solely to foundations, although the *Chronicle of Philanthropy, Chronicle of Higher Education,* and a handful of other publications report on them. But these are small and read mainly by practitioners in colleges, universities, and other nonprofits who usually understand foundations to some extent—better than the general public, at least. David Rockefeller, one of the giants of foundations, said (1973) that the public is the *constituency* of foundations and as such deserves a dialogue with them, a privilege they do not generally enjoy; he thought the initiative belongs rightly in foundations because they have been inaccessible for so long. Dean Rusk, president of the Rockefeller Foundation and secretary of state in the Kennedy administration, made similar comments (1961).

The Competition for Foundation Grants

Wherever foundation officials turn, it seems that managers of non-profits complain of being desperately underfunded. Foundations receive thousands of grant proposals each year, and grantseeker demand for information about grantors is accelerating to such an extent that the Foundation Center is running out of chairs in its libraries (Kirkman, 1995). In 1991, more than 578,000 people used the center's libraries in New York City and regional facilities in Cleveland, San Francisco, and Washington, D.C., up 24 percent over 1990 and 43 percent over 1989. Many such users are fund-raising neophytes preparing their first grant proposals; in 1991, 40 percent of visitors to the four libraries were first-timers. According to Anne J. Borland, Foundation Center vice president and director of public service, "We're getting people who have had cutbacks in state funding and looking for more foundation support. We're getting people who were fully funded by the government and never sought foundation support. And then we're getting our regular audience of non-profits who are being squeezed" (Millar, 1992, p. 20).

As the number of grantseekers has risen, foundations have become much more exacting in their evaluation of proposals, sharpening their program interests and applying more rigorous grantmaking criteria. For example, in 1996 the Pew Charitable Trusts stopped making grants for operating support to the Philadelphia Orchestra, a well-connected and long-time grantee, saying it had failed to meet "high standards of fiscal, administrative, and programmatic performance" (Dundjerski, 1996a, p. 12). Pew had enacted a new policy: no more grants to organizations with budget deficits of more than 5 percent of operating expenses. In the future it plans to eliminate grants to arts organizations that are operating in the red—a clear message to such grantseekers that they must have their fiscal house in order if they expect to receive grants.

The competition for grants coupled with the tightening of grantmaking policies has created what might be called a *grantor's market,* an environment of substantial (perhaps unprecedented) foundation selectivity. Foundations historically have funded only a handful of the many proposals they receive; today most find it increasingly difficult to respond to the growing number and diversity of requests. The percentage of grant proposals that receive funding has been variously estimated at different times: Cuninggim (1972) indicated it was less than 5 percent, Broce (1979) concluded it was about 1 percent, Lefferts (1982) said about 10 percent.

The ratio of accepted to rejected proposals varies depending on the foundation. The Sloan Foundation funded about 6.7 percent of the fifteen thousand proposals it received in the early 1980s (Perry, 1982); in both 1994 and 1995, the Carnegie Corporation funded about 5 percent of those it received (Carnegie Corporation, 1994; Famiglietti, 1996). The Ford Foundation's acceptance rate has declined; it was 11.2 percent in 1987 (*Chronicle of Higher Education,* 1988a), but by 1994 the number of incoming requests had nearly doubled to 33,700, of which only 5.3 percent were funded (Bailey, 1995).

Increased numbers of proposals are causing problems for some foundations. The MacArthur Foundation received 5,400 proposals in 1991, an increase of almost 50 percent in three years. The volume of requests at well-known foundations such as MacArthur, which awards the controversial MacArthur Fellowships, is staggering, according to Margaret E. Mahoney, a trustee of the foundation and president of the Commonwealth Fund (Bailey, 1992). The Hitachi Foundation has been receiving more than 2,500 unsolicited proposals annually, forcing its program officers to spend a great deal of time reviewing them even though only 1 to 2 percent can be funded. This has reduced the time that foundation staff can spend with prospective grantees to talk about needs, and it has significantly decreased grantseekers' chances for funding (Regelbrugge, 1995).

The Employment and Education of Fund-Raisers

Another indication of the stiff competition for foundation grants is the brisk job market for fund-raisers. Membership in the National Society of Fund Raising Executives, the nation's premier association of fund-raisers, more than tripled to 16,000 between 1984 and 1994. Between 1980 and 1990, membership in the National Association for Hospital Development, which represents fund-raisers in health care, rose nearly 106 percent (Hall and Murawski, 1995; *Chronicle of Philanthropy,* 1990a). A randomly chosen 1995 issue of the *Chronicle of Philanthropy* (July 27) contained nine pages of advertisements—virtually all for fund-raisers—from organizations ranging from a Quaker preschool to the University of California.

Like the job market, the education of development officers has exploded in recent years in response to the competition for foundation grants and other private funds. About thirty colleges and universities now offer courses in the administration of fund-raising, with institutions as prestigious as the University of Chicago having entered the market with its certificate program called Managing Institutional Advancement (*Chronicle of Philanthropy,* 1995b). Some organizations, such as Yale's Program on Nonprofit Organizations, focus on research; others, such as Saint Mary's University of Minnesota, concentrate on training. Such schools offer a variety of degree programs, and other organizations (for example, the Grantsmanship Center and the Council for the Advancement and Support of Education) conduct noncredit seminars on proposal writing, managing annual funds and capital campaigns, and similar topics.

More than half the colleges offering courses in fund-raising began after 1990, and the majority of these courses descended from the Association of American Colleges' Program on Studying Philanthropy, which began in 1986 (Gorman, 1988). Education in fund-raising has grown so rapidly that colleges and universities are having trouble meeting the demand. The University of Washington, for example, has ninety to a hundred applicants yearly for its fund-raising certificate program, which can take only thirty-five (H. Hall, 1995a).

Though very popular, such programs draw complaints from some students that they do not focus enough on fund-raising per se. Some colleges require only one course in fund-raising to get a master's degree in the management of nonprofit organizations; others have no fund-raising requirement. Tim Homan, who earned a master's degree in nonprofit management from Case Western Reserve University, said, "More and more, you just do not get an executive director's job without fund-raising experience, [but] many of the master's programs haven't caught up with reality" (H. Hall, 1995a, pp. 41–42). However, at least some academic officials doubt the need to redesign curricula. Al Abramovitz, director of the Mandel Center for Nonprofit Organizations at Case Western, said that the university's faculty do not consider fund-raising a scholarly discipline, even though it is essential to managing a nonprofit organization. Fund-raising still lacks a body of systematic research, without which few academics are persuaded that it is worth studying in higher education, let alone deserving of an advanced degree.

The Growth of the Nonprofit Sector and the Diversity of Problems Confronting Foundations

A major cause of intense grant competition and the lively market for fund-raisers and the programs that educate them is the growth of the nonprofit sector. The number of nonprofits in the United States rose from 766,000 in 1980 to 1,024,766 in 1990, nearly 34 percent, and in 1994 the Internal Revenue Service approved more than forty thousand new nonprofits. For ten years prior to 1965, the IRS received between five thousand and seven thousand applications yearly seeking tax-exempt status, but in 1965 the number jumped to thirteen thousand and has risen steadily to its current level of more than forty thousand (O'Neill, 1989).

The number of nonprofit employees rose accordingly, from 7.1 million in 1980 to 8.7 million in 1990, almost 23 percent. So, in the same decade, did the charitable sector's share of the gross national product, up from 5.5 percent to 7.1 percent, and private giving from individuals, foundations, and corporations, up from $48.7 billion to $104.3 billion—more than 114 percent (*Chronicle of Philanthropy*, 1990a, 1990b, 1991b, 1992a).

But growth can cause problems. Managers of some of the nation's largest nonprofit organizations, including foundations, identified five problems they believed would represent their main challenges for the 1990s (*Chronicle of Philanthropy*, 1990a, pp. 1, 12).

1. Competition to raise money will be fierce because more non-profits will employ sophisticated development professionals who will use advanced fund-raising methods.

2. Few, if any, charitable organizations are expected to garner more private support, possibly excepting environmental organizations and elementary and secondary educational institutions.

3. The recruitment of managers by nonprofits will intensify, especially executive directors, financial managers, and fund-raisers, and the education of executives in managing nonprofit organizations will continue to be a priority.

4. Nonprofits will face greater pressure for public accountability from Congress and the Internal Revenue Service as a result of evidence of their inaccessibility and in the wake of financial scandals in several prominent nonprofits.

5. Grantmaking by foundations and charitable giving by individuals will continue to be preoccupied by the nation's most intractable problems: AIDS, drug addiction, homelessness, illiteracy, poverty, teen pregnancy, and unemployment.

The diversity of problems facing nonprofits is indicated by the comments of a few leaders who were asked to name *one* problem philanthropy should tackle in the 1990s (*Chronicle of Philanthropy*, 1990a):

- "The epidemic that's hit American teen-agers: drugs, violence, teen-age pregnancy, and AIDS" (Robert Blendon, chair, Department of Health Policy, Harvard University).
- "To help find ways to empower the poor" (Edwin J. Feulner, Jr., president, The Heritage Foundation).
- "Disintegrating communities" (John W. Gardner, professor of public service, Stanford University).
- "The crisis in moral and spiritual values" (James Osborne, national commander of the Salvation Army).
- "The grim slide of primary and secondary public-school education" (Tom Wolfe, author).

A sample of titles of recent articles in the *Chronicle of Philanthropy* and other publications also illustrates the diversity of issues confronting foundations:

- "U.S. Grant Makers Are Missing Opportunities to Promote Democracy in Eastern Europe" (Tirman, 1990).

- "The Civil Opportunities of Foundations" (Mathews, 1991).
- "3 Foundations Form New Fund to Focus on Energy Issues" (*Chronicle of Philanthropy,* 1991a).
- "Foundations Urged to Give More Aid to Immigrants" (Gray, 1995).
- "Kellogg Supports Adult Education" (*Chronicle of Philanthropy,* 1996).

Demands from nearly every corner of society are not the only pressures on foundations and other nonprofits. Congress seems determined to balance the federal budget by the year 2002, and in doing so to reduce federal support of many health, social, cultural, and educational programs. Under the House Budget Committee's long-range plan (subject, of course, to the vagaries of politics), federal support of nonprofits by the year 2002 would be 21 percent below current levels. A similar Senate Budget Committee plan would lead to 17 percent less aid. The House plan would terminate, privatize, or convert into block grants three cabinet departments, 284 programs, sixty-nine commissions, and thirteen agencies. The Senate plan would consolidate sixty job training programs, reduce funding for the National Endowment for the Arts and the National Endowment for the Humanities, terminate the AmeriCorps Program, reduce the Community Development Block Grant Program, cut the Social Service Block Grant Program, and hold annual growth rates of Medicare and Medicaid to 6.8 percent and 5.0 percent, respectively, levels significantly below their recent rates of growth (National Committee for Responsive Philanthropy, 1995).

In 1995, Independent Sector surveyed 108 nonprofits in thirty-one states to estimate how they could be affected by the proposed cuts. The study found that federal sources contributed 32 percent of the organizations' budgets in 1994, declining to 25 percent by 2002 if the cuts are made. It concluded that nonprofits would have to increase their private gifts by 70 percent to compensate (Stehle, 1995a). In response to the proposed cuts, 116 nonprofits—including many of the most prominent, ranging from the Girl Scouts to the American Cancer Society—sent a statement to Congress. It said that proposed tax incentives to stimulate private giving would do little to offset cuts in social and educational programs. Charities receive about 30 percent of their revenue from government sources, 25 percent from private contributions, 40 percent from dues, fees, and charges for services, and 5 percent from investment income and other sources. But they cannot increase fees much without putting their services beyond the reach of the very people they are trying to help. Nor can they generate revenue by selling their goods and services; attempts to do so have met with strong opposition from profit-making entities, who claim unfair competition.

The statement also said that the proposal to restore the charitable deduction for taxpayers who do not itemize deductions is likely to increase individual giving by only $3 billion a year, less than 5 percent. That fits recent trends: from 1963 to 1993 gifts from individuals rose an average of 2.4 percent per year after inflation, but from 1988 to 1993 the rise averaged only 1.2 percent. The organizations pledged to do all they can, but "we can only do so much," they concluded. "We cannot begin to do it all" (*Chronicle of Philanthropy*, 1995a, p. 47).

Compounding the problem of federal budget cuts is the likely increase in demand for the services of nonprofits as illiteracy, unemployment, and related problems affect more Americans. Some nonprofits that have lost government funds are turning to foundations for support, but many foundations oppose grants for operating expenses or to replace government aid. They are often reluctant to play the role of rescuer when, in the words of Karl N. Stauber of the Northwest Area Foundation, they "don't see the resources for follow-through beyond the foundation's grant" (Greene and Millar, 1990, pp. 1, 13).

Reduced government funding has caused many nonprofits, especially public universities, to become much more competitive in fund-raising. Anne Alexander, vice president of the AT&T Foundation, confirms that her foundation, for one, is receiving many more proposals from public institutions of higher education. Often these public universities achieve impressive fund-raising results, even compared with those of private institutions that are usually much more experienced at raising money. For example, the University of Texas Southwestern Medical Center in Dallas received four gifts totaling $85 million in four months, and in 1991 a couple who attended the University of Houston gave the institution $51.4 million, one of the largest gifts ever made to a public university. Some schools even exceed their goals: the University of California at Berkeley's five-year campaign that ended in 1990 raised nearly $150 million more than its $320 million goal, for example (Nicklin, 1992).

Grants by 1,020 large foundations to all higher education institutions in 1993 totaled $1.5 billion. Of this amount, private institutions received about three-fifths, a share unchanged from the previous year. Public institutions garnered nearly two-fifths. The share of support to private institutions fluctuated in the 1980s because of several very large awards, but the share to public institutions over the past eight years has risen almost invariably. Private institutions currently receive about three grant dollars for every two given to public institutions, but ten years ago the ratio was three to one (Renz, Lawrence, and Treiber, 1995). Jerry A. May, vice president for development at Ohio State University, said that public universities are well positioned for fund-raising because many of their alumni are entering the 55-to-65 age range and are making or planning to make large gifts to higher education institutions (Mercer, 1997).

Despite these developments, few foundations have responded. The recent report, *Foundations in the Newt Era,* by the National Committee for Responsive Philanthropy, concludes that foundations seem unable to move quickly enough to keep pace with the rapidly changing federal policy environment (Eisenberg, 1995). James Hyman, associate director of the Annie E. Casey Foundation, confirmed the difficulty of responding to a political climate in transition, but June Zeitlin, director of the Ford Foundation's governance and public policy program, spurned the idea that national foundations should be reacting to short-term political trends. "Things go in and out of political fashion," she said. "What Ford does is to stick with its issues over the long haul" (Covington and Parachini, 1995, p. 17). Some foundations are hypersensitive to the restrictions placed on them by the Tax Reform Act of 1969 and are hesitant to appear too partisan in the current political debate, but most are quiet and unlikely to take the lead in responding to political changes (Covington and Parachini, 1995).

There is, in foundations today, an unsettling powerlessness, a pervasive frustration and worry about the forces impacting them and their inability to manage them, an anxiety that resembles the quiet desperation Thoreau said characterizes most lives. Many foundations are uneasy about preserving their privacy in the face of mounting demands for public accountability, developing principles to guide their grantmaking decisions, finding an appropriate role in public debate and in shaping public policy, and maintaining candid and trustful relations with grantseekers. They are concerned about their inability to make much progress in combating some of the nation's most intractable problems, many of which they have been fighting for years. All this has serious implications for nonprofits that have, or want to establish, productive relationships with foundations. But such relationships require understanding what foundations confront and how they operate today. New ways of seeing foundations are therefore needed to enable people to discard their misconceptions and see them in all their intricacy. The first of these new ways is the metaphor of foundations as judges.

Chapter Two

Foundations as Judges
The Art of Deciding Who Gets a Grant

*When you die and come to approach the judgment
of almighty God, when you stand before St. Peter in
supplication at the gates of heaven, what do you think
he will demand of you? Do you for an instant presume
that he will inquire into your petty failures and your trivial
virtues . . . ? No! No indeed! He will brush all these matters
to one side and he will ask but one question: "What did you
do as a trustee of the Rockefeller Foundation?!"*
FREDERICK GATES, *CHAPTERS IN MY LIFE* (1977, P. 265)

I will not give charity. I am not poor enough for that.
FRIEDRICH NIETZSCHE, *THUS SPOKE ZARATHUSTRA*
(1957, P. 3)

The metaphor of the foundation as judge seems particularly apt given that the process and difficulty of grantmaking stem from the central task of foundations, which is to judge the merits of grantseekers and the projects they propose. This is not to imply that foundations perform as judges do in a courtroom, but they do render decisions in a similar manner.

The Metaphor of Foundations as Judges

The major function of foundations is judging grantseekers and the projects they propose, deciding that one applicant but not another shall be funded. Decision making is synonymous with management in all organizations, but it is integral to foundations because it is their technology, the task by which they seek to fulfill their missions. More than any other function—investing funds, selecting trustees, determining program interests, public accountability—the central task of foundations is to *choose*.

Decision making has three steps, which economist and management authority Herbert Simon has called *intelligence, design,* and *choice*. Intelligence is identifying problems or issues that require decisions or, in Simon's cogent words, deciding to decide. Design is developing alternatives that could be chosen in a decision; for example, Option A, B, or C. Choice is choosing one of the alternatives. Rationally, intelligence typically precedes design and design precedes choice, but decision making is far more complicated than this because each step is itself a decision-making process. For example, when making a grant decision a foundation must first decide to decide (intelligence). It then reviews grant proposals from, say, fifty applicants and considers its options (design): fund some, reject others, or request additional information from the applicants. But when identifying alternatives during the design step, a foundation has two choices. It might (at least in theory) examine all alternatives by inviting all organizations in the program area to apply for grants and then pick the best one; this is called *optimizing*. Or it might try *satisficing*, which is identifying only a handful of applicants, say those close to the foundation's location, and then choosing one that meets the minimum rather than the ideal criteria for receiving a grant. Whether it optimizes or satisfices during the design step, the third step, choice, occurs when the foundation selects one or more of the applicants to receive a grant (March and Simon, 1987).

In theory a foundation could proceed smoothly through intelligence, design, and choice, but in reality it rarely does. As any decision maker knows, the seemingly simple three-step process can become a nightmare of complexity, each step a decision-making process that itself requires intelligence, design, and choice. For example, a foundation that has decided to decide to award a grant and has proceeded to the design step by considering alternative grantseekers may face an obstacle and decide not to make a grant after all. That is, it may opt to remain in the design step by deciding that additional grantseekers are needed; if it later determines condition of certainty and the more difficult ones in the condition of risk. An easy programmed decision might be to issue payroll checks every other week; a more difficult one would be to pay foundation bills within thirty days rather than sixty. Nonprogrammed decisions, however, tend to exist in the conditions of risk and uncertainty, the less difficult ones made under the condition of risk and the more difficult ones in the condition of uncertainty. A less difficult nonprogrammed decision might be to award a grant to a qualified applicant in a pool of very unqualified applicants. More difficult would be deciding to make a grant to a qualified applicant in a pool of very qualified applicants.

Goal Ambiguity and "Garbage Cans"

Like most complex organizations, foundations have missions that are difficult to achieve. The goals of many organizations are relatively explicit—manufacturers want to make products, for example—but foundations have vague and elusive goals such as education, socialization, economic growth, peace, or democracy. In organizations with ambiguous goals, which Cohen and March have called *organized anarchies,* decisions are often by-products of unplanned activity, more the residue of events than the reason for them. In such organizations, decisions simply happen as opposed to being made, and managers serve primarily as facilitators, not leaders; in fact, the organization often leads them more than they lead it.

Members of such organizations are said to be "loosely coupled" to each other, more disconnected than connected and sharing few variables because they, their values, and their responsibilities are so different. In foundations, trustees are loosely coupled to the staff because board members often come from a higher social and economic class; in small foundations they may have significant personal or business ties to donors. Foundation trustees enjoy a degree of power staff members can only aspire to and often have allegiances to several, even many, nonprofit organizations because they serve on multiple boards. Their contact with the staff is usually limited to that permitted by the president or executive director and is typically restricted to three or four well-orchestrated board meetings each year. Similarly, staff

that none of the old or new applicants will do, it may ev
to the intelligence step by canceling the grant program a
ing not to decide after all.

According to Simon, two types of decisions exist, *pro*
and *nonprogrammed*; these are not actually distinct but rath
a continuum. Programmed decisions are designed to han
tine and repetitive tasks, so that common situations can
dled without managers having to endure the tedi
inefficiency of making the same decision over and over. Fo
ple, a foundation might decide to issue payroll checks e
weeks, a process that becomes routine as it evolves into s
operating procedure. But because few if any grantmaking d
are routine, they are overwhelmingly nonprogrammed. N
grammed decisions involve unique, extraordinary, or u
dented issues that typically cannot be made using esta
procedures. Such decisions usually are more difficult t
because they require judgment, intuition, knowledge, or
ence (Simon, 1960). The decision to award a grant to on
cant from a pool of very qualified grantseekers, for examp
nonprogrammed decision.

Decisions occur in one of three conditions, *certainty,*
uncertainty; these also lie on a continuum. Certainty and
tainty are *constructs* in that they do not exist in reality. In a tru
dition of certainty, a foundation would have all information
contingencies affecting a grantmaking decision, and thus
be certain (for example) which grantseeker most deserves a
But no foundation actually ever has all such informatio
grantseeker's proposal may have unexplained gaps, its resp
to questions may be less than forthright, or the foundatio
not conduct a very thorough evaluation of the project an
organization proposing it. In a true condition of uncertai
foundation would have no information about the applicant
therefore no idea which one most deserves a grant. Again, no
dation is likely to lack all such information; even the vag
grantseeker usually discloses some information. The most com
condition, then, is risk, where a foundation knows something
not everything about the grantseekers.

Programmed decisions are often made under condit
of certainty or risk, the easiest such decisions being made in

members of foundations are usually loosely coupled to the grantseekers and grantees, as they too are often from different educational or social backgrounds than those seeking money. Staff members are only marginally involved in the work of grantees; the two parties may never actually meet, their business transacted over the telephone or through the mail. If staff members are loosely coupled to grantseekers and grantees, the trustees of foundations are even more loosely coupled to them and even more likely to have different social, financial, or educational backgrounds than they do (Baldridge and others, 1984; Cohen and March, 1974, 1991; Weick, 1984).

When members of organizations with ambiguous goals have meetings, they sometimes attach issues they are concerned about to other items that have little if any actual connection. That is, they air their concerns by throwing them into "garbage cans"; Cohen and March describe this as feelings searching for places to be expressed, collections of choices looking for problems, and solutions seeking questions to which they might be the answer. For example, in discussing a grant request from an antipoverty group, one foundation trustee may voice concern about the decline of capitalism, another may lament the loss of the traditional value of hard work, and a staff member may interject feelings about human rights. Never mind that capitalism, hard work, and human rights are essentially unrelated to the proposal at hand; the proposal nonetheless may trigger such responses and the participants may seize the opportunity to air their concerns or recommendations, regardless of their relevance to the meeting. For them, the meeting is a garbage can beckoning them to throw their feelings into it.

Discussions of organizational goals in, for example, meetings about long-range planning in complex institutions are classic garbage cans, wide enough to accommodate almost any issue and deep enough to hold the concerns of many people. The first item on an agenda is an obvious garbage can because it receives much attention and status at a meeting; also, the participants have no doubt experienced the frustration of being unable to progress in other meetings because the first item on the agenda became a garbage can. Any item on an agenda, however, can be a garbage can if it sparks participants to raise concerns that are essentially unrelated to the meeting. To counteract this tendency, managers sometimes place the most important matters last on an agenda—after the dramatic monologues have been delivered, the enthusiasm for abstract argument has waned, and most of the garbage cans of individual concerns have been filled (Cohen and March, 1991).

Foundations and Decision Making

Decision making in foundations is difficult because grantmaking choices are overwhelmingly nonprogrammed and involve considerable risk or uncertainty. As virtually all grantseekers and grant projects are different from one another, choosing between them can rarely be accomplished by using the standard operating procedures that work for programmed decisions. This leaves foundation officers little to rely on but their personal preferences and foundations' typically ambiguous program interests. Uncertain foundation goals complicate decision making; "improving the condition of mankind" or "advancing the pursuit of truth" are difficult to articulate, let alone achieve. How can donors establish such ambiguous goals? How can trustees interpret them or articulate them as policy objectives? How can program officers create grantmaking programs to achieve such vague objectives? How can staff be expected to fulfill them, or grantseekers to develop projects that serve the proper ends, or anyone at all to evaluate such projects?

Program officers are expected to make wise decisions, but they must often do so based on the necessarily incomplete, often optimistic, and sometimes deceptive information that grantseekers submit. Foundations are vicarious, in a sense; they fulfill their goals through the work of other people or entities, without which they would essentially be pools of unused or poorly applied money. But because they rarely have a complete picture of the interests, intentions, and capabilities of grantseekers, they have to rely on what applicants tell them. Few foundations have the resources to investigate grantseekers or their claims completely and few grantseekers have the courage to be completely honest with foundations. Such circumstances damn foundations to a world of ambiguous goals, vague program interests, loosely coupled relationships, and partial information; confronted with such conditions, many choose to satisfice by funding only the safest and most conventional projects and organizations, trying to reduce if not eliminate the difficulty and ambiguity of making grants.

The Act of Grantmaking

As the central function of foundations, grantmaking is based on the assumptions that judicious funding decisions are possible and that foundations strive to make purposeful, not arbitrary, choices. Grantmaking is not the simplistic measuring of applications by rigid rules or standards, but a complex cultural understanding governed by powerful individual and organizational values. Grantmaking is an art, not a science, and its dimensions are not only intellectual, but aesthetic and moral as well. Grantmaking seeks to be objective, but cannot be wholly impartial because the values, biases, and idiosyncrasies of foundation donors, trustees, and staff members, as well as the attitudes of grantseekers, always influence grant decisions. Nor is grantmaking totally capricious; the process is almost always guided by decision criteria. These criteria are, however, often vague and rarely described publicly by the people of foundations (Barnard, 1938; Friedman, 1973; Odendahl and Boris, 1983).

Many trustees and staff members of foundations have commented on the nature of grantmaking and the special challenges it presents. Robert A. Mayer of the Ford Foundation referred to the "strange world" of giving money away (1972, p. 4); Frederick P. Keppel told the trustees of the Carnegie Corporation that the complexity of grantmaking forced him to "play by ear and proceed by hunch" (Carman and others, 1951, p. 58); and Richard Magat said that grantmaking can be "a rote process, a lottery, a congeries of guesswork, [or] a charade of whim" (1983a, p. 24). The subjectivity of grantmaking causes some foundation officers to attempt to approach their work with detachment, contending that grants should be made with the head, not the heart.

Andrew Carnegie was an early advocate of the enduring assumption that emotions alone are a poor basis for making decisions. Many foundations practice what William H. Allen in 1912 called *scientific charity,* an attempt to ensure that rationality guides grant decisions; this goal was espoused by John D. Rockefeller and his advisor on philanthropy, Frederick Gates, in addition to Carnegie (Whitaker, 1974). But grantmaking with the head alone is not much better than grantmaking only with the heart. To a great extent, foundations already have the coldness of institutionalization, so grantmaking with the head *and* the heart is needed, especially in this age of heartlessness in many of the nation's public and private organizations. During the rite of Baptism in the Episcopal Church, people pray that the child will become a person of "discerning heart," an idea that Alan Pifer, former president of the Carnegie Corporation, thinks would be a good model for grantmakers: objective yet empathetic, analytical yet compassionate (1984d). Foundation officers who practice the grantmaking of detachment try to eliminate all ambiguity from their decisions, progressively attempting to remove contingencies until they have relieved themselves of all burdens of judgment. This can turn them into little more than technicians who hide behind bureaucratic policies that make their grantmaking mechanical and routine.

Objectivity is important for grantmakers, but so too are compassion, humility, and selflessness because foundation officers need emotional as well as intellectual aptitude; they must be able to balance the passion of the moral self with the dispassion of the professional self, knowing when to exercise empathy and when to apply a selective apathy (Joseph, 1986b). Grantmaking requires a rare blend of idealism and skepticism, faith and cynicism, intuition and reason, all tempered with experience, preferably on both sides of the foundation desk. In describing the essential attributes of a good grantmaker, Robert Crane of the Joyce Mertz-Gilmore Foundation, winner of the 1995 Scrivner Award for creative grantmaking from the Council on Foundations, stresses the importance of compassion: "You have to be empathetic, understanding the situation of the people who are coming to you," some of whom are strong, some weak, some prima donnas, and some pitiful (Stehle, 1995b, p. 9).

Although compassion is important for grantmakers, the quality that people in foundations consider essential is *judgment,* an irreplaceable property, partly innate and partly the result of experience. Judgment, which Thoreau called "a genius for charity" (1983, p. 91), is rated higher than any other skill by the staff members of foundations, who speak of the necessary feel or touch, of the "elusive alchemy" of a good grantmaker (Curtis, 1988, p. 42). Grantmakers ask if large or small grants should be made or if safe or controversial projects should be supported. Should actors, writers, artists, or researchers get grants? Should health, science, welfare, or education be funded? Should grants go for operating support or special projects? For buildings, salaries, or endowment? To new or established organizations? For practical or esoteric purposes? For current or future needs? To radical or conservative people? To relieve suffering or to attack the causes of problems? For social change or the preservation of the social order? To empower the powerless or sustain the powerful? To schools, museums, hospitals, libraries, agencies, churches, civil rights groups, professional societies, advocacy organizations, clinics, day care centers, think tanks, parks, universities, or shelters for the homeless?

The Difficulty of Grantmaking

Philanthropists and philosophers have joined foundation officers in commenting on the difficulty of grantmaking. Prior to the Christian era, Aristotle said in words paraphrased by modern authors that to give money away is easy, but to decide to whom to give it and when, why, and how much is neither in every man's power nor an easy matter (Anderson, 1992; Macdonald, 1956). Carnegie was frustrated with what he called the "supremely difficult art" of grantmaking, confessing that he had not worked one-tenth as hard at making money as he had at giving it away. In 1906 he was so disheartened that he wrote, "You have no idea of the strain I've been under. Millionaires who laugh are very, very rare indeed"; in 1913 he added, "Pity the poor millionaire, for the way of the philanthropist is hard" (Wall, 1970, pp. 880–881; Carnegie, 1913). The Carnegie Foundation's Henry S. Pritchett (1922, p. 12) said that grantmakers "must sweat blood with gift money, if its effect is not to do more harm than good." Giving away money is a wearisome and complicated task, Dwight Macdonald candidly admitted, "vexing to the soul and wearing on the liver" (1956, p. 109).

Many foundation staff members complain that their work has a peculiar sense of unreality because its effectiveness is very difficult to evaluate. The work is so ambiguous that many foundation officers have trouble even describing what they do; "the necessary words," says Nielsen, "are not available" (1985, p. 419). A staff member of the Ford Foundation said that working there was like being in never-never land because there was no competition and no criticism: "You won't get fired if you fail," he said, "and anyway nobody could be sure that you were failing. No one ever got fired from a foundation for doing a bad job—only for sticking to a principle" (Macdonald, 1956, p. 124).

One reason that grantmaking is not conducive to evaluation is that grants to fields such as education, the social sciences, and the arts and humanities do not readily lend themselves to measurement. Foundations are removed from the natural flow of evaluative information that most other organizations receive from their customers or constituents, and some foundation staff are reluctant to engage in objective evaluation, satisfied instead with just enough assessment to reassure the occasional suspicious trustee or outside critic. "You never know what people think of your work," said a program officer of the Ford Foundation, "because no one will tell you with any frankness. Even the people you turn down won't criticize you to your face" (Macdonald, 1956, p. 125). Tirades against foundations are common, but applicants rarely display them as long as a grant, or another grant, seems possible. Foundations are the Santa Claus for adults; people make their lists and live in hope—and no one screams at Santa (Andrews, 1956; Cuninggim, 1972).

Unlike foundations, a business can use the market as a measure of its success; if people do not buy the business's product or service, the firm quickly knows it has gone wrong. Kenneth Boulding has called this phenomenon *Edsel's Law:* when the Ford Motor Company introduced the Edsel, it quickly discovered that demand for the auto was too low to continue production, and, responding immediately, withdrew it. But foundations have no such market, so if one were to produce an Edsel in the form of an unsuccessful grant, it might never hear from its "customers" because few grantees would dare admit that a grant had failed, lest they jeopardize receiving future grants. A flawed vision or the utter absence of vision could therefore go undetected and uncorrected until the money ran out. In what Boulding calls the "grants economy," reaction is usually slow, if it comes at all, and it rarely produces changes in behavior; so some foundations, happy in their ignorance, can continue making mistakes indefinitely (Boulding, 1970; 1973).

Another frustration of foundation officers is that they are usually involved only superficially in the work of their grantees. Foundation staff play an essential role in grantmaking, but they do not write the books, manage the organizations, create the art, or conduct the research that they pay for; they function therefore in the nebulous territory between the trustees and the grantseekers. "They are only workers in the vineyard," said Beardsley Ruml, former head of the Spelman Memorial Fund. "They don't plant the vines and they don't drink the wine" (Macdonald, 1956, p. 127). Foundation staff are surrounded by people from the same privileged social, educational, and professional background; there is almost no exchange of personnel between foundations and little new blood from outside their tight circle. Congress and the Internal Revenue Service have occasionally challenged their independence, but even these regulators have not posed a deadly threat, despite protests to the contrary by foundations. Foundation officers have a great deal more autonomy than do managers in most other organizations because they are not evaluated by voters, customers, patients, journalists, parishioners, audiences, or stockholders; for them, there is no bottom line, batting average, power rating, or return on investment by which their performance can be assessed.

Also, foundation staff rarely have honest relationships with applicants or grantees. When a person goes to work for a foundation, the frequent tease is, "Congratulations, you'll never have another bad lunch or hear another honest word." A foundation officer volunteered: "If you say something stupid at a cocktail party, people aren't going to say you're wrong. They'll bend with you. I've seen professors who have worked on a subject for years bring their proposal to a program officer who will usually make some inane suggestions. But the professor usually agrees, even if it means substantially shifting the focus of his work" (Branch, 1971, p. 16). Foundation staff are seldom on a person-to-person basis with grantseekers because they both create zones of protection around themselves. Foundations guard against giving undue encouragement lest grantseekers get the impression that grants are imminent; grantseekers are very good at picking up signals real or imagined from foundation staff, and quick to point out the happy coincidence that a foundation seems interested in doing the *very* thing they want to do. Grantseekers, too, always guard against saying something that might damage their prospects for getting grants.

An unexpected pleasure for new foundation officers is being the center of attention at gatherings where people take them aside to talk about projects, their advice accorded unaccustomed respect because they are surrounded by the aura of power that the wealth of a foundation creates. The reverence bestowed on foundation officers can produce a dangerous degree of arrogance as well as illusions of omniscience or omnipotence or both (Keppel, 1930), and it cannot be healthy psychologically for foundation people to have all their jokes laughed at and all their opinions immediately and completely agreed with. The power to make grants is corrupting, and it is a rare foundation officer who has never abused it: "We can say to the supplicant across the desk any outrageous thing, crack any terrible joke. He must nod sagely and laugh at the right places" (Miller, 1984, p. 19). In their defense, however, foundation staff often feel that everyone wants something from them. At a dinner party, Mr. and Mrs. H. Rowan Gaither, he the president of the Ford Foundation in the mid-1950s, were introduced as the *Gaitskills,* and they had a good time until the hostess discovered her error and reintroduced them, after which everyone began to pitch projects to them. "It's a nice job," the sardonic Robert M. Hutchins used to say when he was associate director of the Ford Foundation. "You meet so many *interested* people" (Goulden, 1971, pp. 85–86).

Another hazard of working in a foundation is having to reject many more proposals than can possibly be funded. Day after day, foundation managers listen to grantseekers talk endlessly about themselves and their projects, only to have to tell almost all of them that funds are not available or that their requests are "out of program." In a single morning, a program officer at one of the nation's twenty-five largest foundations rejected by phone, by letter, or in person all of the following (Goulden, 1971, pp. 85–86):

- An Ivy League college seeking a grant for a professorial chair that had been established years earlier by an alumnus but that was now without funds
- A college that wanted money for computers

- A university whose medical school would not be receiving an expected grant from the National Institutes of Health and wanted the foundation to replace the funds
- Requests from nine other organizations whose proposals did not match the foundation's program interests

Every day, foundation officers are reminded how badly things are going in organization after organization, and it is easy for them to become depressed, especially if they are idealists. Grantmaking places special burdens on the altruistic; its psychological costs include regret, self-doubt, and an enormous need to be liked. Keppel said that the world's woes can easily become an oppressive obsession for foundation officers, turning them into "altruists who are melancholy, reformers who are mournful, 'low-spirited humanitarians,' [and] saints who are spoil-sports instead of being 'happy warriors'" (Carman and others, 1951, p. 40). Another problem for them is that grantmaking can be a two-edged sword, sometimes doing enough damage to counteract the good it does. Grants for social programs, for example, can encourage dependence in the same people whom they try to make independent. People worthy of assistance, Carnegie said, seldom require it, and alms giving often does injure its recipients, especially if it rewards vice, intentionally or not. Carnegie believed it would be better if fortunes were thrown in the ocean rather than given in such a way as to encourage "the slothful, the drunken, the unworthy" (1983, p. 105). To foresee that a project will produce only its intended effect and not results contrary to its purpose, to be able to identify the real causes of problems, to distinguish between remedy and treatment or cause and effect—these skills require true genius. For what can be used as the basis for grantmaking? Common sense? The advice of friends? Experience? These are shifting sands. Can we turn to science to guide us? Is there a science of doing good? (Stephens, 1895; Todd, 1930).

Despite the claims of foundation officers about the difficulty of grantmaking, few others would agree that giving money away is tough. Most members of the public must think that grantmaking is a breeze; they believe it is just getting rid of money, and they have no trouble getting rid of theirs. But to people who doubt the difficulty of giving money away, Alan Pifer points out that managing a foundation is a huge responsibility, although he admits that it is one of the most agreeable ways to make a living and has no sympathy for foundation people who do not appreciate just how lucky they are, especially when the difficulties of their work are compared to the "agonies" of being a grantseeker (1984d, pp. 18–19).

Principles of Grantmaking

One of the most interesting questions about foundations is whether they use principles to guide their grantmaking decisions. It is surprisingly difficult to say because foundation officers seldom openly discuss the tenets they apply in grantmaking or commit them to writing for others to see, especially people outside foundations. With almost a hundred years of experience making grants, foundations might be expected to have developed a widely held set of such principles, but most of their judgments are based on the inclinations of their managers and a few maxims and traditional wisdom shared among foundation officers, all of which is "very soft stuff," according to Orville Brim (1973, pp. 217–218). Because so few foundation managers have talked publicly about the principles they apply in grantmaking, serious misconceptions exist about the grantmaking process. Some radical critics challenge even the most fundamental underpinning of foundation grantmaking, the principle of rationality, claiming that grantmaking is not at all purposeful, but a purely random process in which foundations, like slot machines, may or may not pay off depending on their erratic mechanical logic (Macdonald, 1956). This suggestion is not true, of course, but does have just enough credibility to make it appealing (and dangerous), as the testimony of one foundation trustee confirms:

> Well, we don't know much about what we're doing, but we sure have a nice time doing it. Every December the chairman invites all of us to dinner. We have a few drinks and a good meal and a lot of laughs. After dinner he tells us how much money we have to give away, and we all pitch in with ideas on who to give it to. I usually suggest my college. Somebody else will tell about his niece who is working for a charity. I've always liked the girl, so we include the charity. And of course somebody's wife is always on the board of something or other, so we include that. It doesn't take much time (Goulden, 1971, pp. 81–82).

Confronted with such capriciousness, many grantseekers have confessed to rolling and kneading their proposals to try to make them match the arbitrary interests of some foundations. But even if the grantmaking principles of foundations could be discovered, many grantseekers would still believe that they are far less influential than other factors such as friendship, family, business connections, or IOUs (Young and Moore, 1969).

An Early Grantmaking Philosophy

One of the earliest examples in the history of the development of grantmaking principles occurred in the Rockefeller Foundation during discussions between John D. Rockefeller, his advisor Frederick Gates, and the trustees of the foundation. Five months after the founding of the foundation in 1913, Jerome D. Greene, one of the original nine trustees of the foundation and the board's first secretary, presented a "Memorandum on Principles and Policies of Giving" to the board that had a profound effect on the philosophy of the foundation. Greene's memorandum established the grantmaking framework that the foundation followed, with relatively few exceptions, in subsequent years. Greene (1913, pp. 7–9) stated seven farsighted principles in his memorandum:

1. Individual charity and relief are excluded, except as the indirect result of aid given to other institutions well organized for such purposes.
2. Applications for the aid of institutions or enterprises that are purely local are excluded, except as aid may be given to these establishments as models to other localities and as part of a general plan for the encouragement or improvement of similar institutions . . . .
3. It may be said that when an individual or an institution goes into a community with the intention of making a contribution to its welfare, no gift of money, however large, and no outside agency, however wise or good, can render a service of unqualified good and permanent value except so far as the gift or the agency offers the means or the occasion for evoking from the community its own recognition of the need to be met, its own will to meet that need, and its own resources, both material and spiritual, wherewith to meet it.

4. In general, it is unwise for an institution like the Rockefeller Foundation to assume permanently or indefinitely a share of the current expenses of an institution which it does not control. Such a continuing relation inevitably carries with it a continuing responsibility for the conduct of the institution that is aided . . . and the implied continuing approval of management tends to make the receiver subservient to the giver, thus detracting from the receiver's independence and self-respect. . . . When giving to the support of institutions or movements for which the community, whether general or local, ought to make itself responsible, the Foundation will, as a rule, assume less than half of the cost of current expenditure.

5. On the other hand, the Rockefeller Foundation must carefully avoid the dangers incident to gifts in perpetuity. Having the qualities of permanence and universality it is better able than any private individual to adapt its gifts from generation to generation . . . to the most urgent needs of the time. It should therefore be careful not to hamper its own trustees or the trustees of other institutions by gifts in perpetuity narrowly limited to particular uses.

6. As between objects which are of an immediately remedial or alleviatory nature, such as asylums for the orphaned, blind, or crippled, and those which go to the root of individual or social ill-bearing and misery, the latter objects are preferred—not because the former are unworthy, but because the latter are more far-reaching in their effects. Moreover, there are many charitably disposed persons to whom remedial and alleviatory agencies make the more effective appeal.

7. As a general rule it is not expedient to entertain applications for the aid of projects, however meritorious, that have not been carefully thought out by their promoters, so that the purposes to be accomplished, the form or organization to be employed, the persons prepared to assume the permanent responsibility for the project, the precise programs to be followed and the amount of financial support already secured, may be stated with precision as to the basis of the application. . . .

Early in the Rockefeller Foundation's history, the trustees recognized that the foundation's limited funds, coupled with the vast

possibilities for their use, necessitated a choice between two policies: to engage in projects that were remedial or to try to find the
solution to human problems. The distinction seemed to the
trustees to be the difference between the less important and the
fundamental, between a policy of scattered activities and a policy
of concentration (Andrews, 1956). However, an original trustee of
the Rockefeller Foundation (who has gone unnamed) recommended his own imaginative philosophy for the new foundation:
"Our policy," he said, mindful of the foundation's enormous wealth
and the nation's considerable problems, "should be to have no policy" (Weaver, 1967, p. 114). The trustees of the Rockefeller Foundation split into two factions in its early days. The liberals wanted
the foundation to address criminology, alcoholism, drug addiction,
mental illness, venereal disease, family problems, income policy,
and juvenile delinquency. They were opposed by the conservatives,
led by Frederick Gates, who believed that the foundation should
deal with fewer issues and award a handful of large grants instead
of many small grants (Kohler, 1991).

These principles were bolstered by another idea from the early
days of the Rockefeller Foundation: the doctrine of concentration,
the notion that foundations should focus their grantmaking to
avoid what Gates, who was rarely unable to find the words to
describe one of his newly developed principles, derisively called
"the sin of scatteration." He explained scatteration as the difference between "wholesale" and "retail" giving. Carnegie scorned
this too; to a nervous applicant who estimated that his project
would cost as much as $5,000, Carnegie snapped, "I'm not in the
retail business" (Coon, 1938, p. 23). The trustees of the Rockefeller
Foundation agreed with Gates and chose to focus on a few large
problems, attacking their causes instead of their symptoms. But the
choice was not easy, and it remains difficult today because projects
that tackle problems at their core are always difficult to develop
and manage, and the temptation for foundations is to take the easy
road of treatment rather than the often long and winding road of
cure. Scatteration does not discriminate between the good and the
mediocre, but, like the rain, falls on the just and unjust alike. This
type of grantmaking is more of a drizzle than a good, solid farmer's
rain; with scatteration, it does not rain hard enough anywhere to
make anything grow (Macdonald, 1956).

Despite Gates's strong opposition to scatteration, Rockefeller's General Education Board, like many foundations then and now, was guilty of the practice; in the early years it made what it called "major grants" to forty-nine southern white colleges and twenty-eight Negro colleges, thus covering with a philanthropic sprinkling almost all the institutions in that region. In the same year, the board made 137 other grants that ranged from a high of just $4,100 to a low of $300 (Embree, 1949, p. 30). Even today many foundations spread their grants across multiple fields; undoubtedly Gates would label this practice scatteration, just as Nielsen has called it "cafeteria philanthropy, a little something for everybody" (Bailey, 1992, p. 6).

A West Coast millionaire, whose generosity must be admired even as the rationality of his giving is questioned, provided a modern example of scatteration when he told Odendahl: "I give to the ballet, the opera, the symphony. I give to hospitals. I give to universities. . . . We give to everything" (1990, p. 16). Adopting the principle of concentration, not scatteration, the Rockefeller Foundation for years placed the following notice in its annual report: "The Rockefeller Foundation does not make gifts or loans to individuals, or finance patents or altruistic movements involving private profit, or contribute to the building or maintenance of churches, hospitals, or other local institutions, or support campaigns to influence public opinion on any social or political questions, no matter how disinterested these questions may be" (Coon, 1938, p. 52). The foundation also endorsed a policy of building on strength rather than weakness. "Make the peaks higher," Wickliffe Rose, an original trustee of the foundation, used to urge, so that grants from the foundation would go only to first-class institutions, and, in theory, the positive effect of these awards would spread so that the influence of a Johns Hopkins University or a University of Chicago would reach every college and university (Fosdick, 1952, pp. 100, 296).

Frederick Gates became associated with Rockefeller in 1892 and quickly realized that Rockefeller, like many rich and powerful people, had few advisors with the courage to tell him exactly what they thought. Gates had an eloquence that could be passionate; Rockefeller, when he spoke at all, did so in slow, measured terms without raising his voice and without gestures (Fosdick, 1952). Gates, whom Rockefeller himself described as "the guiding genius in all our giving," quickly introduced what he called *scientific giving* to Rockefeller's philanthropy, borrowing perhaps from the principles of scientific management developed at the same time by Frederick Winslow Taylor, father of American management. To illustrate his idea of scientific giving, Gates told the story of how Rockefeller had been responding to hundreds of appeals from individuals, including many Baptist missionaries all over the world, sending each a small contribution. Gates recommended that Rockefeller stop making donations to individuals; he used the Baptist missionaries as an example, referring each of them to their headquarters in Boston to which Rockefeller, a devout Baptist, then gave not thousands of dollars as before, but hundreds of thousands (Fosdick, 1952, p. 7).

A shrewd administrator, gifted with a remarkable feel for the ways of the world and its most worldly inhabitants, Gates was educated as a Baptist minister and was painfully sensitive about his role as gatekeeper of Rockefeller's fortune. Before he began working for Rockefeller, Gates said that he had known "only pleasant acquaintances, delightful companionships, (and) intimate friendships," but after becoming Rockefeller's advisor, he soon learned that whoever guarded Rockefeller's fortune and investigated appeals to him would be "surveyed with no friendly eye," especially because Gates found many of Rockefeller's habitual charities to be worthless and practically fraudulent (Gates, 1977, pp. 160–161). Gates was fond of maintaining a philosophical discourse with Rockefeller through letters (even though Rockefeller rarely wrote back), and after 15 years of working for Rockefeller, Gates wrote him a letter in which he proposed that Rockefeller create six permanent philanthropies:

- A fund to promote a system of higher education in the United States
- A fund to promote medical research throughout the world
- A fund to promote the fine arts and refinement of taste in the United States
- A fund to promote scientific agriculture and the enrichment of rural life in the United States

- A fund to promote Christian ethics and Christian civilization throughout the world
- A fund to promote intelligent citizenship and civic virtue in the United States

According to Gates, the foundations should be large enough to attract the attention of the world; nothing less, he wrote to Rockefeller, "would befit the vastness of your fortune and the universality of its sources" (1977, pp. 208–209). Rockefeller, too, struggled to define a philosophy to guide his philanthropy. The best philanthropy, he decided, is a search for finalities, an attempt to cure evils at their source (Rockefeller, 1933, p. 177); to this end, he identified six priorities:

- Progress in the Means of Subsistence
- Progress in Government and Law
- Progress in Literature and Language
- Progress in Science and Philosophy
- Progress in Art and Refinement
- Progress in Morality and Religion

Rockefeller developed these six ideas twenty-eight years after Gates proposed that he establish the great corporate charities, and three of them are identical or very similar to the six objectives Gates had suggested in 1905: art and refinement, morality and religion, and government and law.

Other Prominent Grantmaking Philosophies

Like Rockefeller, many other early philanthropists and their advisors sought to develop principles to guide their charity. Andrew Carnegie struggled to define a philosophy to direct the distribution of the $300 million he would give away in his lifetime and, with the help of only one secretary, searched tirelessly for worthy causes. Unlike Rockefeller, though, Carnegie did not rely on an advisor such as Frederick Gates, but immersed himself in ideas on the distribution of wealth. According to Carnegie, there were but three such methods: first, wealth could be left to the family of the decedent; second, wealth could be bequeathed for public purposes; and, third, wealth could be given away by its owner during his lifetime. Carnegie did not like the first method because he did not believe that people should leave their money to their children. "If this is done from affection, is it not misguided affection?" he asked. "I would as soon leave to my son a curse as the almighty dollar." The second method, leaving wealth for public purposes, Carnegie said is merely a way to dispose of wealth, and he believed that people who left their money this way "would not have left it at all had they been able to take it with them." Thus the third method was Carnegie's choice: dispensing wealth during a donor's life, considering wealth a trust for the people of a community, doing for them better than they could do for themselves because of the philanthropist's superior experience. The man who dies leaving behind millions of dollars will pass away unhonored, Carnegie said. "Of such as these, the public verdict will then be: 'The man who dies rich dies thus disgraced.' Such is the true gospel concerning wealth" (1983, pp. 101, 106).

Henry Ford's philosophy of philanthropy was the "wholesome, saving power of work," an idea based on two principles that he applied first in his company: money was not to be used to solve a problem that could be solved by work, and no project was to be undertaken that would not become self-supporting. "The track itself should be fixed," said Ford. "Charity and philanthropy are the repair shops and their efficiency, however high, does not remove the cause of human wrecks" (Whitaker, 1974, p. 60). Ford believed that the best thing money could do was to create work for people. He once told a vagrant at the gate of his company, "You go to the employment office, tell them that I sent you there, and that they are to give you a job. . . . If you would prefer work to begging, you are going to have your chance" (Marquis, 1923, pp. 38–40, 94). The inscription "Chop Your Own Wood and It Will Warm You Twice" appears over one of the great open fireplaces in Ford's Dearborn, Michigan house. Ford hated charity and all it stood for; he paid people generously, but only for work, not for seeking alms. Samuel S. Marquis, his executive assistant, once heard him say that the only man on whom he bestowed charity was ruined by it; the amount involved was about $17 (p. 108).

At the Russell Sage Foundation, one of the nation's oldest foundations, two grantmaking principles were fundamental from its outset in 1907: funds should be given only to projects that promise good returns and only if they could not be funded by other sources. At a meeting of the foundation board on May 10, 1907, Robert W. de Forest, counselor on philanthropy to Mrs. Olivia Sage, wife of the deceased donor, suggested that three areas should be declared beyond the scope of the foundation. First, the foundation should not attempt to relieve the financial needs of individuals or families; to do so would use funds that should be applied to eradicating the *causes* of poverty. Second, the foundation should not support colleges and universities because the board believed that higher education was sufficiently funded by other agencies; however, elementary education was exempted from this restriction. Third, the foundation should not support "churches for church purposes" (Glenn, Brandt, and Andrews, 1947, p. 26; Russell Sage Foundation, 1907). A meeting of the trustees of the foundation was called in November 1931 to discuss whether the foundation should make grants to alleviate problems caused by the Depression. A memorandum presented the arguments on both sides of the issue, and a telephone call brought last-minute word that another foundation was curtailing its regular programs in favor of supporting the New York Emergency Unemployment Relief Committee, formed to provide aid to people victimized by the Depression. After extensive discussion, a resolution was presented and passed: "Resolved, that the policy of the Russell Sage Foundation in the present emergency, as always, is in its permanent contribution to the improvement of living and social conditions by its studies and its wide co-operation with agencies, rather than by contributing directly to relief. Therefore, be it resolved that the Russell Sage Foundation make no contribution to the Emergency Relief Committee" (Glenn, Brandt, and Andrews, 1947, p. 489).

Julius Rosenwald, founder of Sears, Roebuck and the Rosenwald Fund, was emphatically opposed to establishing foundations in perpetuity and believed that a foundation should end with the life of the donor or, at most, one generation thereafter. Rosenwald thought that to establish foundations in perpetuity implied a lack of confidence in the future, "which I do not share," he said, and that injecting the fortunes of one period into another time five hundred or a thousand years later was inappropriate (1929, p. 12). Carnegie felt the same way, although he did not restrict his foundations to the length of his life. "No man of vision will seek to tie the endowment which he gives to a fixed cause," said Carnegie, recommending that the donor leave to the judgment of the trustees the question of changing the mission of a foundation to meet the requirements of the time and that "they shall best conform to my wishes by using their judgment" (Pifer, 1984a, p. 202).

F. Emerson Andrews suggested that foundations could spend their money in a hierarchy of three ways. First, at the lowest level in the scale, they could make grants to help people *in trouble*, for example, if a person lost his job, a foundation could award a grant to replace his lost income. Second, foundations could make grants to help people get *out of trouble* by supporting the rehabilitation of a person who suffered an accident. Third, foundations could make grants to help people *avoid trouble* by funding efforts aimed at prevention. In his speeches, Andrews (1973, pp. 113–114) often cited five principles of grantmaking that many foundations espouse today:

- Give adequately, but not lavishly; give in ways that stimulate giving from others.
- Give toward rehabilitation rather than relief, toward cure rather than treatment; still better, give toward prevention.
- Give toward research and discovery, especially the discovery of the conditions of health and well-being.
- Give so that the gift will not confirm a feeling of inadequacy, but stimulate the recipient to help himself.
- Finally, give thought, for with thoughtful giving, even small grants may accomplish great purposes.

The Council on Foundations encourages foundations to establish principles of grantmaking and policies that define their interests and objectives. According to the Council, grantmaking principles should provide a framework for stable practice, afford the public a view of the ethical and philosophical values on which grantmaking is based, and give foundations a symbol with which to understand what is fundamental when deciding on priorities, choosing among grantseekers, and committing resources in the public interest (Council on Foundations, 1980, 1984; Joseph, 1986a). Many of the nation's earliest grantmaking philosophies were developed by businessmen who were committed to rationality and efficiency in their businesses and their foundations. They saw no reason that their charitable work should be managed any differently than their businesses, and they believed that the principles that had served them well in making money would likewise guide them in giving money away. These men were filled with the scientific ideas of their age, which held that there is a difference between cure and symptoms and that merely treating the signs of illiteracy and unemployment, for example, is inefficient. Eradicating the *causes* of social problems was their objective and that of their foundations.

The Criterion of Realism

Foundations must judge many factors during grantmaking, but two of the most important are the realism of a grantseeker and the feasibility of a proposed project. Judging these begins with questioning whether a program matches a foundation's interests and its other geographic or financial restrictions, but includes an assessment of the proposal's format, the adequacy of its budget, and the achievability of its goals. Foundations equate the realism of a project with the realism of the people proposing it, so a poorly conceived or impractical project often is considered to reflect similar shortcomings in its proposers.

The assets of foundations may appear unlimited, but they are quite small compared to the demands on them. A fundamental policy of foundations, therefore, is to limit their interests, and hence their grantmaking, to certain types of projects or organizations. These priorities are called *program interests* and are established by the donors or trustees of foundations, and grantseekers must meet these criteria as the first step in the grantmaking process.

Program interests can range from a single purpose such as scholarships to multiple purposes such as health care, higher education, and rural development, which are among the interests of the Kellogg Foundation, for example. A foundation may also restrict grants to certain types of projects within its program interests; if education is the program interest, it may make grants only to higher-education institutions, not elementary or secondary schools. Another may fund higher-education institutions, but only private ones. Many foundations further limit their grants to certain states, cities, or communities. Others restrict their grants to specific periods of time, such as one or two years; to certain populations, such as children, the handicapped, or the elderly; or to certain amounts of money, from a few hundred dollars for a project in a small town to multiple millions for an international project.

Foundations are reluctant to make grants for programs that can be financed from a grantseeker's regular budget or by individual donors or government agencies. Many prefer projects that promise significant advances for an entire discipline, not just one organization; this is why some foundations will not make grants toward the operation of colleges and universities, but will fund pathfinding research within them. For every such rule in foundations, however, there are exceptions, and any foundation convinced of the need can make a grant to almost any organization for virtually any purpose even though it may be "out of program."

To compete for a grant, a grantseeker must meticulously delineate how a project matches a foundation's program interests. Questions about that will be first in the mind of foundation officers examining an application. They will also ask: Is the purpose of the project clear? Is the need for it justified? Is the applicant competent to do the proposed work? Is the project well designed to accomplish its goal? Is the time right for the project? Are the proposed facilities sufficient? Are funds available from other sources? Does the project make sense? Is it necessary? (Jacquette and Jacquette, 1973; Mayer, 1972; Townsend, 1974). Many grantseekers send applications to foundations that have no interest in supporting their work, according to a survey by the National Society of Fund Raising Executives. According to almost half the forty foundations that participated in the survey, the first step grantseekers should take is to read foundation application guidelines carefully to be sure that they understand what a foundation is willing to fund. "We get dozens of proposals from organizations that clearly never did a lick of homework, and waste our time and the precious funds of their members sending out hopeless proposals to the wrong funders," said Martin Teitel, executive director of the C.S. Fund in Freestone, California. "I often wonder if these same people try to buy their groceries in the hardware store" (Dundjerski, 1996a, p. 26).

One of the most important factors that foundations assess during grantmaking is the feasibility of grant projects. Ted Townsend of the University of Pennsylvania surveyed one hundred foundations and government funding sources and found that the feasibility of a proposed project is one of five criteria that they consider absolutely important. The others are the purpose of the project, need for the project, competence of the applicant, and accountability of the applicant. Respondents to Townsend's survey defined the feasibility of a grant project as "having enough manpower, money and materials to do the job" and "whether method A can reasonably be expected to achieve intended result B" (Townsend, 1974, pp. 33–34). In judging feasibility, foundations look for a good idea and a practical plan, trying to distinguish between substantive and superficial projects, between those that are articulately written but lack depth, and between those that have merit but suffer major defects. Foundations must also separate applicants who write slick proposals but probably cannot deliver on them from those with good ideas but who are not good at writing proposals (Allen, 1965; James, 1973).

Foundations receive appeals from every conceivable kind of organization, and many of the proposed projects are unrealistic—even humorously so. Foundations have received proposals to melt the polar ice caps and use the runoff to irrigate Death Valley, the Sinai Peninsula, and the Sahara, the latter effort estimated by its proponents to cost $500 million, exactly what newspapers reported the assets of the Ford Foundation to have been when the proposal was submitted. People have sought grants to plant a mile-wide flower bed along the Suez Canal and to promote singing among sailors at naval training stations (Harrison and Andrews, 1946). Foundations have been targets of explorers who wanted to capture the Abominable Snowman, students who thought society would benefit if they completed another year of graduate school, writers only a few thousand words (and dollars) away from finishing the Great American Novel, and soon-to-be-released convicts who asked for grants to prove that comfortable means could suppress their criminal instincts. The Ford Foundation once gave grants to five universities for self-studies, and the main conclusion of the analyses was that each school needed more foundation grants (Whitaker, 1974). A man from Michigan who applied to the Carnegie Corporation said that he was in touch with many spirits from beyond, one of whom was Andrew Carnegie, who endorsed his request, and an even bolder grantseeker told the Carnegie Corporation that he *was* Carnegie and sent his love to everyone at the corporation: "It seems I have been in the fires of purgation for aeons," he commented (Whitaker, 1974, p. 70).

Happily discovering that the Ford Foundation supported programs for world peace, a grantseeker asked the foundation to paint his father's living room yellow so the old man could have peace (Andrews, 1956, pp. 172, 179). A California swindler, arrested for passing bad checks, told the police that he had spent the money to buy uniforms for a boys' football team and expected to be reimbursed soon by the Ford Foundation.

Frivolous or funny requests are legion, but are at least preferable to the ominous: one such request involved flood prevention by killing cats, the idea being that cats kill birds, which can then no longer eat enough harmful insects, which in turn multiply and devour trees, and the treeless hills permit disastrous floods that erode land, destroy cities, and threaten civilization. Politics add another dimension to the ominous. *Pravda* once editorialized that the real business of the Ford Foundation is sending spies, murderers, and saboteurs to Eastern Europe, and the Czechoslovakian Home Service Radio claimed that the purpose of the foundation was to support United States espionage agents (Macdonald, 1956).

To be sure, foundations sometimes appeal to the lunatic fringe, people seeking to invent perpetual motion machines or abolish poverty with a stroke and whose proposals are "often hand-lettered in two colors—and occasionally full four-color jobs with arrows, mottos, flying objects, and exclamation points" (Brim, 1973, p. 218; Goulden, 1971, pp. 91–92). People have asked foundations for money for divorces and to pay their income taxes, and one petitioner sought a grant to implement a new system of economics that would replace not only all economies, but also all religions. Another claimed that sun spots were the primary cause of economic cycles; to offset such trends, the grantseeker wanted to create a magnetic band around the earth to short circuit the sun's rays (Andrews, 1973).

People who submit such proposals are earnest, difficult to shake off, and occasionally right. Galileo would almost certainly have been in this category, with his wacky idea of the earth moving around the sun. "Sometimes I wonder if we give enough attention to the really kooky ones," a foundation officer confessed. "What would we have done . . . had a sailor walked in here five centuries ago and asked for money to make a voyage to prove the world is round?" (Andrews, 1956, p. 177). Directors of research projects funded by grants have been compared to Christopher Columbus, who set sail for America not knowing where he was going, arrived not knowing where he was, and returned not knowing where he had been, all at someone else's expense (Whitaker, 1974). But another foundation officer doubted if the explorer would have been rejected out of hand: "We would probably have financed a university study to survey all available evidence on whether the world could be round—and then turned him down, for his idea was contrary to existing knowledge" (Goulden, 1971, p. 94–95).

Dwight Macdonald, who defined the Ford Foundation as "a large body of money surrounded on all sides by people who want some," said that when the foundation relocated to New York, the entertainment quality of the proposals it received declined precipitously. "We don't get the kind we used to in Pasadena," he lamented, where the foundation's staff used to call their headquarters "Itching Palms" (Whitaker, 1974, p. 197).

All foundations, especially well-known ones, receive a bombardment of applications by mail, telephone, or personal contact. In 1909, for example, a British syrup manufacturer sponsored a contest for ideas on how Carnegie should give his money away, and of the forty-five thousand suggestions received, the largest category (more than 27 percent) was individuals begging on their own behalf (Whitaker, 1974). Requests to the Rockefeller Foundation in its early days came in multitudes from all over the world, many asking for small amounts of money that, the grantseekers almost always pointed out, John D. Rockefeller would never miss. Frederick Gates once counted the requests for a month, recording fifteen thousand the first week and more than fifty thousand for the month (Gates, 1977; Whitaker, 1974).

People who submit such appeals usually have a poor understanding of foundations, and the format of their proposals, which ranges from mimeographed mass-mailed letters to gold-embossed brochures with expensive art work, often tips their hand. Proposals with fancy paper, printing, or binding do not impress many foundations, especially when these fancily garbed applications attempt to disguise projects with unrealistic goals, padded budgets, or weak justifications. Despite this caveat, one grantseeker reported great success, mostly among family foundations, with thirty specially-printed proposals in gold-embossed imitation leather covers at a cost of over $1,000 (Quay, 1952).

In addition to judging the feasibility of grant projects, foundations must assess the achievability of the projects' goals. They seem to disagree about these, however. One respondent to Townsend's survey, whose view represents that of many other respondents, said that he usually accepts the goal of a grant project "whether or not it can be achieved," but another told Townsend that he tends to discount project goals because they are "usually set too high" (Townsend, 1974, p. 34). Explaining these conflicting views, Townsend says that foundations and government grantors appear to be willing to support projects even though their goals seem only partially achievable. "Not all things worthwhile necessarily lend themselves to measurement," said one respondent. An officer of a government agency, though, said that if a proposal does not contain a plan to evaluate goal achievement, he considers the application incomplete. But in Townsend's survey, the feasibility of goals fell only about midway in importance among twenty grantmaking criteria identified by foundation and government grantors (Townsend, 1974, pp. 34–36).

Robert M. Johnson, former president of the Wieboldt Foundation, saw that many applicants had such a poor understanding of foundations that he created a fictitious course, session three of which, entitled "Coping with the Pressures of Goals," discusses the different perceptions of goals by foundations and grantseekers. Johnson's course teaches applicants to anticipate that some foundation people live in and for the future and are enamored with goals, unable to respond meaningfully to projects when they become a reality. At the same time, grantseekers are urged to depart from the "Mr. Fixit Syndrome" in which they pledge to solve every part of a problem, and some foundations readily accept the offer (Johnson, 1975a, p. 14).

The realism of project budgets is another factor that foundations judge during grantmaking. They look for budgets that are adequate but not wasteful, assessing the competence and trustworthiness of an applicant's financial personnel, the reliability of its financial systems, and the strength of its financial position as illustrated by financial statements. Such statements may also disclose administrative competence; managerial incompetence is usually reflected in financial mismanagement. Financial statements often reveal if an applicant has depended on only one or two funding sources or on many sources, the latter normally indicating wider interest in the organization and its programs. Financial support from many sources usually means less financial volatility for the applicant and less risk for a foundation. Financial statements may also show reserves so large that a foundation may decide that a grant is simply not needed. Among the questions asked by a foundation about an applicant's finances are these: Does the organization have a budget? What are the applicant's major expenditures and relative percentages for program and administrative areas? How do actual expenditures compare to line items in the budget? Do adequate internal controls exist? Are there reliable reporting systems? Do any of the organization's trustees have a financial background? (Goodwin, 1976, p. 32). F. Lee and Barbara Jacquette, he of the Carnegie Foundation for the Advancement of Teaching and she of the Foundation for Child Development, studied the grantmaking criteria of foundations and found that a *realistic financing plan* and *soundness of the budget* are two of the most important factors. According to the Jacquettes, foundations look for budgets that include projected revenue and expenses in generally accepted categories such as salaries, benefits, rent, supplies, equipment, and utilities. A perplexing problem for grantseekers is whether to pad budgets by requesting more money than is needed on the assumption that foundations may cut budgets by some amount or percentage. Foundation managers can usually recognize padding, so they do not recommend this practice. Instead, they prefer budgets that estimate expenditures realistically, asking for neither too much nor too little money because either tactic shows poor management and reflects poorly on the budget, the grant project, and the grantseeker (DeBakey, 1977; Jacquette and Jacquette, 1973; Lefferts, 1990).

The Criterion of Competence

The second major factor that foundations judge is the ability of grantseekers to do the work they propose. Many consider the competence of applicants to be the single most important grantmaking criterion. One reason is that success often depends less on the design of a plan than on the competence of the people who do the work. Competence was one of five factors that Townsend's survey rated as "very much" to "absolutely" important in grant decisions (Townsend, 1974, p. 33); Lindsley F. Kimball of the Rockefeller Foundation identified twelve criteria that foundations apply in grantmaking, foremost being the persons to be involved. This tenet was the basis for the Rockefeller Foundation's Fellows Program, which searched worldwide for the ablest people it could support; every Rockefeller Fellow was handpicked, and among the 10,000 fellowships awarded over the years were thirty Nobel laureates and leaders in every field (Kimball, 1974).

F. Lee and Barbara Jacquette report that foundations expect proposals to be explicit about the positions, duties, education, and experience of project staff. Foundations use several methods to evaluate the competence of grantseekers, including the opinions of foundation trustees and staff and outside reviewers, and many applicants fail to show that they understand the problems they seek to address or have sufficient competence to carry out the projects they propose. This suggests that the part of proposals that describes the capabilities of the people to be involved, not the budget section, often creates the most trouble for applicants (Lefferts, 1990).

Much of grantmaking consists of sizing up people, essentially betting on a person to do a job. The most ancient and useful rule of foundations, said John Gardner, president of the Carnegie Corporation from 1955 to 1965, is to "find the good men and back them"; competent people can perform well even though their plans may be faulty, but the best plans cannot ensure success if the people involved are incompetent. Not surprisingly, therefore, foundation officers confess that most of their mistakes are due to errors in judgment about the promise of people and organizations, not plans or goals. One problem with assessing competence is evaluating people who have promise but little experience or reputation. First, inexperienced people are often less predictable and therefore more prone to controversy, which is anathema to many foundations; second, people without a reputation are sometimes more prone to failure, if only because they lack the credibility to *declare* their projects a success. "I see it every day," said a staff member of the Ford Foundation. "If a dean calls up from the University of Kansas, he is lucky to get listened to at all. [But if a dean from Harvard calls], you unconsciously respond more. . . . I do it myself, even though I promise not to" (Branch, 1971, p. 14). To assess inexperienced people, foundations often seek the advice of grantees, trustees, members of advisory boards, editors, and professors.

Americans have had great faith in the power of money to solve problems, but experience has taught some bitter lessons about the limitations of throwing money at problems. Money does not do research, create paintings, teach students, cure diseases, write music, produce plays, or care for the elderly. Money is no substitute for competence; the major difficulty in foundation grantmaking is not so much a lack of money but a shortage of people with the drive to accomplish goals. This policy can be risky, however. When an individual is essential to a project, that person's participation often determines its life span. But change often comes from one person, so, according to David Rockefeller, foundations have to be willing to take risks to identify such people (1973). Mediocrity cannot be transformed merely by money, but many people persist in the belief that money makes the difference and that enough money can correct any problem. Money is enabling, but only people produce (Embree, 1930; Kimball, 1974).

Implications for Grantseekers of Foundations as Judges

The inescapable reality of foundations, their very context, is the necessity of deciding between competing grantseekers. Grant decisions are implicitly uncertain, and foundations are always seeking information that may bring some measure of objectivity, however small, to the subjectivity of their task. Program interests can reduce some of the uncertainty, but they usually are too general to add much objectivity. Grantseekers should expect impersonal treatment from foundations because the subjectivity of grantmaking causes some program officers to approach their task with detachment. Standard operating procedures are not especially adaptable or useful in grantmaking, so foundations have little alternative but to rely on their own judgment, certain of its uncertainty.

Like all organizations, foundations are fallible in their judgment, so it is possible that some grant proposals may be rejected for all the wrong reasons, unhappy grantseekers understandably claiming in response that little or no rationality was exercised. Grantmaking is art, not science, and sometimes the art is high and sometimes it is low. Although grantseekers are entitled to complain about illogical decision making in foundations, few should be eager to trade places with them; giving money away wisely is very difficult, and though it may lack the intensity of raising money, the task has its own unique challenges. Grantmaking is not a lottery or a slot machine, and although a few foundations are capricious, most apply little-known and seldom-articulated principles when making grants, six of the most important of which follow:

- Foundations expect grantseekers to interpret their program interests conservatively and to meticulously delineate exactly how projects match the priorities of foundations; many grantseekers show a complete disregard or ignorance of program interests.
- Grants for local projects are best sought from community foundations or family foundations prominent in a locality. Nonetheless, many inexperienced grantseekers turn to national foundations for small grants with the mistaken impression that "they will never miss the money"; such foundations almost always reject small projects because they are too limited in scope or too tied to a single institution to have much adaptability.
- The feasibility of a grant project is extremely important because the feet of most foundation donors and trustees are planted firmly on the ground. Offbeat, impractical, or poorly conceived undertakings are unlikely to get foundation grants,

despite all that has been said about them supporting maverick
people and organizations.

- Foundations assert that projects depend on the competence
  of the people to be involved because grantmaking is a bet that
  people can do what they say they can do, and the design of a
  project alone hardly guarantees success. Neither does money,
  which is merely enabling; only people produce.

- Foundations are reluctant to make grants for palliative purposes because they prefer to try to cure evils at their source.
  For example, foundations prefer to eradicate the causes of
  poverty instead of giving money to beggars, believing that
  it is better to cure a disease than to treat its patients.

- Foundations expect grantseekers to help themselves, especially by raising money from other sources; few respond
  positively to pleas such as, "If you do not give us the grant, we
  will go out of existence." Grants can encourage dependence,
  and most foundations deplore making people or organizations dependent. Nor are foundations interested in being
  shackled to the same grantees year after year; long-term
  grants may constrain initiative and impede response to
  other compelling causes.

Recommendations to Foundations as Judges

Foundations should try to resist applying rigid measures to evaluate grant proposals in an attempt to remove some or all of the subjectivity from their decisions. They therefore already have the
coldness of bureaucracy; they face the depersonalization of foundation philanthropy, a process dependent on *written* documents
with little or no personal contact between foundations and applicants. Eliminating the personal touch in philanthropy and replac-
ing it with what has been called scientific charity are inappropriate
because mechanistic grantmaking is inconsistent with the concept
of partnership between grantmaker and grantseeker.

Foundations should periodically reassess their missions and
program interests, examine the successes and failures of their
grants, and consider new directions that may better serve the intentions of their donors, the preferences of their trustees, the capabilities of their staff, and the needs of their communities. More

evaluation of the effectiveness of grantmaking is needed by people inside and outside foundations. Foundation trustees should insist that evaluation be a part of grantmaking, just as foundations require that evaluation be a component of the projects they fund. Many foundation staff are removed from the problems of their grantees, and many grantseekers have almost no idea of what it is like to be a foundation. More interaction between these parties is recommended. Foundations should also communicate more with each other, and younger foundations should establish a mentor relationship with older foundations to benefit from their experience.

Principles of grantmaking are an indication that a foundation has thought rationally about the best use of its funds. Illogical, random, or capricious grantmaking serves no one's interests—neither those of the donors, trustees, and staff nor those of their grantees. Scatteration, spreading grants over a multitude of purposes and organizations rather than concentrating on one or two problems, is not particularly effective even in small foundations; more foundations should concentrate their grantmaking. Concentration allows trustees and staff to become expert in an area and to identify the best people, strategies, and organizations in that arena. "A thousand points of light" is a charming idea, but an intense beam is much more effective. Foundations should increase their support of research on themselves and other nonprofit organizations in philanthropy. They should also fund the education of development officers and the organizations that provide such training to help increase the professionalism of this occupation and to raise the level of understanding of foundations among people in nonprofits.

Chapter Three

Foundations as Editors
How the Quality of Writing Affects Grant Proposals

*"When I use a word," Humpty Dumpty said, in
rather a scornful tone, "it means just what I choose
it to mean—neither more nor less."
"The question is," said Alice, "whether you can make
words mean so many different things."*
LEWIS CARROLL, *THROUGH THE LOOKING-GLASS*
(1982, P. 136)

Publishing houses have editors who evaluate the quality of manuscripts as a major indication of their potential for publication, linking the caliber of the author with the quality of the writing. Likewise, foundations evaluate the clarity of grant proposal writing as an indication of grantseeker quality.

The Metaphor of Foundations as Editors

Foundations and editors perform similar functions, one of the most important being to determine the clarity and readability of other people's writing. Editors are essential in publishing, especially acquisitions editors, who acquire the manuscripts that become books. Such editors serve as intermediaries between publishers and authors, oversee copy writing and editing, advise on advertising and promotion, and monitor the production of books from the initial stages of copy editing and typesetting to the final steps of printing and binding.

Editors must stay current with the leading scholars and lines of research in their fields. They talk with professors, researchers, representatives of scholarly associations, and editors at other publishing houses about authors and ideas for books. They establish relations with reviewers who help them evaluate the quality of manuscripts, and they keep in touch with authors whose books they have published. Editors are always looking to the future, trying to identify the next good author and the next important book. They need a broad intellect and good judgment because editing involves trusting one's instincts. "You read something and have a strong feeling that this is bad, he missed something here, [or] you disliked this," said one editor, who explained his job as giving authors his objective opinion, much like a therapist (Powell, 1985, pp. 72, 87).

Foundations determine which few of the many grant requests will be funded; in this they have much in common with editors. Editors determine if manuscripts are well written, evaluating their content and organization, checking their logic, and looking for concise presentation of ideas. In judging the clarity of a manuscript, editors evaluate the quality of its author, linking clarity of expression in the manuscript with clarity of thinking by the author. They assume that a well organized manuscript indicates a well organized author. Foundations go through the same process with grant proposals. Just as editors may judge the quality of authors by the clarity of their writing, so may foundations judge grantseekers by the clarity of their proposals. For editor or foundation, the decision-making process can take months, or a snap judgment may be made in seconds. Unsolicited manuscripts and unsolicited proposals are the most frequently received but get the least attention; well-known authors and well-known grantseekers get the most. Authors and editors, like foundations and grantseekers, are often mutually contemptuous; they may question each other's competence, sincerity, loyalty, even integrity. Yet they are mutually dependent as well, for one could not exist without the other.

In either case, serendipity is a factor. Poorly written books may still be accepted for publication and poorly written grant proposals funded. A bad book might sell well while a good one goes unread; an apparently sensible project may be funded but fail, while one that seemed doomed to all but those who proposed and paid for it succeeds wildly. For those who hope to sell a book or get a grant, however, serendipity is a poor substitute for clear logic, structure, and writing.

Grant Proposals and the Importance of Clarity

The earliest description of a grant proposal that I have found is from a fourteenth-century administrative handbook. Even then, fund-raising by the written word was so important that one educational organization conducted what today would be called a course in writing grant proposals. At the time, monasteries conducted most formal education; this course was given by a highly regarded Cistercian monastery in Austria where monks trained laymen to become administrators for kings and nobles. One aspect was writing fund-raising letters, which the monks said should have five parts (Phillips, 1969, pp. 158–159):

- *Salutation:* "Give greetings and praise. Make tactful recognition of rank and virtues."
- *Exordium:* Introduce the proposal.
- *Narration:* Describe the problem.
- *Petition:* Present the request, the "supplication."
- *Conclusion:* Bring the letter to a "graceful end with a form of peroration."

To accompany grant proposals, the monks developed twenty-two cover letters, each citing a different reason for the desirability of philanthropy, including "Be Generous to Avoid Ridicule," "By Giving Joy You Receive Joy," "Do As You Would Be Done By," and "To Be Kind Is Better Than Being an Animal." These letters are so worldly that it seems most likely the monks modeled them after the entreaties passed to them by the rich uncle of a ne'er-do-well student at the University of Paris. One such letter, on the theme, "The Obligation of the Wealthy to Give," has a ring of truth as clear today as in the Middle Ages, especially regarding the poverty of scholars:

Most upright in life and upright in all dealings, salutations to my most honourable master with my deepest respects. Oh fortunate businessman! Oh noble merchant! Oh much admired financier! The Kingdom of Heaven could be compared to your estate, for it could be so easily transformed into eternal wealth. Truly there is nothing more miserable than the miserable poverty of the scholars. Among these I am to be most pitied, for I am overwhelmed by my labours, broken by misery, and sapped by the gnawing of harassing debts. I therefore beg and beseech your laudable interest in such a worthy cause. I pray and implore you, let me, your loyal clerk in squalid misery, enjoy some benefit of your treasure, which neither thieves steal nor moths corrupt (Phillips, 1969, p. 160).

More contemporary (but no more insightful) descriptions of grant proposals have been made by grantseekers and grantmakers alike. Alan Gregg, former director of the Medical Sciences Division of the Rockefeller Foundation, said that a proposal should perform three functions:

1. Define the problem and its significance.
2. Present the qualifications of the people to be involved.
3. Discuss the circumstances that favor undertaking the work.

The circumstances to which Gregg refers can include the applicant's facilities, the degree of collaboration from the grantseeker's colleagues, the attitude of the sponsoring organization toward the project, and the likelihood of support from other funding sources (Penfield, 1967). Robert Lefferts, a professor, administrator, and consultant on fund-raising, says that a grant proposal serves five purposes (1978)]: written representation of a program, request, instrument of persuasion, plan, and promise. The proposal as a promise is a somewhat unusual idea, but not without precedent; DeBakey (1977, p. 27) describes it as a "promissory note."

In the same vein, Richard Johnson (1985) says that a proposal should address what he calls the Five P's: problem, plan, person, place, and price. Manning M. Pattillo, once president of the Danforth Foundation and the Council on Foundations, prefers covering six points:

- The purpose of the project and its significance
- How the purpose will be achieved
- What results are expected
- Who will direct the work
- How much it will cost
- Why the applicant is qualified to do the work (1965, p. 90)

Like most foundations, the Carnegie Corporation does not have an application for grants, but instead asks applicants to submit a "clear and straight-forward" proposal describing the significance of a proposed program and its duration, methods, personnel, and budget (1994, p. 156). Thomas Broce, who has insight from both sides of the grantmaking table, says that foundations want to know, Who are you? What are you doing? Why? How can we help? How much money do you need? Why is your project or institution a good investment? A grant proposal, therefore, should describe the following:

- The objectives and benefits of the project
- The relationship of the project to the goals of the applicant organization
- The amount of money needed (Broce, 1979, p. 131)

Scholar Jacques Barzun spent a lifetime observing the interplay of grantseekers and foundations, and few of the ironies of the process escaped his wry notice. "We all know what a project is," he says. "It is something neatly clamped in a folder, not too thin and not too bulky. . . . The last page consists of figures, headed 'Estimated Budget' and divided into three- or five-year slices." A grant proposal, according to Barzun, is a "literary form" whose composition is an "art not vouchsafed to everyone"; to be successful, a proposal must be different from all others, yet "in line with current programs" and "widely applicable" (1959, p. 183).

The Mystery of Grant Proposals

Grant proposals have a certain mystique, and many grantseekers have been mesmerized by the process of writing them. Albert Szent-Gyorgyi, who won the 1937 Nobel Prize in physiology for his work on vitamin C, confessed that he agonized over them his entire scientific life (DeBakey, 1977). Many others have had similar reactions. Proposal writing instills "madness," said McGuire (1981, p. 41); no, said Broce, the word is "terror" (1979, p. 129); at any rate, says Barzun, it is a task so difficult as to require not just skill but "an indefinable fitness" (1959, p. 183). But from the fundraiser's perspective of Broce, there is no magic to writing proposals: the skills required are mainly planning, organization, and common sense (1979). From the foundation perspective, Pattillo agrees: the main point is to have a good idea, a sound plan, and a realistic goal (1962).

To the academician, writing grants can be difficult or easy. Laurence Peter of *Peter Principle* fame once claimed he was so good at getting research grants that he did not have time to use them. Less humorous professors also write proposals, and for some grantseeking can become a passion more consuming even than their disciplines. Writing grant proposals can keep one intellectually busy, and may bring adulation (and certainly jealousy) from colleagues, some of whom admire the glamour they perceive in grantseeking, while others envy the rarity of the researcher's association with foundations. A researcher can even become addicted to grantseeking, perhaps hiring research assistants to do the work on grant projects so the scholar can concentrate on his main skill: getting grants. The pursuit of money, Barzun said, can be as much an obsession as the pursuit of ideas, and few people have the energy to be preoccupied by both (Whitaker, 1974).

The Importance of Clarity

As the competition for foundation funds intensifies, grant proposals are becoming increasingly important, and proposal quality is thus essential. It may not be the single most important factor in getting a grant; personal, public relations, financial, and ideological principles also affect grantmaking decisions in foundations. However, the grantseeker-foundation relationship is usually *written* as opposed to face-to-face. In that case the proposal may be the only link between the two parties, making it essential that the grantseeker be able to explain complex ideas about work to be done in the future in simple, here-and-now terms and express the often murky concepts of the social and behavioral sciences in clear, everyday words.

Foundation officers leave no doubt about the importance of clarity to grant proposals. F. Lee and Barbara Jacquette (1973) say it is the first criterion among fifteen that foundations apply in making grants. Foundation program officers interviewed for an article in the *Chronicle of Higher Education* (Perry, 1982) list submitting poorly written proposals as one of four frequent mistakes grantseekers make (the other three: failing to understand a foundation's mission, proposing trendy topics, and burying requests for funds in other documents submitted). Pam Horst of the Fund for the City of New York looks at the clarity of a proposal before any other factor: "There are too many fuzzy-headed ideas" in grant proposals, she says (Duca, 1981, p. 51). Even if an idea is clear, however, the words used to describe it may not be. And to foundations, the clarity of a proposal indicates the ability of the applicant to write clearly, think clearly, articulate project rationale clearly, and show it is capable of performing the work proposed. "If people can't write in English," said E. Alden Dunham, retired director of the Carnegie Corporation's higher education program, their proposal is "probably not worth funding," and any application full of jargon is "automatically discarded as far as I'm concerned" (Perry, 1982, p. 25).

Program officers, like editors, are usually well informed on the specialties of their employer. Many are authorities in their field, having been hired by foundations from universities, research centers, and think tanks. They know the literature, the latest developments, innovations, and lines of research, and they spend days interviewing applicants and reading countless proposals. Applications that are vague, hyperbolic, or ignorant of the literature do not impress many program officers, and ambiguous proposals portend unrealistic, contrived schemes that often will accomplish little or nothing. Grantseekers may well be capable of sound reasoning, productive research, and competent management, but if they cannot persuade foundations of this *in writing*, they may never establish their potential as grantees (DeBakey, 1977).

As editors mediate between authors and publishers, so do program officers serve as intermediaries between foundations and grantseekers. On the applicant's behalf they interpret a foundation's program interests as well as its unpublished preferences and policy changes, the little-known predilections of trustees, and the interests and biases of other staff members who may have a say in grant decisions. Foundations and grantseekers need each other, but the former have the money and the power. Grantseekers and potential authors are numerous, foundations and publishers considerably less so; program officers and editors thus do not overly fret if one candidate fails to please, for others are always waiting in line to be considered.

Like manuscripts received cold by publishers, grant proposals that come over the transom at foundations have little chance of acceptance. Unsolicited book manuscripts have less than one chance in a hundred of being published; unsolicited grant proposals probably face the same odds. The oft-cited 5 percent funding rate in foundations includes solicited proposals, those from prior grantees, and those from new applicants who make prior contact. The funding rate for applicants with *no* prior contact is certainly less than 5 percent and perhaps less than 1 percent. Even a phone call or letter of inquiry before sending a proposal improves the odds. According to John Jensen of the George Gund Foundation, "I can think of a number of proposals I would have declined if I didn't first have a phone conversation that gave me a positive opinion about the person on the other end of the line." John Tirman of the Winston Foundation for World Peace adds that phoning a program officer before sending a proposal is "infinitely better" (Robinson, 1996, pp. 38–39). Better yet if the caller has something in common with the person called. John Graham, executive director of the Giraffe Project, a nonprofit that recognizes people who stick their necks out for the common good, served in Vietnam; so had the foundation executive he called. "[That] helped break the ice," says Graham. "The call led to an appointment, and we later received a grant" (Hall, 1989, p. 18).

A lesser but still important factor for proposals is length. According to Richard Johnson, succinctness counts because few program officers are willing to plow through page after page of verbiage to try to figure out what an applicant is trying to say (Perry, 1982). Wordiness can indicate a deficiency of substance or a failure to see clearly the essentials of one's plan. Nor will fancy words usually impress, though some foundation people *are* swayed by jargon and become the victims of illusion. Foundations want a simple, clear description of what is to be done, why, and how the grantseeker intends to go about it. Such clarity is rare, however, and we now consider part of the reason.

Proposalese: The Grammar of Grantseekers

Many proposal writers persist in using a flowery (and funny) language I call *Proposalese*. Proposalese uses words that are obscure, not familiar; vague, not specific; and big, not small. Philosophical attunement, perceptual parameter, innovative stimulation, concerted effort, and self-programming modular interface—all these are Proposalese. No wonder the Carnegie Corporation reported that some proposals it received had "an other-world quality" (Whitaker, 1974, p. 69).

In Proposalese, proposal writers are not mere fund-raisers; they are advancement officers, development directors, grants administrators, external support directors, resource procurement managers, and directors of foundation relations. At Seton Hall University, where I worked as a fund-raiser in the 1980s, my title was director of university advancement. Long before that, though, when I initially encountered Proposalese in my first job as a proposal writer, phrases such as "interactive relevance" were new to me. At first I thought my vocabulary was too limited, but I soon realized that my coworkers, in effect, wrote in a foreign language. Eleanor Elliott, chair of the boards of Barnard College and the Foundation for Child Development, recounts an almost identical experience with grant proposals: "At first I thought I was too dumb to understand what I was reading," she confesses. "But now I say flatly if you can't understand it, it isn't your fault. It's the fault of bad writers" (1984, p. 40).

The Proposalese duties of proposal writers? They are responsible for formulating "germinal concepts as on-going seminal opportunities," building "interdisciplinary catalyzed models," evaluating "trailblazing demonstration projects," and convincing foundations that their grants will have a "multiplier effect" and "make the peaks higher" (Whitaker, 1974, p. 195). In Proposalese, grantseekers do not get ideas; they conceptualize, develop a concept, or construct a conceptual framework.

Why, a reader asked William Safire of the *New York Times,* does no one have an idea anymore? Now it is always a notion. Tongue in cheek, Safire explains that for a while *idea* had its day, but now it is just another thought. A *thought* is a brief idea, usually modestly derogated as "just a thought" but deserving of respect because it is more than a mere "feeling." A *concept,* though, is "an idea with big ideas" (1981, p. 185). Grantseekers writing in Proposalese never just say that they are interested in foundations and would like to study them. That is far too explicit—even dangerous—for a grant proposal; its edges need to be sanded and its corners rounded, so applicants learn to say, "By deploying a team of experts from varied disciplines under the close supervision of the undersigned, the proposed study will shed light on a problem of urgent immediacy and global importance" (Barzun, 1959, p. 184).

A "Perspicuous" Language

Proposalese makes clear ideas unclear. The authors of one study admitted they had used a "private language [of] special words" in their report, but when preparing to release it to the public realized they needed to use "perspicuous" language so people could understand them. What they needed was a clear language, but they did not say so; instead they used an unclear word for clear (Macdonald, 1956, p. 55).

The Social Science Research Council once did a study on the problems of foreign students attending colleges and universities in the United States. The report identified "varieties of cross-cultural experience," but made no "firm conclusions about causes and effects" and recommended more studies to "test hypotheses . . . discerned in the initial phase of [the] research." Dwight Macdonald of the Ford Foundation, no stranger to Proposalese and other grantee tactics, translated: "We didn't find out anything [so] we're starting the whole thing all over" (1956, pp. 105–106).

"Exceptional Organizational Capability"

Proposalese features interchangeable words: one word can make about as much (or as little) sense as another. Betty McGuire, who read thousands of proposals at the Kresge Foundation, noticed what she called a "universal proposal language" so similar that entire paragraphs could be switched from proposal to proposal (1981, p. 44). Take two Proposalese phrases, "commonality and similar cognitive framework to problem-solve" and "operational definitions on learning behavioral objectives." The words that make these up can readily be used to create ten (or more) new phrases with no loss (or gain) in meaning. Here are three easy ones:

1. Cognitive learning objectives
2. Behavioral framework to problem-solve
3. Commonality of operational definitions

Try a few yourself. Behavioral commonality of learning objectives, similar cognitive learning behavioral objectives, operational cognitive objectives of a behavioral learning commonality . . . the possibilities seem endless.

The dedicated student of Proposalese can use what I call the Proposalese Unparalleled Fluff Finder. Simply choose one word from each of the following three columns. For example, number 1 from column A, number 2 from column B, and number 3 from column C gives you just the right words to assure suspicious foundations of the "exceptional organizational capability" of your employer. Words 8, 9, and 10 from columns A, B, and C might convince skeptical foundations that you will work hard because of your "synchronized transdisciplinary task-orientation." Choose several combinations of three words to create a thousand phrases—almost enough for the most prolific proposal writer (Moore, 1995).

Proposalese Unparalleled Fluff Finder

Column A	Column B	Column C
1. exceptional	1. nondisadvantaged	1. productivity
2. sequential	2. organizational	2. flexibility
3. systematized	3. monitored	3. capability
4. parallel	4. reciprocal	4. mobility
5. functional	5. logistical	5. dissemination
6. responsive	6. transitional	6. time-phase
7. optimal	7. stimulational	7. projection
8. synchronized	8. heterogeneous	8. accountability
9. compatible	9. transdisciplinary	9. programming
10. psychosocial	10. management	10. task-orientation

An "Innovative Research Methodology"

Proposalese is also versatile; it lends itself not only to the arts, sciences, and humanities, but even to sports. When I watch a boxing match on television, I like to turn down the volume and use my Cosell impression to call the action in Proposalese: "The Champ circles the ring using an *innovative research methodology* to measure the Challenger. Dancing, he develops a *monitoring system to assure sound educational programming* for his opponent. The Kid, new to the rigors of the ring, counters with his own *short-term programming pattern*. But the Champ *implements the learning process* by delivering a series of *performance-oriented, competency-based* blows! Stunned, the Challenger falls, his *supportive human resources* expended."

Early in my career, a small-town group asked my help in getting a community development grant. At our first meeting, the leader handed me a proposal, a single page with this sentence written on it: "We need $5,000 to fix our sidewalks." Unfortunately, I was unable to help; the tedious proposal process soon caused the group to give up. In a dream, however, I imagined their request in Proposalese:

> As the legitimate representatives of a multi-ethnic, heritage-based, rural living unit, we seek an innovative yet viable solution to the ills plaguing our community. Through a concerted programmatic effort, we have identified our target area and have established a sound relational analysis of the operational dimensionality of our dilemma. We have articulated the rudiments of traditional manners of providing the services we require and have determined that our plan reflects a substantial philosophical shift from the characteristics of projects which have preceded ours. Accordingly, we note with certainty both the behavioral commonality and dissonance of cataloged programs that are the springs from which our project sips. Our estimated request of $500,000 will sow the seeds of an ongoing program, but represents only a minimal commitment to the development of a performance-oriented model demonstrating the multiple capabilities of our project. If such an endeavor is consistent with your philosophical attunement, we would enjoy the opportunity to engage in a joint evaluative dialogue together in concert with you.

At the end of my dream, an elderly member of the group seated next to me compared my proposal to the original. She shook her head and whispered in my ear: "Too much baloney."

The Precursors of Proposalese

Just as English is derived from the Romance languages and German, Proposalese also has precursors: Impressionese, Educationese, Foundationese, and Redundancese.

Impressionese

Impressionese is the lingo of making a good impression, the slanguage of Washington, Wall Street, and Hollywood, of schmooze, euphemism, and feigned sophistication. In Impressionese, taxes are revenue enhancements, life jackets are personal flotation devices, and boarding houses are personal care facilities.

Examples abound. The president of New York City's public television station, announcing the station's decision to accept advertising, called ads "enhanced corporate underwriting credits" (*Time*, Mar. 15, 1983, p. 92). A vice president of the parent company of Pennsylvania's Three Mile Island nuclear power plant called the accident there "a normal aberration," and, after investigating, the chair of the Nuclear Regulatory Commission concluded: "It would be prudent to consider expeditiously the provision of instrumentation that would provide an unambiguous indication of the level of fluid in the reactor vessel" (Kanfer, 1980, p. 90). In the language of weather reporters, rain is "precipitation," "precipitation activity," "a precipitation condition," or, among hip weather forecasters, "a precip event." One weather reporter warned of "encroaching clouds" and "enhanced cloudiness," and another observed that clouds were beginning to "crescendo a bit." The Metropolitan District Commission in Boston told people to keep off the ice by urging that "all persons terminate using any body of water under MDC control for any ice-related recreation" (Newman, 1979, p. 43).

Almost innumerable other usages of Impressionese can be cited (for a few, see Safire, 1981, 1983, 1988; Friedrich, 1984). Even sports has been overrun by it: NBC once explained that New York Jets quarterback Joe Namath, who was arguing with the referees, was "holding a detente with the officials" (Newman, 1975a,

p. 80), and other analysts favor this dubious style as well. Less surprisingly, perhaps, Impressionese is the mantra of New Age organizations and their followers. The spokesperson for Guru Ma, leader of the Church Universal and Triumphant, warned that the United States was entering "a general trend of accelerated negative karma" (Lacayo, 1990, p. 20), for example, and one groovy groom's self-written wedding vows announced, "It is therefore our glorious and divine purpose to fly mountains, to sow petalscent . . . to glorify glory, to love with love. . . . This is the purest double helix of our us-ness" (Morrow, 1983, p. 78).

Educationese

Educationese is the language of all educational organizations, but especially colleges and universities. It is not new; it was called "Pedigese" many years ago by Wallace Buttrick, who served as secretary, president, and chair on Rockefeller's General Education Board (Flexner, 1952, p. 89). In Educationese, students are talented, faculty dedicated, and administrators invariably effective. Questions from students create "hypothetical learning modes," enabling "transpersonal teaching" to yield "expected student outcomes."

Educationese is the language of academic committees, and at the first meeting of a search committee, I heard the following conversation. "Our objective," the chair began, "is to develop a framework of commonality to guide the selection process." "Pardon me," asked a political science professor. "Don't we need some operational definitions before we problem-solve?" "I agree," said a psychology instructor. "We can't do a thing without a cognitive framework." "You're right," said the chair. "I think we have commonality." Lest you think I made this conversation up, Barzun (1945, p. 54) witnessed a similar exchange over fifty years ago. At a college meeting, a professor asked the admissions director why more music students were applying. "Well," the director replied, "I should say that the forces undergirding the process are societal." The professor wondered how to respond. "I think we should go on to institute actual implementation," he mumbled.

Edwin Newman once received a news kit from an Ivy League college that claimed a study contained "arresting conclusions of almost watershed quality," but "no easy panaceas." Joked Newman: "No hard ones either" (1974, pp. 142–143). The headmaster of an academy told his faculty, "There should always be something on-going going on" (1974, p. 142), and the president of the University of Miami tried to explain (or explain away) a budget deficit by saying, "We will divert the force of this fiscal stress into leverage energy to pry improved budgetary prediction and control out of our fiscal and administrative procedures" (1975b, p. 138). A professor who analyzed the characters in the television program *The A-Team*, which featured, essentially, a bunch of tough guys hanging around, described them as "ubiquitous in colonizing the conventional spheres of interpersonal activity as a self-sufficient autonomous unit" (Sykes, 1988, pp. 111–112). One can only imagine what the professor would have said about television tough guys such as Mike Wallace, Sam Donaldson, or George Will.

In Educationese, to know oneself is to have self-awareness, people are indigenous populations, and families are homogeneous socioeconomic units. Reasons are causal linkages, disagreement is dissonance, relations are interpersonal, and conditions are inevitably favorable. Research may be either multidimensional or multidisciplinary, but objectives must always be measurable. Some of the multidisciplinary papers given at the first International Symposium on Humor, for example, were measurably humorless. One educator was asked if he thought certain persons were "inherently teaseworthy." "No," he said. "I believe the matter is entirely situational, teasewise." One researcher read a paper entitled "Phylogenetic and Ontogenetic Considerations for a Theory of the Origins of Humor," referring to "intra-humans," "arousal fluctuations," and "stimulus discrepancies." His point: if you can't think, you won't get the joke (*Time*, 1976, p. 58). At another conference, a researcher who was asked about the role of the scientific method in the social sciences replied, "It supplies knowledge that can be transmitted from person to person *qua* knowledge, here called 'intersubjectively transmissible knowledge,' or briefly, 'transmissible knowledge.'" According to Newman, the scientific method must then be "a bridge over the River *Qua*" (1975b, p. 140).

Educationese even appears in ads for college jobs. Illinois Benedictine College (1992, p. B37), apparently mindful of the rising cost of advertising, sought a vice president for development to be responsible for "all the usual institutional advancement activities: alumni activities, corporation and foundation relations, planning giving, the annual fund, etc." The etc. covered all the bases—and saved money on the ad, too. Seeking a president, the

College of Saint Mary (1995, p. B66) informed candidates that it had begun "meaningful" long-range planning—not just the ordinary, routine, or regular kind. The San Francisco Art Institute (1982, p. 43) even tried to anticipate the dangers of Educationese in its ad for a new academic dean, asking candidates to send a statement of their "educational philosophy." Taking no chances, the institute wisely defined educational philosophy as "what you think an Art School should be."

Foundationese

Foundationese is the language of foundation trustees and staff members. Its chief purpose is to assure everyone that everything is well in hand; its cardinal principle is to accentuate the positive and, at all costs, to avoid confrontation. Foundationese ever seeks the lowest common denominator, the words that will offend no one and on which everyone can agree—a point that is often well below sea level.

For example, one foundation board chair began a meeting this way: "Now, I'm not quite sure how the discussion ought to roll. But let's just bat it around a little and see where the ball comes out. No holds barred and we *do* want to have a real meeting of minds" (Macdonald, 1956, pp. 99, 102). Users of Foundationese are masters of the obvious; they believe that ideas not worth stating bear repeating. The Ford Foundation said it tries to "strengthen its grantees and enhance their ability to accomplish (their) purposes." Instead of trying to weaken them and impede their ability, apparently. Foundationese words, like those of Proposalese, are interchangeable: "The Trustees of the Ford Foundation believe that a healthy economy is essential if American democracy is to function effectively" might as easily have been stated as "Democracy is essential if a healthy economy is to function effectively." It's as reversible as a trench coat; jokes Macdonald, "Gives just as good wear either way" (1956, p. 103).

Foundations are as prone to using Foundationese as grantseekers are to using Proposalese, so the publications of foundations are filled with "flexible relevances," "changing fluxes," "germinal interfaces," and "self-liquidating leverage." As one foundation officer lamented, "In our world, you have to have 'leverage' even to get out of bed in the morning" (Whitaker, 1974, p. 207).

Redundancese

The fourth and final precursor of Proposalese is Redundancese, the art of using more words than necessary to make a point. For example, only redundant banks offer free gifts; by definition, *all* gifts are free. Similarly, researchers seek human volunteers, engineers design mechanical robots, and disk jockeys play old songs to evoke nostalgia for the past. Tax evaders submit falsely padded expense accounts acting under false pretenses, and police officers seek positive identification of alleged suspects who committed senseless murders. Investment counselors plan for the future, hoping that the stock market sets another new record high.

The *New York Times* identified playwright Saul Levitt as a "lifelong native of New York" (Kanfer, 1978, p. 36), ABC Radio reported that an earthquake in Armenia had created the danger of disease from "dead corpses," and United Press International said Tip O'Neill was the "apparent heir apparent" to the House speakership (Newman, 1975a, p. 159). A local eatery once claimed that "Lafayette's Most Unique Restaurant Is Now Even More Unique" (Kanfer, 1980, p. 90), but a mere double redundancy is nothing to the U.S. Department of Labor, which turned a rare triple negative by declaring, "No lost time injuries that do not result in a medical expense should not be reported to the OWCP" (Kanfer, 1978, p. 36).

International affairs, filled as they are with major catastrophes and diplomats meeting in close proximity, are also wellsprings of Redundancese. In late 1983, President Reagan sought to break the deadlocked Strategic Arms Reduction Talks by offering the Soviets a "build-down" of nuclear weapons; not to be outscored by the Gipper, Congress sweetened the deal by proposing a "double build-down" (*Time*, 1983, p. 16). A U.S. Senator voiced concern not only about nuclear proliferation, but about "the spread of nuclear proliferation" (Newman, 1979, p. 41), and another Senator opposed what he called a nuclear waste "suppository" for his state (Gorey, 1988, p. 31). When negotiating with the Russians, President Bush said he enjoyed "dialoguing" or, when three Superpowers were involved, "trialoguing" (Dowd, 1990, p. 48).

Redundancese also prevails in sports. During game four of the 1990 World Series, CBS reported that the Oakland A's had won "six consecutive post-season games in a row." Some athletes use a language even more twisted than Redundancese. Heavyweight boxer King Levinsky, accounting for his poor showing against champion Joe Louis, explained that he had been in a "transom" against the champ (Newman, 1975a, p. 89). Magic Johnson, formerly of the Los Angeles Lakers, marveled at how well he and teammate James Worthy played together: "It's almost like we have ESPN," he said (*Sports Illustrated,* 1986, p. 18). A boxing manager once invited radio listeners to "reminisce about tomorrow night's fight" (Newman, 1975a, p. 88), and when rumors circulated that a baseball manager might be fired and replaced by Yankee great Yogi Berra, a sports reporter for the *New York Times* phoned Berra for his reaction. "Yogi," he asked, "have you made up your mind yet?" "Not that I know of," Berra replied (Eskenazi, 1985, p. 12).

Implications for Grantseekers of Foundations as Editors

Because foundations equate the quality of applicants with the quality of their proposals, grantseekers should not underestimate the importance of clarity in grant proposals. At the very least, this means avoiding Proposalese.

Grantseekers should begin writing applications as early as possible, for although fund-raising folklore abounds with stories of successful proposals written in less than twenty-four hours, many more take weeks or months to research and write. Proposals must communicate clearly and quickly because few program officers have the time to wade through fifty pages before the plot unfolds. Get to the point fast; a proposal is not a history lesson. At the beginning of the proposal, briefly state *what* is to be accomplished, *who* expects to accomplish it, *why* the work needs doing, *how* it will be done, *where* it will be done, *when* it will be finished, and *how much* it will cost.

Do not submit other documents with a proposal; the college catalog, admissions viewbook, job descriptions, union contract, president's resume, minutes of the faculty senate, or applications to other funding sources are not relevant. Do not promise more than can be delivered; exaggeration rarely attracts a foundation's attention or wins a grant away from the competition. A proposal is essentially a promise to do certain work for certain pay, and as it may become binding, overstatement is unwise. Besides, program officers are professional skeptics who can usually spot people who exaggerate or do not know what they are talking about.

Trying to make a proposal reflect a foundation's philosophy by borrowing from the language in its publications or praising its "innovative contributions" is unlikely to be beneficial. Also, trying to appeal to the political ideology of a foundation is unwise; conservative foundations have supported liberal programs and vice versa.

Do not generalize in a proposal and do not ramble. Eliminate all but essential adjectives and adverbs. Use familiar nouns and verbs, shorter sentences, more paragraphs, and frequent section headings. Avoid jargon, abstractions, and footnotes. Do not use gimmicks such as expensive paper or embossed binders with metal foil type; foundation staff have seen just about every trick, and such tactics do not pull much weight with them.

Do not send the same proposal to several foundations at the same time; instead, send a letter of inquiry to see if a project matches a foundation's program interests and if the foundation is accepting proposals. A letter of inquiry will yield a faster response and can be sent to several foundations simultaneously with little risk of embarrassment. Do not drop in on foundations without an appointment, and do not present a proposal to a trustee behind the backs of foundation staff; the latter practice usually comes back to haunt applicants because most trustees refer requests to the staff anyway, knowing that one of the purposes of staff is to reduce favoritism and quid pro quos in grantmaking. Foundation staff are human, and their reaction to an applicant who has gone over their heads is likely to be understandably inhospitable. Do not use emotional appeal or provocative or inflammatory language; facts and documentation should be stressed. If a proposal challenges accepted ideas and practices, explain why in an objective and low-key way.

Finally, however many people are involved in preparing a proposal, only one should edit the entire application to ensure consistency of style. A proposal written by a group usually looks disjointed and reads poorly.

Recommendations to Foundations as Editors

Foundations, like editors, should not place so much emphasis on the quality of writing that they overlook good ideas hidden within poor prose. Some grantseekers lack the ability to describe in writing work that they are fully competent to perform; others are good at describing work but unable to do it. In their role as editors, foundations must be able to discern the difference. Anything less is an abdication of their responsibility to discover promising people and beneficial projects. Writing good grant proposals is not as easy as some foundation officers say, and some people, even very intelligent people, cannot write clearly and persuasively. Writing ability alone should not qualify—or disqualify—applicants for foundation support.

Chapter Four

Foundations as Citizens

How Accessible and Accountable Are Foundations?

> *As a group, [foundations] are institutions like no others, operating in their own unique degree of abstraction from external pressures and controls, according to their own largely self-imposed rules. They are private, and yet their activities cut across a broad spectrum of public concerns and public issues. They are the only important power centers in American life not controlled by market forces, electoral constituencies, bodies of members, or even formally established canons of conduct, all of which give them their extraordinary flexibility and potential influence. Yet they remain little known and less understood, shrouded in mystery, inspiring in some the highest hopes and expectations and in others dark fears and resentments.*
> WALDEMAR NIELSEN, *THE GOLDEN DONORS* (1985, P. 4)

Foundations resemble citizens in a democracy because both have legal and voluntary responsibilities to their fellow citizens. A foundation's fellow citizens are grantseekers, other foundations, the federal government, and the American people. Citizens are legally

Note: The research for some of the information in this chapter was supported by a grant in 1991–92 from the Lilly Endowment and the Indiana University Center on Philanthropy. Much shorter versions of this chapter appeared as "The Public Accountability of Foundations: Private Organizations in the Public Interest" in the Spring 1994 edition of *Philanthropy Matters,* and as "The Privilege of Privacy: Twenty-Five Years in the Public Accountability Record of Foundations" in the Summer 1995 issue of *Nonprofit and Voluntary Sector Quarterly.*

required to do certain things, such as pay taxes, and also have voluntary responsibilities, such as contributing to the betterment of their communities. Foundations, too, have legal and voluntary responsibilities, many having to do with public accountability.

The Metaphor of Foundations as Citizens

The idea that citizenship carries obligations as well as rights is one of the most fundamental tenets of a democracy, and it applies to both individuals and organizations. People are responsible for voting, paying taxes, obeying the law, respecting the rights of other citizens, keeping abreast of current events, and contributing to the betterment of their communities. Foundations, beyond whatever responsibilities they assume themselves, are mandated by legislation to be publicly accountable in certain ways.

Foundations are obligated to be accessible to grantseekers and the general public and to be accountable to the federal government. They must pay certain taxes (as enacted by the Tax Reform Act of 1969) and disclose certain information on their assets, grants, trustees, and staff members. The legislated public accountability responsibilities of foundations include the following:

- Pay an annual 2 percent excise tax on net investment income.
- Award at least 5 percent of assets each year in grants.
- Complete the annual Internal Revenue Service return (Form Annual Return 990–Private Foundation) and make it available for public inspection. The return includes information on income, expenses, assets, grants, and liabilities, questions on whether funds were used (in violation of federal law) to influence legislation or participate in political campaigns, and a controversial public information section, discussed later in this chapter.
- Place an advertisement each year in a newspaper with general circulation stating that the annual return is available for public inspection in a foundation's principal office during regular business hours within 180 days of publication of the notice. The annual public notice must state the address and telephone number of the foundation's office and the name of its principal manager, and a copy of the advertisement must be

submitted with the IRS return as proof of publication
(Commerce Clearing House, 1994, pp. 6,424, 6,500).

Beyond legal requirements, foundations best serve the public when
they voluntarily assume other responsibilities—standards and practices to encourage civil behavior in their relations with people and
organizations. These could be summarized as follows:

- Respond to requests for information from individuals such
  as grantseekers and organizations such as the Foundation
  Center.
- Publish annual or biennial reports and other publications
  such as newsletters, statements of program interests, or guidelines for applicants.
- Place a listing in the *Foundation Directory,* the *Foundation Directory: Part 2* (for small foundations), or other such sourcebooks.

Foundations and Federal Regulation

The federal government has shown remarkable restraint in regu-
lating foundations and the people who establish them. Despite
three major Congressional investigations in this century, only the
Tax Reform Act of 1969 subjected them to considerable regulation.

The relationship of foundations and Congress began with the
Revenue Act of 1913, which exempted from taxation those organizations that operated exclusively for religious, charitable, scientific, or educational purposes. Congress permitted donors to take
a charitable deduction for their contributions to such organizations in 1917, but passed no other law affecting foundations until
the Revenue Act of 1943, which required foundations and certain
other nonprofits to file annual returns with the IRS listing income
and expenses. From then until the Tax Reform Act of 1969, no
other major regulations were placed on foundations.

Congress did, however, keep a watchful eye on foundations
during this period. A 1952 investigation sought to determine if
foundations were engaged in un-American activities; it concluded
that they were not supporting Communism but were vulnerable to
subversive influence. The committee recommended better public
disclosure by foundations and suggested that the annual Internal

Revenue Service return include more information, especially the contributions which foundations received, names of grantees, and administrative expenses. A follow-up investigation and subsequent 1954 report expressed concern that foundations were encouraging "moral relativity" and "collectivist" political opinions, but the methods used to arrive at this conclusion were criticized and no legislation resulted.

In 1961, however, Representative Wright Patman of Texas announced yet another investigation, this one by the Subcommittee on Foundations of the Select Committee on Small Business, both of which he chaired. In what amounted to a one-man, eight-year crusade, Patman identified what he considered to be five abuses by foundations:

- Their assets and economic power were increasing rapidly.
- Some people were using foundations to avoid paying taxes, to control businesses, and to channel money illegally to themselves, their friends, or their relatives.
- The IRS had been lax in its oversight of foundations.
- Foundations that owned or controlled businesses created a competitive disadvantage for other businesses, especially small businesses.
- Foundations spent too much of their money overseas.

Patman recommended that foundations be limited to a lifespan of twenty-five years and be prohibited from operating businesses and from owning more than 3 percent of the stock of a corporation. He asked the IRS to deny a tax deduction to people who established foundations until the assets of the foundations were spent for charitable purposes. Patman also recommended that foundations be prohibited from influencing political campaigns and conducting voter registration drives. In response, the House Ways and Means Committee and the Senate Finance Committee jointly asked the Treasury Department to conduct an independent investigation (Edie, 1987a, p. 50). Treasury did so, examining some 1,300 foundations and concluding that many of them delayed passing their investment income on to grantees; controlled too many businesses; enabled too many donor tax deductions; speculated in questionable financial investments; and engaged in self-dealing with contributors, entities controlled partly or entirely by contributors, the foundation's own trustees or employees, and certain government officials.

Treasury made a number of recommendations about how to deal with the situation, including limiting foundation life spans and donor control over foundations, as well as requiring that foundations give away all investment income or a percentage of their assets each year. The Tax Reform Act of 1969 followed some of these suggestions. It imposed a 4 percent excise tax on the annual net investment income of foundations (reduced to 2 percent) and required them to distribute all their net investment income within a year or pay out at least 6 percent (later reduced to 5 percent) of their assets in grants, whichever was greater. The act also prohibited self-dealing by foundations, regulated their grants to individuals, restricted their ownership of business, and limited their involvement in influencing legislation and participating in political campaigns (Edie, 1987a; Renz, Lawrence, and Treiber, 1995).

The Public Accountability of Foundations

One of the oldest and most controversial issues in philanthropy is public accountability. Democracies have long given favorable tax treatment to foundations and other nonprofits because they are chartered to serve the public good, but in return they have usually expected such organizations to account to the public for their actions. Few nonprofits, however, have escaped public examination as much as America's foundations, whose poor record of accountability deserves the public spotlight.

Public accountability is not discussed widely in the literature on philanthropy. There are few grants for research on the topic and little impetus among foundations to improve, despite legislation by Congress and the encouragement of organizations such as the Foundation Center, the Council on Foundations, and the National Committee for Responsive Philanthropy. A few people in foundations are troubled by the issue, however, because it raises uncomfortable questions about the power of money in a democracy and the ability of wealthy people to influence elections, affect the actions of legislatures, and direct the management of social and educational institutions. But many foundation donors and trustees are quite comfortable with little or no accountability; they believe they should lead the country, with the assistance of their foundations for research on public policy issues. The more contented they are with their privileged position in society, the less likely they are to concede their accountability to the public (Colwell, 1993).

The record of foundations in complying with their legislated public accountability requirements is difficult to assess because few studies have been conducted on it. Their record on voluntary accountability is more extensive, and it has improved in the past several decades. However, this is mainly demonstrated by the increased number of foundations in the *Foundation Directory,* a gain attributable more to the Foundation Center that publishes it than to foundations themselves. Their record of responding to requests for information, issuing annual reports and other public information material, and observing the principles of public accountability endorsed by the Council on Foundations has not improved significantly and is not exemplary.

Privacy Versus Public Interest

At the heart of the issue is the difficulty of balancing two diametrically opposed ideas: the privacy of foundations and the interest of the public. The conflict between the two is as old as foundations themselves. In ancient Greece, foundations were highly suspect because of their political and economic power, and during the Middle Ages in England there was resentment of the Roman Catholic Church's wealth. Henry VIII, having assumed the throne in 1509, attacked the church for controlling approximately half his kingdom's fortune and confiscated its holdings in the 1530s. In the 18th and 19th centuries, critics in England and on the continent charged that endowments held too much wealth and were controlled by *mortmain,* the dead hand of the donor (James, 1973; Kiger, 1954).

Foundations have enjoyed an honored place in the American pluralistic system for a century, but there has always been disagreement about their public responsibilities. Some argue that they are completely private organizations; others say they are private *and* public because they exist to serve the public interest. Exacerbating this debate, some people interpret *public* to mean government control or *private* to mean secret. However, according to James A. Joseph, former president of the Council on Foundations, *private* in this context should refer to an independence of judgment and action and *public* should pertain to the need to serve the public good and remain open to a diversity of opinions about that good (1992).

The public accountability of foundations has been an issue with Congress since President William Howard Taft in his 1912 State of the Union address asked Congress to study the causes of industrial strife, including the role large foundations may have played in creating social problems. In response, Congress established the Commission on Industrial Relations. After three years of hearings, more than seven hundred witnesses, and 6.5 million words of testimony, the commission submitted a report in 1915 critical of foundations, concluding that a small group of wealthy families controlled not only the nation's major industries, but also its educational and social institutions through their foundations, many of which were considered too conservative and even reactionary (Adams, 1966; Cuninggim, 1972).

The commission's recommendations represented many of the concerns addressed later in laws affecting foundations, especially the Tax Reform Act of 1969. The commission recommended that foundations operate under federal, not state, charter because some foundations that had been unable to obtain federal approval because of the controversy surrounding them quickly turned to states, which in most cases eagerly granted them charters, hoping perhaps to benefit from their largess. The Rockefeller Foundation is a case in point: having encountered strong opposition to its request for a charter from Congress, which held up its petition from 1910 to 1913, the foundation approached the New York legislature, which granted a charter on May 14, 1913. Congress denied a charter partly because of the suspicion that John D. Rockefeller would use it as a cover for illegal business activities (O'Neill, 1990; Rockefeller Foundation, 1914). Of ten of the oldest foundations in the United States, only three received their charters from Congress: the General Education Board (1903), the Carnegie Institution of Washington (1904), and the Carnegie Foundation for the Advancement of Teaching (1906).

Foundations' proclivity for secrecy has frequently been a source of friction. During the Congressional hearings in the 1950s and 1960s, many of the worst criticisms concerned their secrecy, leading to the public disclosure provisions of the Tax Reform Act of 1969. The investigations featured intense debate, often laced with stories of abuses by foundations (many exaggerated, some not), that reflected concern about the scarcity of information on what foundations did with their money. From the 1970s to the present, the conflict between the privacy of foundations and the interest of the public has remained controversial and continues to generate debate. The Donee Group issued the report, *Private Philanthropy: Vital and Innovative or Passive and Irrelevant?* (1976), which criticized foundations for their poor accessibility, urged that admission to foundations be widened, and proposed requiring annual public meetings of the governing boards of foundations with at least $250,000 in assets or at least $100,000 in annual grants. John Nason (1977) warned foundations that if they persist in maintaining a "wall of secrecy" (p. 93) around them they encourage suspicion, and if they refuse to report what they do with their money they make more enemies than friends.

Some foundations have adopted communications programs after being secretive for years, persuaded by the recommendations of foundation officers, the examples of other foundations, the encouragement of the Council on Foundations, or the public accountability provisions of the Tax Reform Act of 1969. Despite this progress, many remain secretive and refuse to find the middle ground in the conflict between protecting their privacy and serving the public interest.

Arguments for the Privacy of Foundations

Five main arguments are often made in support for the privacy of foundations:

- Foundations are private organizations created by private citizens and they have little or no responsibility to the public.
- Public disclosure encourages more applications for grants, many of which are far afield from the interests of foundations, wasting the time of both foundations and applicants.

- The "controlling power of competing goods" suggests that foundations function as a kind of philanthropic marketplace, which, like the "invisible hand" of an economic marketplace, checks abuses by individual foundations.
- The tradition of anonymity in philanthropy supports the right of donors, whether individuals or foundations, to make charitable contributions in private.
- Public accountability exposes foundations to potentially embarrassing questions about their grantmaking philosophies and practices.

Foundations Are Private Organizations

If foundations are private organizations created by private citizens using private money, why should they be accountable to the public? If they comply with their legal responsibilities, they fulfill their public obligation completely and government oversight is thus unnecessary. Advocates of this stance point out that foundations, acting privately, are responsible for much of the nation's progress in research, education, and the arts; private enterprise has been successful not only in business but also in philanthropy. Some claim a Constitutional justification for this view, arguing that foundations have a *right* to privacy. William Simon, president of the Olin Foundation and former secretary of the United States Treasury, expressed this view when he defined foundation assets as "private money. It's in private hands. In a free society, the money the government appropriates, through duly constituted legislative bodies, is public money. The rest is private" (Williams, 1983, p. 21).

The view of foundations as private organizations with little or no responsibility to the public has prevailed almost from the beginning. In 1936, Lindeman reported that foundations were "distinctly unwilling" to disclose information about themselves and considered their wealth a "private possession (that) the possessor may dispose of as he pleases" (pp. 5-6). Angered by the assertion that foundation money was public money because it was to serve public purposes, John D. Rockefeller, Jr. is reported to have said that since the government had the power to tax 100 percent of his income, but left a part for him, he regarded this remainder as his own and in no way public (Andrews, 1963).

Public Disclosure Invites More Grant Applications

Foundations fear that publicity will inundate them with applications. Although this argument is one of the oldest, the Foundation Center and the *Chronicle of Philanthropy* confirm that many foundations still believe public disclosure will attract a flood of inappropriate requests (Desruisseaux, 1986b; *Chronicle of Philanthropy*, 1989). This concern is especially prevalent in small foundations, usually the least able to handle large numbers of proposals. Also, small foundations are often managed by attorneys, bankers, or members of the donor's family, who typically have neither the time nor the inclination to process many applications. Some foundations have instructed their bankers and attorneys to avoid contact with the public, and others have gone so far as to direct their staff not to make speeches, write articles, or be conspicuous at public functions (Andrews, 1956; Crossland and Trachtenberg, 1982).

The Controlling Power of Competing Goods

If foundations function collectively as a kind of philanthropic marketplace, would not that marketplace serve to check abuses by rogue foundations? Those who think so maintain that if Adam Smith's "invisible hand" over the foundation marketplace were replaced with government controls, foundations would be socialized, creating an even greater concentration of power that would change philanthropy into a kind of "benevolent absolutism" (Taylor, 1953, p. 123).

The opposing view, however, is that foundations are not part of a philanthropic marketplace. Unlike businesses, they are not dependent on others for their money, do not have to respond to the demands of customers, and are not subject to accreditation or licensing. Thus if they drift into mediocrity or fund outrageous activities, they incur no financial penalty from the government or their own community as long as they break no laws (O'Neill, 1989).

The Tradition of Anonymity in Philanthropy

Many people who make charitable contributions do not seek public recognition; likewise, many foundations consider publicity an invasion of their privacy, an unnecessary expense that diverts philanthropic dollars from charitable causes, an appeal for recognition of good works, or an unsavory practice better suited to show business than philanthropy. For example, the Pew Memorial Trust (now Pew Charitable Trusts) for decades refused to meet with grantseekers or disclose the name of any trustee or staff member, saying that it was observing the Biblical admonition to eschew earthly acknowledgment for charitable acts. Religious tradition has recognized the double blessedness of people who give with no thought of appreciation, but when the philanthropist is a foundation, secrecy usually yields suspicion rather than gratitude (Magat, 1984; Nason, 1977; Taylor, 1953; Whitaker, 1974).

Disclosure Exposes Foundations to Potentially Embarrassing Questions

Does the foundation have a mission? What are its priorities? Is its grantmaking reasoned? Is this a *good* foundation? The answers to such questions are potentially awkward, for they may reveal a weak board, a vague purpose, poor management, flawed decision making, or a list of frenetic grants with little or no rational justification. This might expose their grantmaking to criticism and cause them to fund only the most innocuous projects. Another seldom articulated but nonetheless real worry of some foundations is that disclosure will subject them to inquiry in the intellectual community and force them into a humiliating debate in which they could not defend themselves (Nielsen, 1972).

Beneath all this, however, may be the simple desire of foundations to retain absolute control over what they do with their money. Such diffidence, especially if it deteriorates into secrecy, can taint even the most publicly minded foundations with suspicion. For all their wealth and influence, foundations can be surprisingly timid, and many consider themselves defenseless against political attack. Many were shocked at their lack of defenders during the Congressional investigations of the 1950s and 1960s. Grantseekers are more likely to be a foundation's enemy than its friend, given that foundations reject far more proposals than they fund. Nor are grantees reliable advocates, for gratitude is hardly a universal attribute. The adage, "Give a man something, and you make an enemy of him," often attributed to Henry Ford, seems to apply not only to people but also to foundation grantees. Some grantees resent the foundation's power, still others are bitter at receiving less than they had hoped for—or more than they know they deserve (Henry, 1987; Whitaker, 1974).

Arguments for the Interest of the Public

Four arguments are frequently cited in favor of public interest over foundation autonomy:

- Foundations are both private *and* public organizations, created by private citizens but chartered by federal or state government to serve the public interest.
- People are demanding more accountability from all nonprofits as federal budget reductions require many of them to assume the cost of programs formerly funded by the government.
- Public accountability can improve the representativeness of foundation boards, which are comprised mostly of wealthy, white males with personal or business ties to foundations.
- Public accountability gives foundations an opportunity to condemn corruption in their ranks and set the highest standards of ethical behavior in philanthropy.

Foundations Are Both Private and Public

Proponents of this view believe that the public has a legitimate interest in foundations because people are the ultimate beneficiary of their support, however privately their funds may have been earned and however independently their grants may be made. Foundations are public in that they are required to devote all their resources to charitable purposes and none to the financial advantage of any individual, except compensation for services rendered.

In a democracy, sources of economic power are expected to account for their stewardship of charitable funds, especially when they are governed by self-perpetuating boards. With assets of $200 billion, foundations have considerable economic power and should be accountable for it. To some critics, foundations are inherently suspect because they use their economic power to influence societal values, thereby translating financial power into cultural power. Foundations are elitist organizations in a democratic society, says Thomas Buckman, former president of the Foundation Center, and their need to be accountable to the public is thus especially sensitive. Their half-private, half-public status may exempt them from the sunshine laws, but it does not relieve them of responsibility to account to the public (Coser, 1965; Joseph, 1992; Katz, 1968; Williams, 1984).

Demands for Better Public Accountability from All Nonprofits

Many people want better accountability from all nonprofits, including foundations. They argue that the public indirectly finances foundations by granting them favorable tax treatment, and some wonder if they deserve it. After all, nonprofits have spent millions trying to eradicate drug abuse, poverty, illiteracy, unemployment, and homelessness, but according to virtually every indicator these problems are worse than ever. This makes people question how all that money is being spent.

Elizabeth Dole told the 1992 meeting of Independent Sector that though nonprofits have long been exempt from public scrutiny and free to spend their money as they choose, now they function in a new, more public world in which they must answer to those who foot the bill. But the board meetings of many nonprofits are private, and people thus can find it difficult to learn what charitable organizations are doing with the money given to them, much of it in lieu of taxes. Openness can help foundations lessen this problem, understand the needs of their communities, identify new applicants, and perform better philanthropy. Foundations should discuss their values and grantmaking criteria openly, says Paul Ylvisaker, because secretive foundations are a breeding ground for "personal and institutional botulism" (Desruisseaux, 1987b, p. 34; Williams, 1992, p. 8).

Public Accountability Can Improve the Representativeness of Foundation Boards

Although foundation boards now include more women and minorities than ever before, they remain comprised chiefly of wealthy, white males with personal or business ties to foundations. Today, the typical foundation trustee is not much different than those Lindeman studied many years ago: a man, well past middle age; more often than not of considerable affluence or one whose economic security ranks high; one whose social position is among the higher-income class of the population; and one who is presumably "respectable" and "conventional" and belongs to the "best" clubs and churches, associating with other men of prestige, power, and affluence (1936, pp. 44, 46).

If foundation boards were more representative, it is argued, the arrogance of foundations could be reduced, the gap between foundations and grantseekers narrowed, the elitism of foundations decreased, and the quality of philanthropy improved.

Opportunity for Foundations to Condemn Corruption

Historically, foundations have met scandal in their ranks with timidity, if not silence. Some have violated the laws and ethics of philanthropy, and others have been exposed as "hollow organizations," functioning mainly to enrich their officers and friends (Rosenman, 1990, p. 28). But philanthropy is where the moral agenda of society is put forth, and foundations have a special responsibility to explain how they have advanced it. Simply being inoffensive or meeting the minimum requirements of the law are insufficient; trust should characterize their behavior, and ethics should be the guiding force in all charitable organizations, especially foundations (Boris and Odendahl, 1990; Payton, 1989; Pifer, 1984d).

Advocates of Public Accountability by Foundations

The first advocates of public accountability by foundations were neither grantseekers, government officials, nor critics, but foundations themselves. Since the early 1900s, many articulate leaders of foundations have urged them to acknowledge their accountability to the public.

For example, the Russell Sage Foundation, from its beginning in 1907, supported complete disclosure and maintained records of all known foundations, a task now performed by the Foundation Center. For years Sage was also the premier publisher of research on foundations and philanthropy, a function decades ahead of its time. Harrison and Andrews, Sage officers, frequently warned foundations of the dangers of their secrecy and indicated that serious abuses of power were unlikely as long as their actions were open to public review. Despite vociferous opposition, Harrison and

Andrews (1946) asked Congress to require foundations to publish annual reports on their activities and finances, to tax the income they received from businesses they owned or operated, and to revoke their tax exemption if they failed to devote their assets to charitable purposes.

Frederick Keppel of the Carnegie Corporation spoke for all far-sighted foundation executives when he said that public account-ability was a *duty* and that the public was entitled to the fullest information and widest discussion on them (1930). "If anyone looks closely at us," he confided to a friend in the 1930s, "we'll be in deep trouble" (Lindeman, 1988, p. viii). Foundations should operate with "glass pockets," he added, because the secrecy of one foundation damages the reputation of all foundations, a point on which his propensity for Biblical references led him to quote Saint Paul: "Whether one member suffer, all the members suffer with it, or one member be honored, all the members rejoice with it" (Goulden, 1971, p. 72).

To promote accountability, Merrit M. Chambers (1948) pro-posed a national clearinghouse on foundations to throw light on what he said was one of the most conspicuous blind spots in phil-anthropy. In 1953, what is now the Council on Foundations started one; it has consistently urged foundations to recognize their accountability to the public. With more than 1,300 members, the council monitors legislative and regulatory issues affecting foun-dations, informs the public of the benefits of foundations, provides information about foundations to philanthropists and their advi-sors, and encourages the growth of foundations in other countries. In its first policy statement (1973), the council said foundations should accept the principle of full disclosure and take voluntary steps to reduce their secretiveness so as to learn the interests of other foundations and reduce the number of inappropriate requests from grantseekers. In its second policy statement in 1980, the council urged telling grantseekers about policies and proce-dures and publishing annual reports, newsletters, statements of program interests, and guidelines for applicants. It further said that foundations should acknowledge requests promptly and tell grantseekers immediately if their proposals will not be funded; applicants whose proposals are still under consideration should be told of the steps and timing involved in reaching the final decision.

In its 1984 policy statement, the council said foundations should be accountable to their founders, grantseekers, the public, the IRS, and state government agencies; two years later it added regional associations of grantmakers, the Foundation Center, and local, regional, and national independent sector organizations to the list (Council on Foundations, 1980, 1984). James A. Joseph of the council was a tireless advocate of better accessibility by foundations. Although he recognized the role of government in ensuring the public accountability of foundations, Joseph placed the main responsibility squarely on the shoulders of foundations. "Unless we engage in self-regulation," he said, "we invite increased government regulation. No public presentation by the Council will be as effective as the private practices of foundations" (1983, p. 24).

Despite such encouragement, many foundations have been secretive and unwilling to acknowledge their accountability to the public. Hollis (1938) reported that if he had known it would have taken him nearly a decade to acquire the most elementary information on foundations, he would have promptly abandoned his research. Coffman (1936) found so few foundation annual reports in the 1930s that he was forced to conduct 231 interviews and write over a thousand letters seeking information from foundations, observing that they believed they had no responsibility to the public. The Commission on Foundations and Private Philanthropy concluded in 1970 that a great many inaccessible foundations created suspicion that they were engaged in "secret things done in a dark corner," using their power to promote "obscure, devious, or even sinister purposes" (James, 1973, p. 211). The secrecy of foundations may reveal an "enclave mentality" central to their character, according to Nielsen (1972, p. 305), and although some stories of their inaccessibility have undoubtedly been devised by disappointed applicants, secrecy has long been characteristic of foundations. Many foundations will not complete the Foundation Center's questionnaire to place a listing in the *Foundation Directory* or the *Foundation Directory: Part 2,* and others fail to complete the public information part of the Internal Revenue Service return or purposely leave questions in that section of the form blank. One of the most common complaints about foundations is that they do not answer their mail; Manning M. Pattillo, past president of the Foundation Center, noted that the president of a leading university in 1968 sent letters to 150 foundations but received only two replies (Henry, 1987). Some foundations reply only to applicants they have decided to fund, and many grantseekers have experienced the frustration of submitting a proposal, only to discover later that it was rejected without notice while they waited in "uninformed, prayerful anticipation" (Crossland and Trachtenberg, 1982, p. 20).

Legislated Accountability Practices

In addition to paying a 2 percent excise tax on annual net investment income and awarding at least 5 percent of their assets each year in grants, foundations have three other legislated accountability practices: completing the annual Internal Revenue Service return, making it available for inspection in a foundation's office, and placing an advertisement each year in a newspaper having general circulation.

Completing the IRS Return

The largest and most remarkable investigation of the record of foundations in completing the IRS return was conducted by Wilmer Shields Rich, who, in the early 1950s, traveled to more than sixty IRS offices to inspect the returns of some six thousand foundations (at the time IRS records were kept at district offices, not in Washington). She found so many incomplete returns that she stopped midway through her study and reported her findings to the IRS and other organizations concerned with foundations. In response, she received letters from several hundred irate foundation officials, some of whom ceased filing the IRS return in protest. Nine years later, the Foundation Library Center conducted a second nationwide analysis and continued to find inadequate completion of the form (Rich, 1962). The problem persisted in 1967 when an assistant commissioner of the IRS told Congress that one-third of foundation returns had to be rejected from the agency's computer scanning system because of errors and omissions (Chapper, 1967). Several investigations since then indicate that the problem persists to this day (Andrews, 1973; Gorman, 1983; General Accounting Office, 1984; Nason, 1989).

Placing the Annual Public Notice and
Making It Available for Public Inspection

The Revenue Act of 1950 first permitted public inspection of the
IRS returns of foundations, but only in part; certain sections could
be examined only by executive order of the President of the
United States. Commenting on this arrangement, the Special Committee to Investigate Tax Exempt Foundations and Comparable
Organizations failed to understand why any part of a foundation's
return should not be open to the public: "Its funds are public and
its benefactions, its activities, should be public also" (1954, pp. 20-
22). Early IRS returns revealed little information, and many foundations either failed to submit them or filed returns which were
incomplete.

By 1962, several changes had been made in the return and
more facts were available to the public, including investment holdings; accumulation of capital gains; relationships with contributors;
salaries of officers; names and addresses of grantees; and the number, types, and amounts of grants. Still, many foundations completed only parts of the return and others failed to file it altogether,
although this brought little or no reaction from the IRS (Reeves,
1970). In 1968 the IRS prepared a list of the names and addresses
of the 30,262 foundations then in existence, but it was found to be
riddled with duplication and errors. Commented Congressman
Wright Patman, "If the Internal Revenue Service cannot even come
up with the current addresses of the organizations for which they
have responsibility, I shudder to think of the kind of audit and
review that is being undertaken by them" (Patman, 1969, p. H9389;
Edie, 1987b).

The record of foundations in placing the annual public notice
and making their IRS return available for inspection is difficult to
assess; few studies have been done on it. However, one study by
Richard Magat in 1971 showed that many foundations tried to
avoid public detection and defeat the spirit of the requirement. It
found that 83 percent of New York City foundations had placed
their annual public notices in the *New York Law Journal* while only
17 percent had placed their notices in The New York Times,
despite circulations of 8,969 for the Journal and 846,132 for the
Times—and despite the fact that the same ad in the Times cost

only $4 more. As a publication, The New York Law Journal stretches the meaning of the general circulation clause of the annual public notice provision because it is a periodical for attorneys instead of a newspaper intended for readership by the general public. Also, as Magat pointed out, the circulation of The New York Law Journal in 1971 was less even than the 33,000 lawyers who then practiced in the city. (James, 1973; Whitaker, 1974). Some foundations apparently have even created obstacles for people who want to inspect IRS returns at foundation offices (Nason, 1989; *Chronicle of Philanthropy*, 1992b).

Voluntary Accountability Practices

Aside from their legal obligations, foundations should maintain productive relations with grantseekers and organizations by responding to requests for information, participating in the *Foundation Directory* or *Foundation Directory: Part 2,* and publishing annual reports and other public information material. Their record at these practices is better than their performance in legislated accountability, but it still leaves much to be desired.

Responding to Requests for Information

How well foundations respond to requests for information has been studied for more than fifty years, although rarely with the cooperation of the subjects. In the 1920s and 1930s, Lindeman (1936) spent nearly ten years asking foundations for basic information, but their cooperation was so poor that he could not even determine how many existed although he did discover 202 foundations from which he could acquire no information (1936). Keppel of the Carnegie Corporation reported (1930) that even he, as president of one of the nation's prominent foundations, professionally involved with foundations and in a position to secure information from them, was unable to obtain any information whatsoever from three foundations whose combined assets were $75 million. Such difficulty prompted Keppel to take the unusual step of discussing the problem in the 1939 *Carnegie Corporation Annual Report,* where he described the proportion of foundations operating in secrecy as "disquietingly large" (p. 39). In 1946, Harrison and Andrews of the Russell Sage Foundation were unable to acquire publishable financial data from 255 of the 505 foundations in their records (50.5 percent). Forty-nine foundations (9.7 percent) stated that they would not provide any information and ninety-two (18.2 percent) failed to reply to repeated inquiries (1946).

In 1974, the Grantsmanship Center wrote to the 5,454 foundations in the 1971 *Foundation Directory*, stating that the letter was not a grant proposal but a request for publications for the center's library. The response rate was only 14.5 percent, of which about two-thirds provided useful information (Nason, 1977). In 1979, the National Committee for Responsive Philanthropy revealed how well the nation's 208 largest independent, corporate, and community foundations responded to a request for information. Nearly 60 percent were "below minimum" or "totally unacceptable." Some of this resistance may have stemmed from the fact that the committee had regularly criticized foundations for their secrecy. Still, the foundations that received the request were the richest in the country and possessed the financial wherewithal to reply easily (Bruce and others, 1980; Greene, 1991). Getting information from foundations is especially difficult, of course, if the seeker cannot find them. This has indeed been a problem; for example, about half the 3,363 foundation listings in the 1981 *Foundation Directory* cited no telephone numbers (Magat, 1983b).

Such a lack of candor may help explain why foundations do not receive better media coverage. William A. Henry (1987) said that foundations often seek to generate "cheerful little stories" about their grants, accompanied by a photograph of a "forelock-tugging recipient accepting a check" (p. 46), but the media are suspicious of such stories and are usually unwilling to write about a foundation without knowing its grantmaking priorities, its process for selecting grantees, the contacts (if any) between foundations and grantees, and, above all, the motives of the donors.

Participating in the *Foundation Directory*

One of the best ways foundations can increase their accessibility is by placing a listing in the *Foundation Directory* or *Foundation Directory: Part 2,* the best sources of information on foundations in the

United States. The first directory of foundations was a 1915 guide called *American Foundations* published by the Russell Sage Foundation, a booklet of just ten pages containing brief descriptions of only twenty-seven foundations and a list of books and articles on them (Renz, 1985, p. v). Between 1915 and 1955, fourteen other directories of foundations were published by the Russell Sage Foundation, the Twentieth Century Fund, Raymond Rich Associates, and American Foundations Information Service (Andrews, 1973).

Foundations have long been resisting the directories. In the late 1950s, the Foundation Center began surveying foundations for the first *Foundation Directory* and encountered strong opposition from many, a response that H. Thomas James, once president of the Spencer Foundation, considered "difficult to describe as anything but reprehensible" (1973, p. 211). Many foundations, fearful that a listing would increase the number of proposals they received, threatened to sue the center if even public information about them was released. But the board of the Foundation Center had already determined that the directory would include every foundation that met its criteria, if necessary using information from government records and other sources of public information. To test the validity of the fear of receiving a flood of inappropriate applications, Andrews invented a foundation in 1964 and gave it a small endowment, a deceased donor, and an address at a staff member's home. Andrews listed the "foundation" in the *Foundation Directory* with the notation "not in a position to entertain present appeals of any sort" and recorded correspondence to it in 1964, 1965, and 1966. The three-year listing produced a total of 192 pieces of mail, of which only 17.2 percent were grant proposals, an average of less than one appeal per month, several of which were repeat requests. Arguably, more proposals might have been received if the "foundation" had been given sizable assets or if grant requests would have been welcomed, but Andrews concluded (1973, p. 222) that inclusion in the *Foundation Directory* would not subject a foundation to a burdensome volume of mail as long as it carefully states its purpose and limitations.

The Foundation Center's current policy is to publish available information on all foundations whether they like it or not. Some still do not, and even today the center receives a few irate letters. Sara Engelhardt of the Foundation Center said that about half the foundations in the *Foundation Directory* would probably prefer not to be listed (Millar, 1992, p. 24). Of the 7,292 foundations in the 1995 *Foundation Directory,* only about 37 percent replied fully to the questionnaire for inclusion in the directory; the remaining 63 percent were included by the center, using information from IRS returns. Nevertheless, participation in the *Foundation Directory* and *Foundation Directory: Part 2* has improved noticeably and is better than foundations' record of publishing annual reports and other public information material.

Publishing Annual Reports and Other Public Information Material

Annual reports are an excellent means of voluntary public accountability by foundations, but only about 1,100 of the nation's 38,000 foundations publish them, although approximately 2,500 foundations publish other public information material such as guidelines for grantseekers or statements of program interests.

Foundation annual reports probably began with the Peabody Education Fund, the first American foundation in the modern sense of the term and an important forerunner of American philanthropy. George Peabody established the foundation in 1867, and from the first meeting of its board it published reports of its actions, intending to provide the "fullest information . . . to all who are interested in it" (Murrah, 1990, p. 64). In advocating public reporting, the Peabody trustees declared, "A great Trust of this sort should have a permanent and public record. . . . Reports and Proceedings shall be stereotyped [sic] so that a complete series shall never be wanting in the Public Libraries of the Country" (Peabody Education Fund, 1875). In the mid-1870s, the trustees authorized even wider reporting, taking the remarkable step of deciding to publish the minutes of their meetings and release them to the public.

Other early foundations also published annual reports (Magat, 1984). The Carnegie Institution of Washington (1902) and the Carnegie Endowment for International Peace (1910) published annual reports from their beginnings, as did the Cleveland Foundation (1914), the Commonwealth Fund (1918), and the New York Community Trust (1920). The Carnegie Foundation for the

Advancement of Teaching, founded in 1905, began publishing annual reports the next year, and the Carnegie Corporation, established in 1911, issued its first report in 1921. Rockefeller's General Education Board, founded in 1902, began publishing annual reports in 1914, and at the Rockefeller Foundation full disclosure was the policy when it was established in 1913; its 1914 annual report, with photographs, financial statements, and descriptions of grantees, would be a model even today (Magat, 1984).

Despite the example of these foundations, fifty-five of seventy-five large foundations from 1921 to 1930 did not issue regular reports, and two-thirds of foundations did not publish any kind of report in the 1930s (Hollis, 1938). The number of foundations publishing annual reports between the 1930s and the Tax Reform Act of 1969 increased, but not by much. In 1956, Andrews identified only 107 foundations in the American Foundations Information Service directory that published some type of report. The 1955 edition of that directory contained 4,162 foundations, of which 107 is only 2.6 percent. By 1966 and the coming Tax Reform Act of 1969, the number of foundations publishing annual reports had increased to 127, but the number did not reach 200 before 1969 (Nason, 1977; Richman, 1975). In the 1970s, few large foundations and almost no small ones published annual reports (Friedman, 1973; Goulden, 1971; Nason, 1977).

In 1980, 60 percent of 271 private foundations responding to a survey by the Council on Foundations (1981) said they published reports, and of those who did not, 39 percent said they publicized grants in other ways and 19 percent encouraged grantees to announce grants. But the Foundation Center said that only 14.2 percent of the foundations in the 1985 *Foundation Directory* published annual reports, although 30 percent issued other public information material. In a 1994 survey of almost ten thousand foundations, the center learned that 10.8 percent published annual or multiyear reports; including other publications such as grantseeker guidelines and statements of program interests, the number was 25.5 percent. Although the number of foundations issuing annual reports is rising, the percentage of large foundations (at least $1 million in assets or $100,000 in annual grants) doing so has actually fallen from 16 percent to 11 percent since 1981. The main reason is the addition of over 5,500 foundations to the Foundation Center's survey universe between 1985 and 1994. Most of these are small, have yet to define their grantmaking priorities, and are generally less than accessible (Renz, Lawrence, and Treiber, 1995).

To recognize foundations for publishing annual reports, the Council on Foundations started the Wilmer Shields Rich Award in 1984 (*Chronicle of Philanthropy*, 1990c; Hettleman, 1992). One of the requirements for winning is the inclusion of important information for grantseekers, including the following (Stamp, 1987; *Chronicle of Philanthropy*, 1994; Viscusi, 1985):

1. Address and telephone number of the foundation
2. Names and professional affiliations of trustees
3. Names and titles of staff
4. Statement of purpose and interests
5. Instructions for applying for grants
6. Explanation of how proposals are reviewed
7. List of grants made in the report period
8. Financial statements for the report period
9. List of the foundation's investments

Although annual reports are important, they may not be the best way for foundations to communicate with grantseekers, researchers, or the media. Nielsen says that annual reports are "ill-designed and inefficient" means to accomplish their purposes, rarely providing applicants with the information they need most: how to apply for a grant (1985, p. 416). Nearly fifty years before Nielsen's comments, Hollis criticized annual reports for failing to present the administrative structures of foundations, the procedures for reviewing applications, and the successes and failures of grant projects. To read in an annual report that a grant had been awarded, said Hollis, but never to have read its results is "at the least an unenlightening experience" (1938, p. 70). Some foundations claim they do not publish reports because they can be expensive, using money that could otherwise be awarded in grants. Others fear an increase in proposals received, but clearly stating program interests in a report can actually reduce the number of requests by redirecting those that do not match a foundation's interests. Even the smallest report, therefore, can ultimately save grantseekers from submitting inappropriate proposals and foundations from having to reject them. Some think the IRS return, which some foundations send in response to requests for information, is sufficient public disclosure of their activities. Still others consider annual reports and all other means of disclosure an invasion of their privacy (Curtis, 1987; Desruisseaux, 1986a; Taylor, 1953).

There are, however, excellent reasons to publish annual reports: they tell people what foundations do with their money, and in organizations chartered to serve the public good no rationale can outweigh this principle of accountability. Furthermore, reporting can be a kind of internal compass that helps determine the direction of a foundation and that provides an additional means of evaluation. Annual reports can also help decrease the suspicions people have of foundations, dispelling damaging perceptions and reducing the call for more regulation.

Reporting the results of foundation grantmaking can be exciting, although this benefit may be difficult for low-profile foundations to believe. Featuring grantees in annual reports can give them valuable recognition and strengthen their chances of gaining funding after a foundation grant ends. The Pew Memorial Trust took more than thirty years to issue its first annual report, but when it did in 1979, it was pleased with the results. "It was our hope," wrote the president, "that such a report would attract the requests (to) improve the effectiveness of our work. The response has been gratifying" (Nason, 1989, p. 26).

More foundations are participating in the *Foundation Directory* and *Foundation Directory: Part 2* and publishing annual reports and other public information material, but for every one that has improved its accessibility, many remain stubbornly opposed to the idea that they have any responsibility to the public. Voluntary participation in the *Foundation Directory* and the *Foundation Directory: Part 2* is poor, and compliance with the disclosure provisions of the Tax Reform Act of 1969 is perfunctory and even grudging. Secrecy and isolation are still common in foundations, and their response to regulatory provisions designed to improve their accessibility is often characterized by recalcitrance. More than twenty years ago, David Rockefeller wondered if foundations would ever recognize their accountability to the public or continue to be "austere and mysterious" (1973, p. 24). The answer to his question is yes—and no. More foundations are improving their public accountability, but for many others the lesson is still unlearned: the privacy of foundations is a *privilege* awarded to them because of their contributions to society, not an excuse to ignore the responsibilities of citizenship in a democracy.

Implications for Grantseekers of Foundations as Citizens

The accessibility of many foundations is so poor that grantseekers face an unnecessarily tedious task in getting information from them. Secrecy is prevalent in foundations, and some maintain that they have no responsibility to communicate with the public; others contend that if they comply with the minimum requirements of the law they fulfill their public accountability obligation completely. Some foundations are shy and take very seriously the tradition of anonymity in philanthropy, but the grudging reluctance to provide information was documented by the earliest researchers of foundations and continues to plague the field today. The IRS returns of foundations are often incomplete, especially the public information section, and the IRS has never had enough staff to audit foundation returns to correct this problem and is not likely to examine more returns in the near future because of threatened staff cutbacks.

The privacy of foundations, within certain limits, deserves to be protected just as does the privacy of other nongovernmental organizations. Indeed, the argument that foundations are public organizations because they serve the public good is flawed; if foundation assets were considered public, so could the resources of all other private nonprofits, such that college and museum endowments, for example, could be considered part of the public treasury. The tax benefits foundations enjoy are, in effect, society's payment for the charitable functions they perform, tasks that would otherwise burden the public treasury or, quite possibly, not be done at all. Traditions of personal liberty in this country allow people to save or spend their money that the government chooses not to tax; why should they be restricted if they establish foundations?

Americans have long said that there should be a private counterpart to government aid, an autonomous alternative that allows for private gifts for public needs. Foundations are an important part of that effort, and if we believe in the plurality of society we should defend their right to be private. Foundations do enrich the pluralism of the nation, mainly because they are free from the burdensome reporting and crippling degree of public accountability some people would establish. Among the nation's nonprofits, few possess greater freedom than foundations—and for good reason: they must be free to question any belief or practice, regardless of its popularity. But that is difficult, and sometimes it is dangerous. If foundations were regulated by the federal government, the democratic idea of providing space between private organizations and government would be compromised, and, in response to what they would almost certainly regard as an unwarranted intrusion into their affairs, they might withdraw their support or close their doors forever (Taylor, 1953; Simon, 1973).

There are strong justifications for the privacy of foundations, but their poor record of public accountability raises important questions about the very idea of them in a democracy. Is the inconspicuousness of foundations appropriate, especially when they help finance many of the nation's health, social, cultural, and educational organizations? Why are foundations permitted to have so much wealth and power without being required to publish annual reports, especially when corporations are so obligated? Is their favorable tax treatment warranted in light of their poor record of public accountability? Why should foundations, as organizations chartered to serve the public good, be able to avoid public examination? The answer is that they should *not* because secrecy is inconsistent with democracy and is not tolerated in other organizations that serve the public interest.

Foundations have considerable potential to affect public policy and should not be permitted to operate at the fringes of society. They can claim that disclosure ruins their privacy, threatens their freedom, attracts inappropriate proposals, uses money that could be awarded in grants, and publicizes their charity inappropriately. They have made these excuses since their beginning, but the answers given in the past are still valid today: a certain amount of disclosure is required by law, anonymity is impossible when public records exist, annual reports are required from other corporations, disclosure of program interests can reduce the number of inappropriate requests, and, as public trusts, foundations should not be permitted to isolate themselves from the American people.

Recommendations to Foundations as Citizens

Foundations should acknowledge that they have a responsibility to report to the public on their actions. The guiding principle in public accountability should be to protect the privacy of foundations, but when their privacy interferes with the people's right to know, the interest of the public should take precedence. This position has long been supported by the federal government, associations in philanthropy, and many of the wisest people in foundations; it strikes a balance for private organizations that act in the public weal. The assets of most foundations have been earned privately and are free to be awarded privately, but as long as they are chartered by the state or federal government to serve the public interest, they have a duty to report on how they have fulfilled this commission.

Foundation boards need to be more representative of the communities they serve, and wisdom and experience with problems should be the criteria for selecting foundation trustees, not just familiarity with the donor of a foundation or the donor's business. Foundations should secure the aid of organizations such as the Association of Governing Boards to help strengthen their governance practices. In addition to improving their boards, foundations should hire staff, especially communications staff. Those that are too small to employ personnel, as most are, should consider pooling resources with other foundations to hire staff, retaining communications consultants, or enlisting the aid of organizations such as colleges and universities that have communications staff. The frequent claim by foundations that their limited assets preclude hiring staff, especially communications staff, is no justification for their inaccessibility.

Every foundation should publish an annual or biennial report, regardless of the size of its assets, grants, or staff. Congress has afforded foundations every opportunity to publish such reports voluntarily, but most have not. The time has come for Congress to require them. Without exception, the report should contain the foundation's address, telephone number, the name of its contact person, assets, grants, and grantees for the calendar or fiscal year. A clear statement of program interests and a description of the proposal review process should be included, and so should an explanation of what a foundation does *not* fund. Foundations have assets of approximately $200 billion, so they can hardly claim poverty as an excuse for their unwillingness to publish reports, even though they have often used this very alibi. If most charitable organizations, including some of the smallest and poorest community groups, can demonstrate their accountability to the public by producing annual reports, foundations certainly can too.

The annual public notice provision of the Tax Reform Act of 1969 should be toughened so it reflects the different sizes and geographic service areas of foundations. The current provision allows a foundation to place its notice in *any* newspaper with general circulation in the county in which its principal office is located, regardless of the size of the foundation, its geographic area of operation, or the size of the newspaper. This is an invitation for foundations to fulfill the letter but not the spirit of the law. The general circulation clause should specify that a foundation may not place its notice in a trade publication. Also, the annual public notice (and all other publications of a foundation) should be required to contain the address and telephone number of the foundation—not of another organization such as a bank. Foundations should not be permitted to have unlisted telephone numbers or post office boxes for addresses.

Too many foundations make obvious errors and omissions on their IRS returns, especially the public information section. Individuals are not excused from improper completion of their tax forms, and neither should foundations be. The IRS understandably devotes most of its attention to the tax part of foundation returns, but more attention needs to be given to the public information portion. Congress should direct the General Accounting Office to prepare periodic reports on how well foundations complete that part, thereby assisting the IRS with its monitoring responsibilities. Foundations that repeatedly submit incomplete returns or that continue to make obvious errors on the form should be considered scofflaws by the IRS. Furthermore, the return should be available for inspection by the public in a foundation's office for a year, not just 180 days; it is effective with the IRS for a year and should be available to the public for no less time. Grantseekers should not have to visit a foundation in person to inspect its return, a provision that, ironically, some foundations have used to create obstacles for people who want to get information from them. Foundations should be required to send a copy of their return to anyone who requests it in writing.

The public accountability of foundations should remain on the Congressional agenda until the problem is resolved, and the accessibility of foundations should be monitored continuously. In the past, reports on foundation accessibility were produced mainly during the infrequent Congressional investigations. The accountability studies should document the number of foundations publishing annual reports or other public information material, the performance of foundations in completing their returns (including the frequency of errors and omissions), and unique cases of foundation inaccessibility that come to the attention of the Oversight Subcommittee of the Ways and Means Committee of the House of Representatives. Such information is now collected piecemeal by the Foundation Center, the Council on Foundations, and the IRS, and the proposed accountability report would integrate the disparate information in one document.

Foundation News and Commentary, the magazine of the Council on Foundations, should continue to devote attention to public accountability because many foundations remain unconvinced of its importance and benefits. The council itself should update its *Public Information Handbook for Foundations* (1973) and expand the work into a book on public accountability that presents legislated accountability requirements, advice on publishing annual reports and other public information material, recommendations on relating to grantseekers and the media, and ideas on conducting forums to meet prospective grantees and inform the public of the purposes of foundations. The council should also sponsor seminars on completing the annual foundation IRS return and complying with the annual public notice provision of the Tax Reform Act of 1969; the IRS and regional associations of grantmakers could cosponsor these. In addition, the council should continue to state its advocacy of public accountability in the strongest possible terms.

Chapter Five

Foundations as Activists
How Political Ideology and Influence Affect Grant Decisions

*The major indictment against philanthropy is that it has
ignored the opportunities democracy offers for reforms from
within. It has distracted our minds and attention from
community responsibility for the removal of social defects. It
has encouraged us to leave reforms to the activity of self-
appointed groups. Its reforms have tended to be superficial,
because it has everywhere selected for its leaders those
interested in philanthropy, but not in democracy.*
CORNELIA J. CANNON,
ATLANTIC MONTHLY (1921, P. 294)

Many people think that foundations support social movements to
form or change public policy. But this belief is more myth than
reality; most foundations are involved in the nonpolitical subsidization of conventional, not radical, organizations.

The Metaphor of Foundations as Activists

In some ways, foundations resemble activists who lead social movements to form or change public policy. This image is widely recognized by people in nonprofit organizations and foundations
themselves, many of whom believe that foundations have been at
the forefront of the nation's social movements, especially the civil
rights, peace, and women's movements. The metaphor of founda-

106

tions as activists, however, is more fiction than fact. The evidence shows that the overwhelming majority of foundations, liberal and conservative, have staunchly avoided social activism and the formation of public policy.

Public policy may be defined as the actions of the executive, legislative, and judicial branches of government expressed in laws, regulations, and executive orders, but resting on the most fundamental principles in the Declaration of Independence and the Constitution. The formal enactment of public policy is the responsibility of elected officials, but its formation is open to every citizen and is protected by the principles of the First Amendment: the freedom of speech, the right to assemble peaceably, and the right to petition the government.

Public policy issues are immensely varied: environmental protection, urban redevelopment, health care, campaign financing, inflation, gun control, highway construction, crime, farm subsidies, savings and investment, welfare, education, air traffic safety, foreign policy, taxation, the legal system, interest rates, defense spending, and many more. Advocates of public policy positions seek to disclose, encourage, criticize, or modify actions of federal, state, or local government through lobbying, research, organizing, publishing, demonstrations, and litigation.

Foundations participate in public policy by funding research centers that propose ideas to the legislative branch, suggestions for changes to the judicial branch, or new programs in the executive branch. They provide grants for operating support or special projects in advocacy organizations such as the American Civil Liberties Union and the National Association for the Advancement of Colored People. They fund the education of people employed or about to be employed by government agencies and advocate the appointment of their founders, trustees, and staff members to government commissions and policy groups. They provide scholarships and fellowships to people who want to pursue careers in public service and sponsor polls to measure public opinion on policy issues. They support projects to rectify discrimination and encourage people to register and then to vote. They test the suitability of demonstration programs for wider adoption and disseminate the results of innovative projects through forums, publications, and television programs. They sponsor legal defense organizations and conduct investigations of agencies that misuse their governmental appropriations or private support. They advocate liberal or conservative political policies through think tanks and conferences.

The Issue of Foundations and Public Policy

Some people discourage the involvement of foundations in public affairs, contending that such activity is controversial and that the Tax Reform Act of 1969 restricts foundations to nonpartisan work. Others support it, arguing that foundations exist to serve the public interest and have the right, indeed the obligation, to engage in public policy formation.

This has been an issue since some of the nation's first and most prominent philanthropists entered the public arena. Henry Ford, Andrew Carnegie, and John D. Rockefeller believed that their foundations had the right to influence public policy just as they had that privilege as citizens, but many people then were ambivalent about the participation of the rich in public affairs because though power and wealth were respected, they were also feared. Today, most Americans agree that people have the right to get rich, but many also are concerned that the wealthy have significantly more political power than everyone else. The issue of foundation involvement in public affairs is therefore unresolved, and Dorothy S. Ridings, new president of the Council on Foundations, reports that her travels in 1996–97 confirm that many foundations are "more than a bit nervous" about the role of foundations in public policy (1997, p. 16).

A larger issue is whether elite organizations such as foundations can exist in a democracy without threatening democratic principles. The nation needs highly educated managers for its complex technological institutions, but such elites and the foundations that support them are an ominous presence; conceivably they might use their power and wealth to promote extreme ideologies, to silence people or organizations that oppose them, or to acquire an unfair advantage in their dealings with politicians or government agencies. If instead they avoid the public arena, they may become arcane and irrelevant, abdicating their responsibility to join citizens and other institutions in participating in the democratic process. Involvement in public policy, therefore, is a two-edged sword for foundations: at once perhaps their most substantive opportunity for service and their greatest vulnerability (James, 1973; Pifer, 1984c).

Arguments Against Activism by Foundations

The most common argument against foundation participation in public affairs is that it can be controversial. When foundations enter the public arena, they encounter an often contentious domain in which people who have been subjected to injustice sometimes direct their rage at any convenient target, especially large, wealthy organizations such as foundations. This threat has long discouraged foundations and their trustees from involvement in public affairs; in 1914, Frederick Gates sought to prevent the Rockefeller Foundation's entry into the national debate on social policy by asking its board, "Can you command this material as you can command the materials of investigation in medical science? I fear not" (Brown, 1965, p. 34).

A second argument against foundation participation in public affairs is that the Tax Reform Act of 1969 prohibits it. The law does forbid *partisan* political activity by foundations, but at passage of the Act, Congress said, and has since affirmed, that foundation participation in public affairs within prescribed limits is in the public interest. During investigations in the 1950s and 1960s, Congress as a whole endorsed a public policy role for foundations, although a few members strongly opposed it. The law is somewhat confusing, and some foundation officials, afraid of Congress and the Internal Revenue Service, have forsaken the public arena as a result. However, confusion can provide an excuse for foundations that are already disinclined to support activism, according to John Edie, general counsel of the Council on Foundations, who believes that most foundations have overreacted to the Act's restraints against lobbying (Bothwell, 1984; Edie, 1991; Joseph, 1985; Nason, 1989).

Arguments for Activism by Foundations

The most common argument for the involvement of foundations in public policy is that laws and regulations directly affect many of their program interests, such as education, health care, the economy, and the environment, as well as many of their constituents:

children, minorities, the sick, the old, the illiterate, the unemployed, and the disenfranchised. If foundations were to bypass the public arena, they would avoid many of the problems that they have been chartered to solve and many of the people they have pledged to help. By this way of thinking, the greatest justification for the existence of foundations, or any organization commissioned to serve the public good, is the development of enlightened public policy. Foundations that operate so timidly that they become superfluous fail to do so (Joseph, 1985; Pifer, 1984a, 1984b, 1984c).

A second argument is that pluralistic decision making is essential in a democracy, and all people and organizations have not only the right but the obligation to contribute to the process and thus to the betterment of the republic. No other nonprofit organizations such as research institutes, colleges, and professional societies are prohibited from shaping public policy, so neither should foundations be. The nonprofit sector is indispensable to the public debate because its members have valuable experience in fighting many of the nation's most intractable problems, expertise that would be foolish to overlook. If foundations were barred from the public arena, they might withdraw their support of organizations involved in public affairs and fund only the most innocuous projects. If the freedom of foundations to participate in public policy can be so easily restricted, so can the same right of other nonprofits (Joseph, 1985; Pifer, 1984c, 1984d).

The Political Ideology of Foundations

By one view, foundations are a consistently conservative force, supporting conventional projects in established organizations concerned primarily with maintaining the status quo. That is, they represent a "sophisticated conservatism," espousing the values of efficiency and control, defending the existing system of power and prestige, and avoiding uncomfortable and contentious issues (Arnove, 1980, pp. 17–18).

The conservatism of foundations has its roots in the philosophies of their founders and trustees; in 1936, Lindeman (1988) noted that the great majority of foundation trustees were white, middle-aged, upper-class Protestant lawyers, bankers, and busi-

nessmen who protected the existing political and economic systems and opposed the redistribution of wealth and power. Thirty-
nine years later, Colwell (1993) found that 75 percent of a sample
of seventy-seven foundations had boards controlled by their
donors, who were almost always members of the economic elite.

Advocates of foundation conservatism point out that financial
responsibility is an essential part of a trustee's job, and people competent to handle large sums of money are often conservative. Conservatism in safeguarding charitable funds is certainly
understandable, perhaps even preferable, but the programs of
foundations, if they are to be progressive, need people who are not
satisfied with the way things are. Those who benefit from the current political and economic systems can be formidable barriers to
change. Julius Rosenwald criticized foundation trustees for being
more concerned with conserving foundation funds than in deriv-
ing the greatest possible usefulness from them (Coffman, 1936),
and Paul Hoffman reported that every time the Ford Foundation
received a few letters objecting to something it had done, he had
to spend hours reassuring the board (Macdonald, 1956). "It's hard
to be daring in a big foundation," said Ford trustee John McCloy.
"You're constantly being forced into conventional grooves by criticism or the fear of it" (p. 129).

Another problem is that many trustees are quite removed from
the subjects their foundations address, according to Bill Dietel of
the Rockefeller Brothers Fund (Bothwell, 1984). Educated people
of the sort who serve as foundation trustees are usually well aware
of the need for innovation in society, but they have rarely been personally involved in such advances and are often unwilling to urge
foundations to initiate change. Almost all foundation trustees nom-
inate and elect their fellow board members, so as vacancies occur,
they are likely to fill them with kindred spirits, people who are
wealthy, connected, and conservative—just as they are. As long as
foundations are led by self-perpetuating boards, little more can be
expected of them because the responsibilities of administering
wealth, coupled with the personal philosophies of most foundation
trustees, encourage conservatism.

In the past decade, a few foundations have organized support
of research centers committed to advancing conservative policies
and have played a part in Republican Congressional victories that

have moved public policy to the right. Conservative foundations have long advocated self-sufficiency and economic growth, but they are now concerned with what they believe is the weakening of the moral fabric of society once bound by the threads of community, family, and religion. Midge Decter, director of the Committee for the Free World, a conservative group, accuses foundations of having had a distinctly liberal bent for decades, and conservative leaders, many of whom believe that liberal policies have failed, have encouraged foundations to develop other approaches. The result has been a resurgence of conservative thought in foundations, most notably in the John M. Olin Foundation, the Smith Richardson Foundation, the Bradley Foundation, and the Sarah Scaife Foundation, the last of which has awarded more than $100 million to activist organizations working to move organizations and the government in a conservative direction (Bothwell and Saasta, 1982; Greene and Moore, 1995; McMillen, 1987; Nason, 1989).

The other view of the political ideology of foundations is that foundations have been consistently and predominantly liberal, and have given much more money to liberal organizations than to conservative ones. Althea K. Nagai, Robert Lerner, and Stanley Rothman, authors of *Giving for Social Change: Foundations, Public Policy and the American Political Agenda* (1994), claim that liberal policy centers in the latter 1980s received four times as much money and four times as many grants as conservative policy centers. They examined the grantmaking of 225 foundations that made 4,738 public policy grants worth over $386 million. Of this amount, $170 million (44.0 percent) was considered to be liberal, $163 million (42.2 percent) was said to be politically neutral, and $43 million (11.1 percent) was judged to be conservative. The rest was not classifiable. The trustees of the foundations identified themselves as conservatives (42 percent), liberals (37 percent), or moderates (21 percent). Although fewer in number, conservative grants on average were larger than liberal grants; the average liberal grant was $49,340, while the average conservative grant was $112,756, more than 128 percent higher. Liberal foundations favored women and minorities, immigration, urban affairs, the environment, health, the arts, South Africa, media studies, and population issues, whereas conservative foundations supported religion, economics, aging, health, think tanks, South Africa, war and peace, and human rights (Goss, 1994).

The Capital Research Center, which published the work of Nagai, Lerner, and Rothman, also believes that corporate foundations have a liberal bias and, in its strident words, are "feeding the mouths that bite, while shunning conservative policy advocates who are committed to defending American business." By subsidizing civil rights activists, environmentalists, feminists, and others the center considers hostile to the existing economic order, liberal corporations are violating their fiduciary duty to protect the interests of shareholders. Some of the corporations that the center considers liberal are AT&T, Exxon, General Mills, and Xerox; those denoted as conservative are Dayton-Hudson, Inland Steel, Quaker Oats, and Ralston-Purina. Such classifications, however, have alienated the officers of many corporate foundations: "It's a total bunch of trash," says Peter Spina, general manager of corporate and government relations for Mobil Oil, which placed fifth in the center's "Misgivers List," the top ten so-called liberal corporations. "This is probably the sloppiest scholarship I've seen in a long time," Spina added. According to its critics, the center's mistake in classifying corporations as liberal or conservative is that it focused solely on their public policy grants, which represented only about 15 percent of all their grants (Montague, 1990, pp. 1, 12–13).

Claims of the Capital Research Center notwithstanding, some foundations *are* liberal just as some are conservative, and the Ford Foundation is considered to be the most liberal large foundation. It created or has sustained many advocacy groups, including the Mexican-American Legal Defense and Education Fund, the Legal Defense and Education Fund of the National Association for the Advancement of Colored People, the Native American Rights Fund, the Puerto Rican Legal Defense and Education Fund, the Women's Rights Project, the Center for Law and Social Policy, the Environmental Defense Fund, the Education Fund of the League of Women Voters, and the Sierra Club Legal Defense Fund. The National Network of Grantmakers, a recently formed association of liberal foundations, may have been created in response to the establishment of the Institute for Educational Affairs, the association of conservative foundations. The mission of the National Network of Grantmakers is to expand progressive philanthropy, sustain the movement for democracy, and support groups fighting for women, minorities, homosexuals, and the handicapped (Moore, 1990; Roelofs, 1984–85).

Despite these arguments, claims that foundations are liberal or conservative are not particularly accurate. Foundations span the political spectrum, and their grantmaking is generally much less about promoting a political agenda than about trying to solve problems and support nonprofits. Conservative critics accuse liberal foundations of engaging in partisan political activity, of creating dependence rather than independence in their grantees, and of injecting left-wing ideology into free enterprise. At the same time, liberal critics charge conservative foundations with advocating social and economic doctrines that control or co-opt their grantees, dulling the edge of grassroots groups by centralizing their authority in the hands of conservatives (Karl, 1986; Ostrander, 1993; Pifer, 1984c). "To the extent that some of us *are* called conservative," says James Piereson, executive director of the John M. Olin Foundation, "you're really talking about a tendency rather than some carefully designed ideology. . . . I don't think it's fair to call us conservative unless you're also prepared to call the Carnegie, Ford, and Rockefeller foundations 'liberal'" (Desruisseaux, 1987a, pp. A74–A75).

Most foundations are neither leftist nor rightist but centrist, and overall their programs and grantees are not liberal or conservative but middle-of-the-road. Most foundation giving reflects personal rather than political interests, and foundations are institutions of social continuity, not social change; their strongest tradition is not social or political advocacy, but a stubborn pragmatism that places politics a distinct second to program. For the vast majority of foundations, leftist or rightist labels are not only unfair but largely irrelevant.

Foundations and Social Movements

Foundations have a reputation for supporting social movements, a guiding principle of which is called *interest group participation,* the idea that the interests of people are best served when they themselves participate in developing policies that affect them. Guided by this doctrine, foundations have funded advocacy organizations such as the National Organization for Women and the National Council of Churches and have supported technical assistance organizations that provide policy research, leadership training, management consulting, organizing strategies, or legal advice to advocacy groups. Such organizations often serve as a buffer between foundations and grassroots groups, reducing the need for foundations to deal face-to-face with noisy activists and the discomfort they create. Unlike many social movements, which are comprised of inexperienced grassroots activists, technical assistance organizations are typically staffed by professionals—often attorneys, public administrators, or retired executives. Foundations do prefer these: from 1960 to 1980, 43 percent of all foundation grants for activism went to research centers and 33 percent to technical assistance centers. Groups that performed actual advocacy work such as organizing and demonstrating received only 17 percent of foundation grants to social movements, and the remaining 7 percent went to churches or agencies that served as sponsoring organizations for new activist groups (Jenkins, 1989).

Foundation support of social movements also derives from two theories of governance proposed by political scientists: a *participation model* based on the involvement of people in decisions affecting them and a *representation model* that appoints leaders to speak for people and holds them accountable for their actions. In their support of social movements, foundations have preferred the representation model, most often funding the leaders instead of the members of movements. They have often required advocacy groups to have management and fiscal expertise, in the process sometimes damaging the sense of ownership by movement members; as grassroots supporters are replaced by foundations and become increasingly dependent on them, they rely less on their members. To ensure their own survival, movement managers have often tempered their tactics to appeal to foundations, confirming Robert Michels's principle of self-preservation in organizations. The civil rights movement is a case in point; by funding *reasonable* people and organizations in the movement, foundations promoted moderates as leaders in the black community and served as gatekeepers, granting legitimacy to certain people and organizations and encouraging palatable reforms such as voting rights while discouraging more militant goals and tactics. By declining to fund radical people and projects, foundations withheld needed nourishment from those organizations, few of which survived (Ostrander, 1994).

Mitchell Sviridoff, former head of the Ford Foundation's Division of National Affairs, confirms that the foundation supported the "moderate middle" in the civil rights movement, organizations such as the Urban League and the National Association for the Advancement of Colored People instead of more radical groups (Reeves, 1970, p. 16). According to Peter Skerry, visiting fellow at the Brookings Institution, the upheaval in 1994 at the NAACP that led to the ouster of executive director Benjamin Chavis was not orchestrated so much by its membership as by the Ford Foundation, which withheld a major grant until the NAACP put its administrative and financial houses in order. William Raspberry, columnist for the *Washington Post,* observed this and questioned how such a venerable organization with 600,000 members could have become so beholden to a foundation (Harwood, 1997).

Foundations, however, cannot be faulted entirely for such policies because without developing managerial and fund-raising skill few grassroots groups would mature and even fewer would survive. Foundations have therefore served as "cooling-out" agencies, delaying and preventing more radical change while maintaining the economic and political order favorable to them and their trustees (Arnove, 1980, p. 1). True grassroots movements are often not accountable to boards of trustees and represent considerable risk to foundations. More professional organizations, however, usually have conventional organizational structures and orthodox management practices and offer greater assurance to foundations that their money will be used prudently. As one foundation officer told Jenkins, "We fund *responsible* militancy!" (1989, p. 298).

Until 1960, foundation support of social movements was almost nonexistent, but such funding increased during the 1960s and 1970s to its peak in 1977 and then declined through 1980. But even at the peak, foundation support of movements comprised only seven-tenths of 1 percent of all their grantmaking; of the 22,000 foundations at that time only 131 had funded an activist project or organization, and of those only 39 had contributed more than a third of their annual giving to activism, whereas 66 had never given more than 10 percent. From 1960 to 1980, the largest recipients of foundation grants to activism were organizations representing blacks, which received $56.9 million (22.9 percent of the total); environmentalism, $25.2 million (10.2 percent);

women's rights, $16.6 million (6.7 percent); Mexican Americans, $15.8 million (6.4 percent); and consumerism, $12.8 million (5.2 percent). Peace, students, the poor, the aged, and homosexuals received the rest. Foundation grants to social movements during these twenty years ranged from a high of $5.5 million (by the Ford Foundation to start the Mexican-American Legal Defense and Education Fund) to a low of $150 (for take-back-the-night marches); the average was $24,534 (Jenkins, 1987, 1989).

Ironically, foundations have rarely funded organizations that most need the money. More than sixty years ago, Coffman (1936) noted that the majority of grants went to institutions that were already well funded, and in 1968, a year infamous for social and political unrest, nearly 80 percent of foundation giving went to educational organizations (31 percent), health and medical organizations (21 percent), general welfare organizations (14 percent), and cultural institutions (11 percent). The remainder went to religion (4 percent), community services (4 percent), racial or ethnic relations (3 percent), science and the arts (2 percent), technology (2 percent), social sciences (2 percent), and 1 percent each to conservation, recreation, vocational training, housing, individual services, and family programs. Voter registration, voter education, and training for political candidates in 1968 received less than one-half of 1 percent, contrary to the belief that liberal foundations instigated the political activism of that infamous year. Moreover, almost 95 percent of foundation funds in 1968 went to qualified charitable organizations—those to which people could make deductible contributions, such as churches, schools, colleges, museums, agencies, and hospitals, which were already receiving support from the general public. Only 6 percent went to recipients to which contributions were not deductible: 3 percent to individuals and 3 percent to noncharitable organizations, such as social welfare groups, civic leagues, labor unions, trade associations, and foreign organizations (Commission on Foundations and Private Philanthropy, 1970).

Foundations tend to follow rather than start social movements. The civil rights movement began in 1955 with the Montgomery bus boycott, but foundation grants to it were not significant until 1962. The peace movement started in the 1960s, but did not receive foundation support until 1972. The consumer movement began in 1966 with Ralph Nader's work on automobile safety, but his consumer advocacy organization, Public Citizen, was not funded by foundations until 1970. The women's movement emerged as a major force in 1970, but did not receive foundation funding until 1973. Only 17 percent of foundation grants to movements in the 1980s went to groups with a record of conducting demonstrations; the rest went to those using less vocal forms of expression, most prominently law firms (Jenkins, 1989).

Grants to higher education illustrate the preference of foundations for established and well-financed institutions. In 1990, thirty-seven universities received half the $803 million that foundations gave to higher education. The remaining half went to 1,023 colleges and universities, meaning that less than 4 percent of the institutions received 50 percent of the grants. The thirty-seven universities typically had the biggest endowments, the most and largest federal research grants, and the most sophisticated fund-raising operations. The complaint that foundations favor prestigious colleges and universities has been heard for years from public institutions, religious colleges, and historically black colleges, although lately, public universities have become much more successful in raising funds. In the late 1980s, the Andrew W. Mellon Foundation, the Charles Stewart Mott Foundation, and the Pew Charitable Trusts reduced the number of black colleges eligible to apply for their grants by half. Each invited twenty-four institutions to seek grants; nineteen, most of which were members of the United Negro College Fund, were asked by all three foundations. They were considered the most financially viable, and, according to Clarence Jupiter of Xavier University, this policy assured that schools with the most money would be the most likely to get even more (Bailey, 1988).

Foundations have an image of being crusaders for women and minorities, but the evidence repudiates this perception. A Ford Foundation-supported study found that only six-tenths of 1 percent of foundation grants in 1976, one year before the peak of activism support, went to women's programs; the total, $12 million, was less than a single university got that year from three foundations. Only 13 percent of that went to activist programs for women; most went to services (33 percent), research (24 percent), and scholarships (18 percent). Similarly, in 1982 the Foundation Center reported that only 2 percent of the grants of 444 mostly large foundations went to blacks (Bothwell, 1984), and the Latino Institute found that only 1 percent of foundation money in the late 1970s benefited Hispanics (Teltsch, 1981). Such numbers seem to confirm what Andrew Young had told foundations earlier: they should be ashamed at how they neglect civil rights organizations (Bothwell and Saasta, 1981). Until the 1930s, according to Joseph Foote (1990), organized philanthropy seemed to regard minorities only as objects of charity, and as late as 1990 foundation support of minority groups was only about 5 percent of all their giving. From 1991 to 1993, less than 1 percent of all foundation giving went to programs for American Indians and less than half of that went to groups run by Indians.

Despite limited direct support of women and minorities, an argument could be made that many foundations benefit women and minorities indirectly. Grants to hospitals, colleges, and universities, for example, could be said to help women and minorities, even though they do not go directly to organizations supporting or advocating for these people. Many kinds of grants encourage change in the relationship between groups or individuals, change that often involves economic or political power; thus, virtually every grant, including those which are merely ameliorative, could be said to produce social change of some sort and affect the public interest (Simon, 1973). Perhaps so, but foundation grants to organizations directly serving women and minorities have been minuscule, dispelling the myth that foundations are crusaders for social change and contradicting the descriptions that foundations have given of themselves. Richard Lyman, former president of the Rockefeller Foundation, candidly observed that foundations often talk about diversity, but practice "the herd instinct and conformity." Of the nation's 38,000 foundations, less than three dozen, most of them relatively small, give all or most of their grants to activism, and the number of foundations willing to fund community organizing, voter registration and education, advocacy, social justice litigation, and other initiatives intended to bring disenfranchised people into the debate about public priorities is "pathetically small" (Bothwell, 1984, pp. 1–4; Covington and Parachini, 1995, p. 2).

When deciding whether to support social movements, foundations often seek the advice of consultants because activist groups usually have little, if any, record of performance. Before making its landmark grant to the Cleveland chapter of the Congress of Racial Equality in 1967, for example, the Ford Foundation conferred with the editor of the *Cleveland Plain Dealer* and several of that city's prominent business figures. Activists themselves have sometimes become consultants to foundations (Jenkins, 1989). To pave the path to foundation grants, some activists have exaggerated the seriousness of problems in their communities, and many foundation officers have readily accepted their assessment, convincing themselves that they are solving grave social issues when they are really not, pleased to be linked arm-in-arm against injustice with exotic types from the ghettos and barrios (Hart, 1973).

But many public policy research centers, dependent on grants, have learned to focus on issues that interest foundations because groups that challenge the economic or political order have not been supported widely (Colwell, 1993). The reason foundations do not support challenges to the status quo, say some experts, is that they are run by the wealthy. Odendahl contends that elite philanthropy assists mainly in the social reproduction of the upper class, supporting institutions that sustain the culture, education, and status of the wealthy. She says that the rich do not give to the poor, but to institutions they cherish and use themselves: private universities, exclusive academies, art museums, symphonies, theaters, and the finest hospitals. One New Yorker on several foundation boards admitted as much, telling Odendahl, "I feel that I am taken very seriously. . . . I think some people listen to my counsel a little too carefully." The rich belong to a culture, and their philanthropy, far from aiding the poor and the disenfranchised, serves primarily their own interest. "The charity of the wealthy doesn't just begin at home," says Odendahl. "It *stays* there" (Bailey, 1990, p. 4; Odendahl, 1990, pp. 27, 232).

The metaphor of foundations as activists may be thought-provoking—it may even fit common belief about the nature of foundations—but the evidence shows that the chief characteristic of foundations is not extremism but orthodoxy. Grantseeking representatives of minorities and disadvantaged people, and lesser-known advocacy organizations, have limited access to foundations and receive a disproportionately small amount of their grants, "a minor blip on the philanthropic screen" (Eisenberg, 1991a, pp. 41–42). Most foundations do not question or prod the system; *they are the system* and they engage in the distinctly conventional subsidization of colleges, universities, museums, hospitals, galleries, and traditional social agencies.

Yet 57 percent of respondents to a 1996 Gallup poll said they support the role that foundations play in social movements such as civil rights, consumer protection, environmental protection, and equality for women (14 percent opposed it), indicating that people believe that foundations have been active in advocacy work (Dundjerski, 1996c). But far from being the champions of activism, the overwhelming majority of foundations have provided virtually no support to social movements and hardly any impetus to either the left or the right, and both the claims of foundations and the perceptions of the public that foundations are social activists are much more myth than reality.

Implications for Grantseekers of Foundations as Activists

Organizations that advocate on behalf of unrepresented people will find few foundations receptive to their causes. Activist organizations in their formative years typically lack many of the features that foundations expect in applicants: boards of trustees, facilities, equipment, management structures and policies, and financial accounting systems, apart from performance records and wide community support. Then, too, some activists do most of their best work in their early days before they establish formal organizations.

Many foundations are afraid of controversy, controlled by conservative trustees, disdainful (if not terrified) of Congress and the IRS, and too ready to accept the incorrect assumption that the law forbids public policy grantmaking. Foundations are the first aid kits—not the surgeons—of society. They defend the existing economic and political systems and the people and institutions that lead those systems. They are not moved to activism on behalf of people excluded by the systems. They oppose the redistribution of wealth and the people who advocate this remedy for society's injustices. Foundations are not advocates of change; they are barriers to it. Their agenda is not politics, but pragmatism; most foundations are interested in what works. Social programs are now considered by many people to have failed, and some foundations prefer organizations that espouse self-reliance and advocate economic solutions to disenfranchisement.

Recommendations to Foundations as Activists

Foundations should support organizations involved in the formation of public policy because the problems of the public are the problems of foundations. Individual foundations may choose not to be involved in public policy grantmaking just as they may elect not to support higher education, but collectively they should participate in the public debate. Likewise, the Council on Foundations should continue to defend the right of foundations to make public policy grants.

Foundations that opt against public policy grantmaking should do so because they have made a rational decision consistent with their donors' intent and their trustees' guidance, not because they are afraid of publicity, controversy, Congress, or the IRS. As some of the few organizations left in America free from political control, special interests, and financial dependency, they have an obligation to use their special freedom to advocate public policy positions. Foundations that do choose to fund public policy work should increase their direct support of organizations at the forefront of such work instead of funding technical assistance organizations. Admittedly, making grants to movement organizations is difficult; they may lack nonprofit status and even management structure. But foundations should try to the greatest extent possible to fund those at the cutting edge of activism; many fund activists only *after* they have done much of their most significant work. Funding technical support organizations creates a barrier between foundations and social movements and ensures that most of the money will not reach the activists.

Foundations can increase their involvement in public policy issues in many ways according to Dorothy S. Ridings, President of the Council on Foundations (1997, p. 18):

- They can acknowledge that their work has important public policy implications and that public policy issues likewise affect them. If a foundation supports the environment, day care, symphonies, secondary schools, churches, or voter education, it *is* involved in public policy.

- They can encourage people and organizations, including other foundations, to endorse public policy activity by funding policy-oriented research or producing publications on public policy issues.
- They can help form or change public policy by strengthening grantees involved in public affairs or disseminating the results of public policy initiatives.
- They can sponsor forums to discuss public policy issues and bring experts together to talk about issues facing the nation.
- They can facilitate the participation of unrepresented or underrepresented groups in the public debate by funding organizing strategies.

Among the ills that foundations should try to stop are teenage smoking, child labor, monopoly pricing of pharmaceuticals, low-quality children's television programs, unsafe working conditions, and job discrimination. They should be involved in protecting Civil War battlefields, reducing teenage pregnancy, decreasing the school dropout rate, and improving race and ethnic relations. Problems of rural areas, urban decay, drug addiction, homelessness, hunger, productivity, the federal budget deficit, taxation, crime, incarceration, and health policy could all benefit from foundation leadership, as could the problem of the disaffection of Americans from the political process. Foundations should increase—not decrease—their support of women and minorities. The retreat of foundations from funding black colleges and other organizations advocating on behalf of blacks (the voter education project, for example) is regrettable. Foundations were instrumental in the development of women's colleges and black colleges, and these organizations are an excellent investment because they have proven their ability to create paths to prosperity for their students.

Chapter Six

Foundations as Entrepreneurs

How Program Officers View Risk Taking

*We must always remember that there is not enough
money for the work of human uplift and that there
never can be. How vitally important it is, therefore,
that the expenditure should go as far as possible and
be used with the greatest intelligence!*
JOHN D. ROCKEFELLER, *RANDOM REMINISCENCES OF
MEN AND EVENTS* (1933, P. 154)

'Tis not enough to help the feeble up, but to support him after.
WILLIAM SHAKESPEARE, *TIMON OF ATHENS*, I, 1, 107

A common belief is that foundations are risk takers, suppliers of
venture capital to people, projects, or organizations that rarely
receive grants from conventional donors such as corporations or
government agencies. This is more folklore than fact, however;
most foundations fund safe organizations such as museums, hospitals, and libraries instead of dangerous projects or entities.

The Metaphor of Foundations as Entrepreneurs

Like the idea that foundations are activists, the claim that they are
risk takers is more perception than reality. Such a metaphor suggests that foundations are a leading supplier of society's venture
capital and extols their ability to take risks as they attempt to

answer not only today's but tomorrow's questions, weighing the danger of failure against the promise of social, scientific, or educational gain. Remarkably free from pressure groups, political controls, religious interests, and legislative appropriations, foundations have a rare opportunity for risk taking, and with no voters, advertisers, or customers to satisfy, they have the flexibility to adapt quickly to change and to operate on the cutting edge of ideas. Foundations can do what other organizations usually cannot: take the long view, deal with the most difficult problems, support impartial studies, and contribute in a nonpartisan way to the solution of problems. Foundations need not collect funds, maintain memberships, or face the pressures of the profit-and-loss statement; they have few fixed financial obligations, and of all institutions that serve the American people, few, if any, have the assets and freedom that enable them, in theory, to be the venture capitalists of philanthropy.

The concept of venture capital in philanthropy probably developed to a large extent because of the role foundations played in advancing science and education in this century. John D. Rockefeller believed that science and particularly education offered the best hope for improving man's condition, and Lindeman (1936) contended that nearly all donors had education foremost in mind when they established their foundations. The philosophy apparently remains intact today: of ninety-nine elite donors Ostrower interviewed (1995), 92 percent had made at least one of their largest gifts to education, more than any other field, and 57 percent had made their largest gift to a higher education institution.

Foundation grants to science and education, especially through elite universities and research centers, may have helped reconcile a few American intellectuals to some of the contradictions in capitalism, and the advocacy by foundations of the concept of venture capital also may have strengthened the public's faith in both foundations and capitalism. Ernest Hollis traced the development of the idea of venture capital in philanthropy to the years immediately before World War I when some of the nation's leading foundations were established with great assets and aims, according to the doctrine that their funds were best applied to enterprises not likely to be supported by government or individuals, thereby acquiring the connotation of freedom of action. In their formative years, foundations sought to establish their legitimacy and autonomy as organizations and they may have developed the idea of risk capital to try to articulate not only a mission, but a rationale for minimizing legal control and deflecting political criticism. Like the ideas of academic freedom, free enterprise, and other ideologies intended in part to win public acceptance of autonomy for certain organizations, the concept of venture capital is derived from many elements of Western culture, especially English common law on using private wealth for charitable purposes, political and economic theories of self-help and voluntary enterprise, and the idea of progress, particularly the American notion of advancement through education, especially higher education (Colvard, 1964; Colwell, 1993; Lindeman, 1988; Penfield, 1967).

The leading advocates of the role of foundations as entrepreneurs have been the people of foundations themselves. In the 1930s, Frederick P. Keppel (1930, 1933) urged foundations to go where other donors feared to tread, to take risks and make mistakes, even costly ones, in trying to advance the development of mankind. Foundations should demonstrate courage as well as prudence, he said, and he confessed that the Carnegie Corporation had made many errors under his leadership, but never those of timidity. Even the U.S. Treasury Department, in its 1965 *Report on Private Foundations,* said that foundations were uniquely qualified to initiate thought, experiment with new ventures, and dissent from prevailing attitudes—although the department found little evidence that most foundations so acted.

Discovery in the physical sciences, the social sciences, and in the application of knowledge was the operant word in foundations, whose funds were increasingly being used not just for the relief of suffering, but for the more compelling goals of prevention and cure. Philanthropy that does the most good is not charity, according to foundation philosophy, but the investment of money to attack the *causes* of problems and the roots of social pathology, which Alan Pifer defined as the powerlessness of the poor, the undernourished, and the uneducated. Pifer's three decades as a foundation officer were characterized by almost constant turbulence as the nation adjusted to extraordinary economic, demographic, and technological change; looking ahead in 1984, he predicted that foundations would be needed as never before (1984b, 1984d). Criticizing foundations for failing to attack problems at their core, Paul Ylvisaker (1996) said that "dainty dabs of money" are no longer enough, and that, ironically, risk taking is often the safest bet for foundations because it is the only way to produce results comparable to the size of today's challenges. The failure of foundations to take risks, he said, may expose them to an even greater threat: irrelevance as social institutions. Asserting that more is new outside foundations than inside them, Ylvisaker (1996) doubted that they were stretching their resources as far as the needs demanded, stating that the willingness to take risks should be the feature which most distinguishes private from public philanthropy. However, according to Ylvisaker, public philanthropy is often more enterprising than private philanthropy, the latter of which may do what is risky for others to do, but rarely what is risky for it to do.

Many people in foundations approach grantmaking in the same careful way as they make financial investments, and the process of giving money away has often been described as a kind of investing. John D. Rockefeller demanded meticulous attention to efficiency in his businesses and applied the same standards to managing his foundations: "Certainly one's ideal should be to use one's means, both in one's investments and in one's benefactions, for the advancement of civilization. Our investments not less than our gifts have been directed to . . . multiply [and] diffuse as universally as possible the comforts of life. . . . These are the lines of largest and surest return" (Rockefeller, 1983, pp. 115–116). John M. Glenn, one of the original executives of the Russell Sage Foundation, also referred to opportunities for grantmaking as "lines of philanthropic investment" (1947, p. 34), and Julius Rosenwald, who learned the value of money early in his life, said, "Whether a dollar is paid out for necessities or luxuries, in wages or philanthropy, I am desirous of seeing as full returns for it as possible" (1929, p. 136).

Russ Alan Prince and Karen Maru File developed a seven-part typology of donor personalities, one of which, the Investor, has a philosophy similar to that of many foundations. The *Investor* is interested in a well-conceived and well-managed program of philanthropy and tries to reduce the risk of giving through careful planning and selection. According to Prince and File, about 15 percent of donors are Investors, and a typical Investor is well educated, male, and a business owner, characteristics that incidentally are very similar to those of foundation trustees (Prince and File, 1994).

Like the investors they resemble, foundations can be placed on a continuum of grantmaking philosophies ranging from liberal to conservative, and most foundations lie at or near the conservative end, funding low-risk, socially and politically acceptable projects and organizations (Curti and Nash, 1965; Nielsen, 1985).

The Reality of Foundations as Entrepreneurs

Although the idea of foundations as entrepreneurs is one of the most prevalent themes in the literature, the performance of foundations as venture capitalists does not support the theory. Most foundations have demonstrated a marked aversion to risk, nonetheless proclaiming their readiness to support unknown people and unconventional projects so often that they and many of their constituents have come to believe the myth.

But not everyone has so readily accepted the claim. Keppel consistently urged foundations to be entrepreneurial, but observed that most of their trustees had a natural tendency to restrict their grants to the "safe and sane" and were interested more in the *respectability* of their grants than in their results (1930, pp. 35, 42). Devereaux Josephs, who served as a consultant to the Ford Foundation in the 1950s, boasted to the *Wall Street Journal* that foundations fearlessly championed the cause of venture capital and operated at the "edge of social change." But according to Dwight Macdonald, the project that Josephs espoused operated not at the edge of social change but in the very center of the status quo. Like giving turkeys at Thanksgiving, Macdonald said, the program was one to which "no humane person could object and no imaginative one could applaud"(1956, pp. 168–169). Indeed, in 1952 only 1 percent of foundations said that any of their grants were risky, and twenty years later 68 percent of foundations admitted that their role as venture capitalists existed more in theory than in reality; other studies have revealed more of the same (Commission on Foundations and Private Philanthropy, 1970; Branch, 1971; Bothwell, 1984). Goulden summed up the situation by asserting that foundations "build cuckoo clocks and pass them off as cathedrals" (1971, pp. 317–318).

The Commission on Private Philanthropy and Public Needs determined that the smallest foundations had made almost no controversial grants. Of those with assets of $100 million or more, however, 38 percent had made some chancy grants, but these represented only 3 percent of their total giving. The risk-taking record of large foundations is important because critics have traditionally judged the foundation community by the performance of its most prominent members. But by their own admission, large foundations have had a bleak record in innovation, and they have rightly been sensitive to criticism on this point.

Robert Maynard Hutchins of the Ford Foundation facetiously estimated the impact of a foundation grant to be in inverse proportion to its amount (James, 1973)—and, one might add, to the size of the foundation. In the 1960s, the Ford Foundation became embroiled in a controversy over how controversial it was, trying to defend itself in a memorandum that cited eleven examples of controversial grants it had made, the memo itself indicating the foundation's sensitivity to the issue. Some of the examples in the memo show that what the foundation considered to be controversial was actually quite mild and what may have been contentious yesterday may not be so today: a grant to the Arkansas Department of Education for teacher training caused a bitter argument and was characterized as the "Arkansas Purchase," and a grant to a ballet company brought accusations from proponents of modern dance that the foundation favored traditional schools of dance (Friedman, 1973, p. 172; Rudy, 1970, p. 46). But in a way, every grant is inherently controversial; grantmaking by its very nature is the act of deciding in favor of one organization over another. Making a grant to a museum may seem safe enough, for example, but museums sometimes attract negative publicity for what they exhibit, or for having too few young people on their boards or too few black artists in their collections.

Moreover, some people think the needs of museums pale in comparison to the importance of combating diseases, homelessness, illiteracy, or other formidable problems. But giving money to museums and schools at least appears safe, and foundations want to avoid making mistakes, embarrassing themselves, or wasting their limited funds. Consequently they tend to prefer the concrete and the accepted to the obscure and the exotic, which may be why, as Waldemar Nielsen put it (1992, pp. 33–35), that most foundations have failed to make "even a detectable dent" in society's larger problems despite their millions in grants and billions in assets.

The National Committee for Responsive Philanthropy criticized foundations in 1995 for funding too many research projects instead of those that deal with real problems. When foundations fund only research, especially on esoteric topics, they fulfill just part of their potential; Congressman Wright Patman condemned the Bollingen Foundation of Pittsburgh for funding research on the origin and significance of decorative medieval tombstones in Bosnia and Herzegovina rather than programs to alleviate poverty in its hometown (Simon, 1973).

A major principle of the idea of foundations as entrepreneurs is that if they do not fail occasionally, they are not taking enough risk. But very few foundation projects have been complete disappointments, indicating a lack of daring. Even when projects do fail, some foundations have developed a rhetoric of convenient rationalization that releases them from responsibility for it. But for a foundation to state that "the agency failed because it couldn't survive" is like a psychiatrist saying, "My patient committed suicide because he was crazy" (Kostelanetz, 1989, p. 36).

Failure need not stigmatize a foundation or its grantees; there are often hidden benefits to failed projects, such as learning that a particular program design causes problems or that the public is not ready for an idea, however impressive it seemed to those who thought of it and funded it (Brim, 1973; Harrison and Andrews, 1946). Success and failure are relative, measured differently by different people on both sides of a foundation's desk, and the results of grant programs are rarely unequivocal, especially in the short term. Frank Karel, who has worked in foundations for more than twenty years, says that the effects of many projects take fifteen to twenty years to see and that the majority of programs that foundations fund cannot be proven to have succeeded or failed because many grants are given to support the on-going work of established organizations (S. G. Greene, 1990, p. 10). Philanthropy essentially has no clear bottom line, says Nielsen; people in foundations understand the ambiguity of their work, and those with self-confidence are not bothered very much, but some less assured program officers worry that if their grants were to be reported as failures, their credibility and even their jobs might be jeopardized. "God help you if you say publicly that several of your grants didn't work out," warns Nielsen. "That will zip around the circuit, and you've got to live with it the rest of your professional life" (S. G. Greene, 1990, p. 10).

When grants do fall short of their goals, foundations seldom acknowledge it publicly. They may not wish to embarrass the grantee or expose themselves to litigation by an organization claiming that its reputation has been damaged or its ability to raise funds constrained. Not that they are likely to know a failure has occurred: the Commission on Foundations and Private Philanthropy (1970) reported that 41 percent of foundations never took steps to monitor their grantees or evaluate the results of their grants, over half never made field visits to their grantees, 72 percent never required grantees to submit reports to receive installments on their grants, and 91 percent never insisted on independent audits of grantees' expenditures. The commission concluded that most foundations apparently found the process of *making* grants more satisfying than evaluating them. Although few foundations want to throw good money after bad, they should encourage grantees to tell them about their problems and not wait until it is too late, says Colburn S. Wilbur, executive director of the David and Lucile Packard Foundation (1993).

Although many foundations and their donors have long had an aversion to risk taking, some young philanthropists are more venturesome. George S. Pillsbury, Sr. financed so many things at Yale University he cannot remember where all the money went. For his son George, though, Yale was "never in the picture"; the 1992 Yale graduate has created a network of social change foundations and has chosen to support "change, not charity," funding organizations that fight pollution, apartheid, and discrimination against gays and lesbians. "If we just gave money to a school, that's not going to solve the problem of access to higher education for most people," said the younger Pillsbury (Greene, 1989, p. A27). Rob McKay is taking a much different approach to his giving than his father, who founded Taco Bell and sold it to PepsiCo in the late

1970s. McKay is making grants to organizations that advance social justice and community renewal and sees himself as more of an activist than a philanthropist. So do other young foundation leaders; see Fix, 1994.

Reasons for the Aversion to Risk Taking

It is well documented that foundations usually have conservative trustees who believe that social stability is good and that the burden of proof rests with those who advocate economic and political change. C. J. Cannon (1921) described foundation trustees as belonging to a class on which the injustices of society have not borne heavily—as the bulwark of the status quo, ready and eager to apply palliatives as the great patchers-up of society. Study after study since then have agreed; with few exceptions, foundations are extensions of America's banks, brokerage houses, law firms, and business leaders, and they act accordingly, sticking to the political, philosophical, and economic center, if not to the right. Also, foundation boards are sometimes plagued by the presence of one or more bully trustees who are accustomed to getting their way without question or argument. Such people can easily intimidate their more timid colleagues in the genteel world of philanthropy, where most trustees quickly learn to get along by going along and to reject any proposal that may provoke an eruption from a reactionary trustee.

Dangerous problems are not likely to be tackled by foundations controlled by centrist boards, especially when asked to do so by applicants who make trustees uncomfortable; Harold Laski (1930) knew of a project killed by foundation trustees who believed it would be displeasing to Mussolini. Also, foundations have learned from experience that some politicians and members of the public are uneasy about allowing them too much influence in determining society's direction. Some have turned this criticism to their advantage, defending their timidity by pointing out that Congress attacked them when they supported risky programs.

Few foundation staff members have done much better than trustees in encouraging risk taking. Many are quick to laud the benefits of venturesome grantmaking, but in practice they are conventional and orthodox, preaching the values of nonconformity while practicing conformity. After all, homogeneity—a similarity of education, professional background, economic status, social perspective, and political persuasion—is so dominant a feature of foundation staff that few of them are likely to challenge the assumptions underlying grant decisions or the strategic direction of their employers (Pifer, 1984c). Defensive about the inability of foundation grants to create real change in organizations, an apologetic program officer tried to reassure Macdonald: "We don't want to play God. We only want to diffuse creativity and thought" (1956, pp. 127–128).

Foundation staff might be called *financially marginal:* associated with money but rarely wealthy themselves, ambitious perhaps but lacking the security that comes from having money. Grantmaking is not considered a profession based on education and skill, but a job acquired through personal or family connections, business IOUs, or favoritism. This is not completely true; foundation employment is slowly becoming a profession, but it has not yet arrived. The job market is minuscule, with no clear requirements or skills, limited lateral and upward mobility, and no professional association or recognized training program. Grantmaking is not a talent widely accepted as transferable to other jobs, and there is no code of conduct for it apart from the *Principles and Practices for Effective Grantmaking* of the Council on Foundations, a set of guidelines for foundations, not so much the people who work in them (Bennett, 1990; Nason, 1989; Ylvisaker, 1987a).

Even foundations that do take risks often lose the zeal for daring grantmaking as they mature, becoming more impersonal and routine, no longer energized by the vigor of their founders. If foundations have an "irremediable defect," as Turgot believed (Stephens, 1895), it is the difficulty of maintaining enthusiasm for fulfilling the high aspirations of their donors. "There is no body that has not in the long run lost the spirit of its first origin," observed Henry S. Pritchett (1929, p. 517), who warned donors that they were deceiving themselves if they thought that their fervor could be communicated from age to age, especially to people employed to perpetuate its effects. Julius Rosenwald must have anticipated this eventuality when he urged that all foundations cease to exist at the death of their founders or shortly thereafter.

Pifer said that foundations are characteristically paralyzed when it comes to taking a stand, especially on social and moral issues, and he cautioned that their fearful approach might lead to a decline of morale among foundation staff and the end of foundations as a force in philanthropy (1984c; 1984d). Not only do foundations tend to become bureaucratic with age, but they typically develop partnerships with established organizations and begin to represent the past rather than the future. A scholar who had received grants from the Ford Foundation said the foundation was daring and imaginative in its early days, but "now [a proposal] has to go through all sorts of committees. They don't make the mistakes they used to, but they don't take the chances, either. It's become a well-oiled operation, smoothly conveying the dough from the trustees to the grantees" (Macdonald, 1956, p. 165).

Foundations and Individuals

The truly entrepreneurial foundation supports creative people, but few foundations actually do, though they may aspire to. As early as 1912, William H. Allen said that foundations believed it more productive to fund people than to endow institutions. For that matter, Benjamin Franklin established the Franklin's Friends trust through his will in 1790 (His Majesty's Commissioners, 1834); it was set up to loan $300 at 5 percent interest to "young married artificers of good character" and it did so until its final distribution in 1991. Simon Guggenheim established a foundation in 1925 that has made all its grants to individuals, and in the 1930s the Rockefeller Foundation launched a program that, for just over $1 million, brought to the United States 178 scientists, including several Nobel Prize winners, who were threatened by the rise of Nazism (Williams, 1989).

Despite these early examples, foundation grants to individuals today are rare. In 1993, according to the Foundation Center, only 1.7 percent of the $11.1 billion foundations gave for all purposes went to individuals (Hall, 1995; Renz, Lawrence, and Treiber, 1995). Most foundations make grants to individuals only through institutions such as universities that serve as an IRS-approved control responsible for a person's future after a grant ends. Eccentrics who are intolerant of institutional rigidity are thus not likely to get many grants. Ironically, foundations are the best hope for such people; conformists can find a home in organizations and get funding from the government. Einstein, for example, said, "I am a horse for single harness, not cut out for tandem or team-work," and he, no different than Hegel, Weber, or Galileo, undoubtedly would have terrified most foundations, which prefer precisely defined problems and equally exact performance expectations (Whitaker, 1974, p. 203). One disadvantage of making grants to individuals is the greater need for staff to evaluate potential recipients; Charles Dollard (1953) told Congress that it can take more work to make a grant of $5,000 to one person than to give $500,000 to a university, and H. Rowan Gaither of the Ford Foundation said, "We do try and take care of the individual, but it's hard in a foundation of this size. It's very hard to support individuals without a staff of about 1,000, so we prefer to rely upon other institutions to provide this service for us" (Whyte, 1956, pp. 231–232).

Some infamous grants to individuals were awarded by the Ford Foundation to seven staff members of Robert Kennedy after he was assassinated in 1968. They were the idea of McGeorge Bundy, then president of the Ford Foundation and a friend and former colleague of both John and Robert Kennedy: "I was moved by a sense that this was an enormously talented group of young people, a group that had suffered a brutal shock. With Bobby dead, what were they going to do?" Bundy's solution was to give each senior staff member a "travel and study" grant. Some trustees expressed concern, and a member of the House Ways and Means Committee questioned the grants' legitimacy. Bundy replied that they were "fully justified in educational terms." But through the Tax Reform Act of 1969, Congress placed tough restrictions on foundation grants to individuals: they are now allowed only if the procedures for making them are approved in advance by the Treasury Department (Hall, 1995, p. xi).

The Tax Reform Act of 1969 requires foundations to ensure that their grants are used for charitable purposes, not the personal advantage of any individual. Grants for travel and study are not permitted unless they are awarded on an objective and nondiscriminatory basis in the form of scholarships or fellowships, awards in recognition of achievement, or funds for a specific purpose such as to improve the skills of a recipient. The law requires that something tangible emanate from a grant to an individual, minimally that a report be obtained by foundations at least annually, although the reporting requirement can be lessened when a grant is made to an educational institution for the benefit of a person instead of directly to that person. These provisions reflected widespread stories, some apocryphal, of foundation presidents swapping grants so their sons and daughters could attend college tuition-free, of supposedly competitive scholarships awarded to relatives of donors or trustees of foundations, and of travel and study grants made on the basis of who the recipients knew rather than what they could do (Edie, 1987a, 1987b; Hall, 1995; Williams, 1989; Zurcher and Dustan, 1972).

Today's most famous grants to individuals are from the Fellows Program of the John D. and Catherine T. MacArthur Foundation. These "Genius Grants," established in 1978, differ from most others in that people cannot apply for them and they have no strings attached—no book, report, research, or other product is expected from a recipient. The foundation each year invites leaders from many professions, whose names are not made public, to identify promising people. Staff then research the nominees and a committee selects twenty to thirty of them. The grants are based on the age of the recipients and range from $150,000 to $375,000 paid over five years. The Fellows Program is one of the most controversial in the United States; common complaints are that it rewards rather than stimulates creativity and that its grants go mainly to white male academics at prestigious eastern colleges and universities. More grants are made in science than in any other field except the arts. Adele Simmons, president of the foundation, says the grants often go to people who probably would not win awards through the peer review process in federal agencies. Catherine R. Stimpson, director of the Fellows Program, wishes more foundations would provide grants to individuals: "We can't refuse to support . . . the individual person who is building an institution, building an organization. I really take seriously individual possibilities, and we can't cut back on the safety net for creativity" (Bailey, 1992, p. 12; Greene, 1995, p. 8).

The Principle of Discontinuity

One of the most steadfast principles of foundations is what might be called *discontinuity*, the idea that they should provide only start-up funds and then sever their support and pursue other opportunities as soon as practical. "The aim is to give as little as possible for as short a time as possible," Edwin Embree explained (1930, p. 329), a philosophy he considered the essence of foundation philanthropy and the antithesis of traditional almsgiving.

If foundations do not observe the principle of discontinuity, the venture capital concept will suffer, as John D. Rockefeller, Frederick Gates, and other trustees of the Rockefeller Foundation clearly realized. Gates (1977, p. 234) warned the board that progress quickly leaves old needs—and old charities—behind, and therefore new opportunities will always be the "most important, exigent, and imperative." Any policy to the contrary, he said, places the dead hand of the past on philanthropy of the future. Jerome Greene thought it unwise for a foundation to assume part of another organization's costs indefinitely because it "tends to make the receiver subservient to the giver, thus detracting from the receiver's independence and self-respect . . ." (1913, pp. 7–9).

Perhaps to avoid restricting recipients' freedom, foundations generally have avoided actively helping to reshape the policies of their grantees in favor of offering arm's-length advice, according to William M. Dietel, former president of the Rockefeller Brothers Fund. But John Heyman, president of the New York Foundation, suggests supervising grantees to the same extent that an investment bank supervises the holdings in its portfolio: minimal if they are blue chips, maximal if they are small start-ups. "Obviously, a grant of $2,000 to the American Red Cross should call for nothing more . . . than the reading of reports," says Heyman. But venture capitalists in business—and in foundations—should not hesitate to intercede in the management of organizations they have invested in, saying, as it were, "We're not going to throw our money away without doing everything we can to try to save this organization" (S. G. Greene, 1990, p. 11). To some grantees, however, there is a fine line between offering advice and telling people what to do, and they criticize foundations for crossing it. President A. Lawrence Lowell of Harvard once demanded in a letter to the Rockefeller Foundation, "Who do you think runs Harvard, you or me?" (Kimball, 1959, p. 125.) Grantees may also resent the quick withdrawal foundations sometimes make from projects they have funded, but foundations recognize that grants occasionally encourage organizations to grow out of all proportion to their normal rate—"organizational cancer," Macdonald called it (1956, p. 118).

Foundations may worry about the effects of their grants on recipients, but grantees rarely seem concerned about how grants affect foundations; they tend to be mainly, if not exclusively, interested in how much, not how long. But to most foundations, how long is at least as important. "What hardening of the arteries is to the human body, getting loaded up with future commitments is to a foundation," said Macdonald (1956, p. 115). The problem is most acute when a grantee assumes that getting a grant this year means getting one next year—and the year after that. Prudent foundations try to disabuse them of this illusion; otherwise a grantee "will never learn to forage for himself," said Macdonald. Raymond Fosdick asserted that the work of foundations is *demonstration*, not administration, and that their only proper function is to "prime the pump, never to act as a permanent reservoir" (1952, p. 294). To maintain their independence, he said, they should ensure that other funding sources or the grantee itself will continue the work that they helped start, and their grants should not be so large as to "dry up the springs of popular giving."

However, foundations should not stop funding a project or organization so suddenly as to destroy it; they can ease the transition by, for example, telling the grantee up front that it will receive awards for three years with lower payments each year and to expect "no future commitment," a phrase familiar to most grantees. Consequently, long before a grant ends, "a chill wind has begun to blow on the necks of the grantees," encouraging them to raise money elsewhere (Macdonald, 1956, p. 116). The Markle Foundation did this to one of the donor's favorite charities, and in response the organization angrily returned Mr. Markle's portrait, which until then had hung in its reception room (Russell, 1977). With only a few exceptions, the Russell Sage Foundation observed the policy of discontinuity from its inception, making grants for one year only and with no commitment for renewal, explaining in 1908 that its role was to "help start the machine." Later that year, though, signaling a problem that occurs in almost all foundations to this day, John M. Glenn of the foundation reported to the trustees that he was forced to make "a stiff resistance" to many requests for extensions or second awards, despite the foundation's well-known policy against such grants. Frustrated, he asked the board, "Are we to continue these appropriations indefinitely?" (1947, pp. 44-47). However, not even this foundation followed the doctrine of discontinuity completely; in its formative years, two consultants to the foundation insisted that grants should be made one time only. But for all their stringency in applying these restrictions to applicants, these same consultants had no problem exempting themselves: they were officers of an organization that requested and received grants from Sage for the next *thirty-six consecutive years* (Andrews, 1956).

Many organizations outlive their usefulness, lose their effectiveness, or exist in declining form. Sometimes they even succeed in solving the problem they were set up to fight. Also, grantee income can increase to where it no longer needs a foundation grant, or decrease to where it becomes a poor investment. John D. Rockefeller, Jr. felt that there was nothing sacred about organizations and, in a letter to Raymond Fosdick, advised him to see them for what they are: "Machinery and personnel . . . the instruments by which objectives are reached," adding that unless foundations kept themselves "clear-eyed," they would "run the risk of dry rot" (Fosdick, 1952, p. 294). Wise foundations reject the role of grantor of last resort when other funding sources, especially government ones, withdraw their aid. "We refuse to be triage agents" for the government, said Lance E. Lindblom, president of the J. Roderick MacArthur Foundation (Goss, 1989, p. 5). But if federal cutbacks continue, foundations should expect to hear the argument from applicants that foundations *should* make long-term commitments. Also, the traditional role for foundations of starting projects and then passing them to other funders may apply less and less: "First it was going to be government, then government slowed down," says Kirke Wilson, executive director of the Rosenberg Foundation. "Then it was going to be corporations, then corporations slowed down. Now it's going to be individual funders . . . [but] individual funding is no panacea" (Leonard, 1989b, p. 46).

The Principle of Continuity

Countering the doctrine of discontinuity is the principle of *continuity*, the idea that foundations should stay with projects and organizations long enough to give them a chance to be completed or become self-sufficient. Grants should have impact beyond their immediate purposes. For example, if a foundation endows a professorial chair in a college, it should benefit not just one professor and his or her current students, but all the students over the professor's career. If a foundation uses its money to try to discover a miracle antibiotic, as the Rockefeller Foundation did with penicillin, it will save *millions* of people if the effort succeeds. As Lindsley F. Kimball said (1959, p. 122; 1974, p. 44), "It is better to lick yellow fever than to build hospitals to take care of the patients."

Although there is wisdom to discontinuity, continuity also makes sense because projects often require not only initial support but extended funding. Some foundations speak deridingly of grantees that rely on them lifelong and adopt the policy of making grants for a maximum of one or two years. But that is often based on neither excellence nor the needs of nonprofits, says Pablo Eisenberg (1983); he argues that it is a denial of innovation and risk taking, and that it would be more productive to support organizations for the long term. How can foundations impose a two-year limit on the search for a cure for cancer? Or diabetes? Or cystic fibrosis? As Embree said, grants must be large enough—*and long enough*—to accomplish their purposes: "Rich rewards do not spring from poor tools or underpaid men in philanthropy any more than they do in other fields" (1930, p. 329).

There are many occasions when long-term support makes sense. A project can take longer than expected or an organization longer to mature than anticipated. The early results of a project may be so impressive that it is worth a larger or longer grant to try to achieve even more promising outcomes. A project may be greatly needed but lack enough popular support to acquire funding from other sources. The person responsible for an organization may be qualified in every way except in raising money, causing a foundation to support an agency longer than it otherwise might. Supposedly, a new organization touched by the magic wand of a foundation receives such an infusion of vigor that it soon becomes "self-sufficient and a recognized element of the community," in the jargon of foundations and nonprofits.

But many grantees never become self-supporting, even when they claim they will be by the time their grants end. Some foundations know this; they have seen the predictions by prison counselors about the rehabilitation of hardened criminals and the claims of imminent enlightenment of recalcitrant people returning from one-day management seminars. To insist that grantees become self-sufficient can force them to replace reliance on foundations with dependence on other funding sources, substituting, as it were, one addiction for another. To some foundations, therefore, a self-sufficient nonprofit is merely one that is independent of *foundations,* even if still dependent on other grantors.

Unrealistic expectations of self-sufficiency by grantseekers do create anxiety in foundations, many of which have fallen for more than one hopeful story; in 1968, the Ford Foundation gave $500,000 and the Rockefeller Brothers Fund $100,000 to the Center for Inter-American Relations, which sought to increase North American interest in Western Hemisphere policy issues. Three years later, the center was appealing desperately for funds just to stay alive with letters that said, in effect, "We started this project for you, and now you should come up with the money to save it." An administrator of the center confessed that he could persuade so few people to come to its seminars that it had raised doubts about whether anyone (besides the center and a couple of foundations) thought it served a useful purpose (Goulden, 1971).

The Voter Education Project, however, clearly served a useful purpose; thanks largely to it, five and a half million Southern blacks have registered to vote, and the number of black elected officials in the South has risen from less than 100 to more than 4,400. Yet in 1991, foundations ceased to support it, and it is going out of business even though its mission is far from complete: four million Southern blacks eligible to vote are still not registered. Its only apparent sin is failing to become independent of foundation support. Ed Brown, the project's director since 1989, tried to raise money from other sources, but like so many in his predicament he did not succeed. Brown puts much of the blame not on foundations, however, but on the people who have benefited most from the progress the organization made possible: black political leaders and the black middle class, who have failed to provide the money to keep the organization going. "In the final analysis," says Brown, "nobody else pays for your freedom. You have to pay for it yourself" (White, 1992, pp. 38–39).

Operating Support or Project Grants?

A question related to the issue of continuity is whether foundations should offer *operating support grants* for the ongoing administration of organizations, or only *project grants* for special time-limited programs. The debate has persisted since the beginning of organized philanthropy, and today as in the past foundations prefer project grants.

In 1993, 44 percent of foundation giving went to project grants; operating support garnered just 12 percent. (The remainder was for capital support, research, student aid, and other smaller purposes.) Furthermore, the average project grant was about $94,000 and the average operating support grant was about $68,000, a gap the Foundation Center says has widened since 1980, when project grants were 33 percent of foundation giving and those for operating support were only 12 percent. Keppel noted this trend as early as 1925 and approved of it because he thought it would force grantees to identify other funding sources and encourage foundations to withdraw from projects before their work becomes "ruts and routine" (1930, pp. 53–54). Project grants reflect a more targeted approach to grantmaking, a greater concern for accountability to trustees and the federal government, and an increase in the number and professionalism of foundation staff, whose expertise in strategic planning has pushed foundations toward special projects. But this has not satisfied the financial needs of nonprofits that suffer from government cutbacks; they hope that foundations, however unlikely they may be to reverse their preference for project grants, will help make up the difference (Leonard, 1989b; Renz, Lawrence, and Treiber, 1995).

Many foundations do not provide operating support because they believe it will involve them in the management of nonprofits, exposing them to criticism from constituents, the federal government, or the public. Others claim it is more difficult to terminate operating support grants than project grants, which usually have a natural end or a cutoff point beyond which foundations have no commitment. Project grants may also be easier and cheaper to evaluate, which may appeal to some trustees or donors who restrict their foundations to one or two program interests. Project grants often have potential for publicity or recognition, which may help grantees attract aid from sources that prefer the high visibility that comes from sponsoring art exhibits or making the largest gift to a capital campaign. Project grants allow a foundation to support a program even if the agency running it is otherwise displeasing or does work inconsistent with the foundation's program interests. A college where I worked received a grant for a project to educate deaf students from a foundation that otherwise would probably not have considered the school for support.

Wise foundations know that project grants can undermine a grantee's financial health by allowing it to carry out extraneous functions that do not improve its day-to-day management or increase its fund-raising. Aware of this problem, some foundations make grants to strengthen fund-raising or insist that fund-raising be a part of all projects. Susan Berresford, president of the Ford Foundation, says foundations should be concerned about the overall financial health of their grantees; some foundations that agree are helping through matching and challenge grants, which require an organization to match the amount of the grant from other sources. Matching grants are not new: the Peabody Education Fund offered a grant of $1,000 to the public schools of Rome, Georgia if the city would levy a tax of $3,000 and convert some private schools into public schools, and the Carnegie Foundation for the Advancement of Teaching required colleges which sought its pension funds to achieve curriculum standards established by the foundation (Harrison and Andrews, 1946). But matching grants are not common today; they represented only 3.5 percent of foundation giving in 1993, down by half since 1989 even though several large foundations, such as the Kresge Foundation, began to make matching or challenge grants almost exclusively (Renz, Lawrence, and Treiber, 1995).

Matching and challenge grants are an excellent way to measure the commitment of an institution to a project, to help stretch scarce resources, and to enable acquiring support from other sources. However, they can pressure an organization's development staff to devote too much attention to raising other money to get foundation grants, and too little to other institutional needs. The most important thing foundations can do for nonprofits is invest in fund-raising, according to Wilson C. Levis, former vice president of the National Charities Information Bureau, because it is a legitimate management function without which few nonprofits can survive. Independent Sector realized as much when it urged foundations to support fund-raising as one of 10 recommendations in its "Daring Goals for a Caring Society" campaign (Hall, 1992; Leonard, 1989a).

Although there are no data on foundation grants specifically for fund-raising, grants in 1993 for technical assistance, including fund-raising, represented only eight-tenths of 1 percent of foundation giving, down from 1.8 percent in 1989 (Renz, Lawrence, and Treiber, 1995). To try to improve fund-raising in nonprofits, some foundations are doing the following:

- Making grants for operating support to organizations whose budgets are too small to undertake special projects
- Making endowment grants to provide a continuing source of money when project grants end
- Making technical assistance grants to help nonprofits raise money, especially unrestricted contributions, and manage their money more effectively
- Making grants for consultants to conduct fund-raising feasibility studies (Goss, 1989)

Examples of foundation grants for fund-raising in the 1990s include the following:

- The Frey Foundation in Grand Rapids, Michigan gave $273,000 in 1991 to three local cultural groups to improve fund-raising.
- The Irvine Foundation challenged twenty-two California private colleges and universities to match $8.5 million. Fund-raising at the schools increased an average of 106 percent and they attracted 35,825 new donors, many of whom were recent graduates who might be expected to be contributors to the colleges for years.
- The St. Paul Foundation in 1990 announced a seven-year program to train officials from fifty-five local nonprofits in planned giving.

Even when an organization is succeeding at fund-raising and a grant project is progressing nicely, a foundation supporting it is still likely to receive continuation grant requests or new grant requests (sometimes for another project suspiciously similar to the original). If a project is not succeeding, a request for renewal is almost certain. The foundation must then decide whether to support it longer, hoping that it will become viable, or abandon it, in which case it will probably die. Projects whose grants have ended are rarely incorporated into the budgets of their sponsoring organizations, and those that have been rejected by a foundation are not especially likely to be submitted for funding elsewhere. Studies by the Bush Foundation of 113 applicants whose proposals had been rejected found that approximately one-fourth of the projects were abandoned by their proponents after denial (Archabal, 1984).

Some grantseekers claim that by refusing to make grants for operating support, foundations encourage applicants to submit proposals that claim to be for special projects but actually are not; Brian Hofland, vice president of the Retirement Research Foundation, confirms that he and other foundation officers have received such proposals (Goss, 1989). When the Minnesota Council of Nonprofits surveyed its 450 members in 1988, their top concern was the unwillingness of foundations to make grants for operating support, and some members even asked the council's executive director to hold a workshop on how to disguise requests for operating support as proposals for special projects (Leonard, 1989b). One reason for such deception is that most foundation grants have what Jacques Barzun called a "hidden tax": unanticipated overheard costs such as space and utilities that must be covered by grantees, causing all kinds of "centers" and "institutes" to become parasitic on their host organizations. For example, when making a grant to establish a research chair, foundations often stipulate that a university bear the costs of locating and hiring the professor and providing office space, secretarial support, furniture, computers, telephones, photocopying, printing, research assistants, laboratory equipment, lab assistants, and a personal library—in perpetuity. One university president reported that twelve years after a foundation funded a $34,000 research project, $500,000 of the institution's own money had been spent to support it (Barzun,

1959). Observing the almost exponential expansion of research projects funded by grants, Goulden observed wryly that stopping the growth of an externally funded research project is "as difficult as rooting out crab grass" (1971, p. 132).

Implications for Grantseekers of Foundations as Entrepreneurs

Foundations extol their role as the risk takers of philanthropy, but very little foundation money is spent as venture capital; the overwhelming majority is invested in established organizations having next to no chance of failure, very nearly as it would be invested by the people who made or inherited it. Risk-taking is more a latent than an actual attribute of foundations, and their record as entrepreneurs is less worthy of the description "venture capitalists of philanthropy" than much of the literature suggests.

In 1930, Edwin Embree predicted with remarkable foresight that courage, independent thinking, and an entrepreneurial spirit would be needed desperately in the nation, although these properties would be in short supply in foundations: "The real danger is that they will have no influence of any consequence in any direction; that they will fritter away their potential power in small and insignificant enterprises . . . (and) that the whole organization will sink into commonplace bureaucracy" (p. 329). Risk taking should be an attribute that distinguishes private from government philanthropy, but federal agencies such as the National Endowment for the Arts and the National Endowment for the Humanities have often been more venturesome than foundations.

Foundations approach grantmaking like banks approach investing, and most are conservative, funding low-risk, socially acceptable projects and organizations. By their own admission, only a handful of foundations—1 to 3 percent—describe their grantmaking as venturesome or pioneering. The aversion to risk in foundations is due partly to their trustees, who are usually conservative in social, economic, and political policy. Failure is anathema to most foundation trustees, who are unaccustomed to failure in their professional lives and uncomfortable with the idea of giving money to people or projects that could fail. The staff members of foundations are usually more supportive of risk-taking than the trustees, but they rarely risk jeopardizing themselves with their board members by openly advocating venturesome grantmaking. Also, foundation staff, though well educated and surely appreciative of innovation in society, have usually led conventional professional lives in the most orthodox of organizations: colleges, research centers, legislative bodies, federal agencies, and government commissions. Foundations often rely on the advice of consultants, few of whom are inclined to support ideas that are unfamiliar to them or that contradict their own recommendations. Even small foundations rarely advocate risk taking because many are little more than extensions of their donors' personal philanthropy, reacting to the many requests they receive from organizations with connections to their donors instead of proactively seeking opportunities for venturesome grantmaking. Furthermore, as foundations age they become removed from the vitality of their donors and tend toward the safe and the conventional, ever mindful of their self-preservation. Grants to individuals are one of the oldest traditions in foundations, but today they are rare. In 1995, the Ford Foundation, the largest grantor to individuals, made 243 such grants for a total of $3.5 million, but that was only about 1 percent of its overall giving.

Most foundations observe the principle of discontinuity and move quickly to other opportunities so that they are not bound to the same grantees indefinitely. Grantees' claims that they will be self-sufficient by the time their grants end are seldom realistic, and foundations are acutely aware of the naivete of these forecasts. To try to preserve their independence, foundations are making multiyear grants in decreasing amounts and establishing firm cutoff dates beyond which there will be no support, and they prefer grants for special projects instead of operating support.

Recommendations to Foundations as Entrepreneurs

Foundations should not be averse to taking risks because they are generally free from external control, but few are fulfilling their responsibility to provide the venture capital of society. One test of foundations should be the number of grants they make on long shots, even knowing many will fail.

Who but foundations will support unproven people or organizations? Will individuals? Corporations? Federal and state agencies? The record suggests not. Who else but foundations would
have funded the education of a generation of black leaders? Who
else would have financed Flexner's study of medical education, the
Conant study of the American high school, and the Public Broadcasting Service? Who else would have made possible the discovery
of penicillin, the cures for hookworm and yellow fever, or Jonas
Salk's research that led to the polio vaccine? Who else would have
started the New York City Ballet or the University of Chicago? Who
else would have supported the early work of 150 people who later
won the Nobel Prize? Who else would have funded *Sesame Street*?
Foundations are perhaps the last American institution whose assets
are sufficiently unencumbered to tackle the most difficult problems. They have been given the freedom to be bold, to support
unproven but promising ideas and people, to fund new or controversial organizations, and to face the thorniest problems head
on. The tragedy is that so few act anything like the entrepreneurs
they could—and should—so effectively be.

Foundations should make grants for longer than one or two
years, which is more an arbitrary standard to allow a quick getaway
from grantees than a thoughtful rationale for discontinuing support. Withdrawing too quickly from organizations virtually guarantees that they will not achieve the oft-touted goal of
self-sufficiency. Foundations should not approve proposals from
grantseekers whose commitment to the projects after their grants
end is questionable; as an indication of commitment, grantseekers
should pledge in proposals to incorporate projects into their operating budgets after the grants that establish them expire. If a grant
project will burden an organization's budget because of the need
to assume administrative costs, that reality should be faced before
a proposal is submitted, with the understanding that a grant will
not ease an institution's overall financial problems and may well
worsen them.

Foundations should reconsider their policy of refusing to fund
organizations that have lost government funding. No longer are
only failed programs losing government aid, but many important
and successful organizations are seeing their federal funding

reduced or eliminated. Foundations should not be afraid to help when the government is no longer able—or willing—to continue its funding; the loss of federal funding is not the stigma it once was.

The search for talent and the support of promising individuals should be the hallmark of foundations. They should broaden their networks of advisors to identify talented people. Funding individuals is becoming a lost art in foundations, although it once represented their main reason for being. All foundations, regardless of their program interests, should set aside some funds to support gifted people; philanthropy today overemphasizes egalitarianism at the expense of excellence.

Chapter Seven

Foundations as Partners

Problems in Building Trust Between Grantmakers and Grantseekers

Someone once said that a foundation executive is a friend who stabs you in the front. Would that it were true.
ORVILLE BRIM, *THE FUTURE OF FOUNDATIONS* (1973, P. 246)

The basic menace of foundations is not their size, although size aggravates the menace. Nor is it the lust of power and fallibility of foundation agents. The basic menace is the attitude of the rest of us toward foundations which are created to give money away. We want some of the power which the money gives. We want the smiles and favor of agents controlling such huge power to help or withhold help. It is what we are willing to do for foundation money not what foundations want or ask us to do that makes foundation giving a social and governmental menace.
WILLIAM H. ALLEN, *ROCKEFELLER: GIANT, DWARF, SYMBOL* (1930, PP. 504–505)

Foundations and nonprofit organizations are often thought of as partners in solving the nation's problems, but the evidence shows that the partnership is troubled at best. Both parties often violate each other's trust.

The Metaphor of Foundations as Partners

Foundations and nonprofits are an alliance in the search for solutions to society's problems, according to this metaphor. But though foundation rhetoric often agrees, the analogy is not especially true because the association is asymmetric: foundations have the money and applicants do not. The metaphor of foundations as partners, therefore, like the metaphors of foundations as activists and entrepreneurs, is more perception than reality.

The imbalance of power gives foundation philanthropy a mystique that is difficult to penetrate and causes considerable apprehension and intimidation in nonprofits, contributing to their perception of themselves as subservient to foundations. There is power in making grant decisions and a certain arbitrariness as well; some grantseekers believe that the more freedom foundations have, the more that prejudice and even abuse enter the decision-making process. To grantseekers, the chair foundation officers sit in is a throne, and the one they occupy across the desk is a pew—handily equipped with kneeler. Some applicants are unwilling to be supplicants and debase themselves, at least in their minds, by having to ask for money. Asking implies need, and need implies inadequacy, and having to seek grants makes many people feel depreciated. Such people often refuse to offer their proposals as applications, but choose to present them—in the most direct manner possible—as select opportunities in which foundations are invited (not asked) to invest (not give) amounts that are expected (not requested).

The imperative of finding funds is inescapable for most nonprofits, but not for foundations; they rarely have to rely on outside parties for their financial subsistence. Although some foundations do try to identify grantees on their own, they are not required to do so to survive. If foundations elected not to seek their own recipients, grantseekers would nonetheless almost certainly find them, as they do in most cases anyway, despite the inaccessibility of many foundations. Their power over grantseekers is obvious, even though some foundations insist to the contrary, and their influence in society is extensive because of the many social, cultural, scientific, and educational developments that bear their direct or indirect mark.

Focusing only on foundations, however, ignores how grantees participate in the philanthropic transaction. The decision of the grantor may be more significant, but the moral currency of the appeals of grantseekers is not without value and the balance of power in foundation philanthropy does not rest completely with foundations. Grantseekers need foundations not only for their money, but also to endorse the legitimacy of their missions, programs, and fund-raising requests. Because philanthropic petitions are affective and designed to appeal to a donor's nonmaterial consciousness, they tend to be less immediately compelling than when the basis of an appeal is votes or money. Petitions in the form of words and images such as grant proposals cannot be accumulated as dollars or votes can be, and consequently grantseekers have little ability to discipline the behavior of foundations in the way consumers can influence the actions of firms and voters can regulate the policies of politicians. Foundations give approval, confidence, and responsibility in addition to money, but grantees contribute time, thought, and action, without which foundations could achieve very little.

Although foundations do not need grantseekers to ensure their financial existence, they do depend on them to help authenticate the moral meaning of their work. In a way, then, grantees are not merely recipients of foundations but donors to them because they help them achieve their missions. The relationship of foundations and grantseekers is therefore one of mutual, if not equal, dependence; foundations and grantseekers both give and get in the social dynamic of power and influence in foundation philanthropy (Ostrander and Schervish, 1990).

Achieving partnership between foundations and grantseekers is difficult because the relationship is all too often like that between banker and borrower: funds change hands, but full participation in the concerns of both parties rarely occurs. Much of the grantmaking process is written rather than verbal and organizational instead of personal, thereby hindering foundations from knowing grantseekers, many of whom are from a different social and financial class. Also, there is a virtual absence of communication between the two except when grants are pending. They rarely talk about their mutual problems or the dynamics of grantmaking and grantseeking, and although communication among foundations has risen, it has not increased appreciably between foundations and grantseekers. They do meet to discuss proposals, but usually in the foundation environment and often involving the one person from the grantseeking organization who best fits that culture. Seldom do foundation staff meet with the people actually being helped by grant projects, and when they do the people are usually so uneasy that little real communication takes place. Further separation occurs because foundations and grantseekers rely on a host of intermediaries to represent their interests and conduct their business. The founder of a foundation, if still involved in its management, acts through the foundation's trustees, who act through its staff, who deal with the grantees, which act through their trustees, who act through staff, who work with the representatives of the groups or problems being dealt with.

Grantmaking creates emotional distance between foundations and grantseekers, and the statements of recipients, when questioning the motives of donors, reflect this suspicion: Something for nothing? What's the catch? What's the quid pro quo? Inexperienced foundation officers are often taken aback by the resentment they sense in grantees, especially if they work for foundations that give money away out of vanity or less admirable motives. The Council on Foundations recognizes the tension and recommends that both parties establish a community of interest through candor and mutual respect to define the purposes of grants, the expectations regarding reports on financial and program matters, and the provisions for evaluating and publicizing the results of projects (Council on Foundations, 1984; Penfield, 1967; Ylvisaker, 1987b).

Foundations are members of the grants economy, as opposed to what economists call the exchange economy. The grants economy consists of one-way transfers of economic goods in which people or organizations make gifts but receive nothing in exchange (although the receiver may reciprocate by doing something the giver wants him to do). Foundations are not the only ones in the grants economy, nor are they even the largest; individuals give one-way gifts too and these far exceed all giving by foundations. However, foundations can be distinguished from business organizations, which operate primarily in the exchange economy and perform *arbitrage,* an exchange of products or services with people or organizations that enables them to increase their net worth (Boulding, 1970, 1973).

Money is the heart of the relationship of foundations and grantseekers, and it can demean, distort, and destroy alliances not only between people but between organizations. For foundations, money is power, and awarding—or denying—it is a means of control over applicants and recipients. For grantseekers, money can be a way to buy approbation or a vehicle to escape dependency and achieve autonomy. In this society, money is often equated with worth, and the words, *net worth,* can be interpreted as an individual's or organization's value—and some people believe that the larger the number, the more valuable the person or entity. By this reasoning, quantity is construed as quality, but this is not necessarily so; indeed, the relationship of the quality of a person and the quantity of his or her money is often inverse (Menninger, 1981). Because people will do almost anything for money, it can corrupt even the most innocent organizations: day care centers, social agencies, hospices, and certainly churches and synagogues, for what priest, minister, or rabbi will knowingly offend a wealthy parishioner? Every grant has a price—sometimes obvious, sometimes disguised, sometimes predictable, sometimes unimaginable—and foundations must expect to receive something both rewarding and punishing in the emotional exchange implicit in grantmaking.

Grantees may be ungrateful as well as ambivalent and even envious, especially after the initial excitement of receiving a grant has subsided and they realize they are passive receivers and foundations are dominant givers (Crawshaw and Bruce, 1978). The gratitude of many grantees more closely resembles the French definition, "the expectation of future favors," than it does sincere appreciation. Ironically, most grantseekers expect their clients to be appreciative, but are not humble enough to be grateful for the money foundations give them. How genuinely altruistic foundations are, however, can also be questioned. Perhaps there is no such a thing as a truly selfless relationship between people in which the gratification of one's own psyche plays no part. Similarly, perhaps there is no genuinely selfless relationship between organizations and people. By taking an interest in gratifying the interests of their grantees, foundations gratify their own interests; in that sense giving is a selfish act, increasing the ego of the giver and making him feel superior to the receiver. Giving is never pure; the most altruistic giving contains elements of narcissism. But the reverse is also true: even gifts that seem blatantly self-aggrandizing include an altruistic element, however small, causing the high aspirations of philanthropy to be inseparable from low technique. Egoism, therefore, is on the same scale as altruism, and the sublime in philanthropy is often deflated by the mundane (Freud, 1948; Menninger, 1981; Payton, 1988).

Violations of Partnership by Grantseekers

Grantseekers violate the spirit of partnership with foundations in ways that reflect the sleazy side of philanthropy, ranging from bestowing feigned deference on foundations to confronting them with outright aggression. Applicants are after something foundations have, and grantseeking can be adversarial, a contest of wills as well as skills, in which grantseekers will whine, wheedle, cajole, manipulate, pressure, exaggerate, and lie to get the money they need, defiantly insulting foundations one moment and obsequiously fawning over them the next.

Bravado in grantseekers sometimes masks disdain, and contempt for foundations is common, especially when grantseekers' proposals have been rejected. But even when they win funds, grantees are hardly universally admiring or even minimally grateful, for many feel they have merely been given their due. Some grantseekers earn foundation mistrust because their ranks include "snake-oil salesmen," whom Richard Landau, a former development officer at Tufts University, called "those suntanned fellows with straight white teeth" who see themselves as manipulators and foundations as the manipulated. These people claim to know all the top officers at big foundations and name-drop endlessly as they tell story after story about summer cocktail parties on Cape Cod with "this one from Ford, or that one from Rockefeller" (Landau, 1975, p. 25).

Fabricating and Inflating Proposals

A major way grantseekers violate their partnership with foundations is by fabricating projects and inflating proposals. Many nonprofits seem to have a few people on staff who are almost professional grantseekers—Whitaker called them "foundation bums" (1974, p. 196)—and who dream up ideas often for little other reason than to get money. Such people pursue foundation money, as George Leigh Mallory said of climbing Mount Everest, "because it is there." Astute foundation executives can usually spot them and sometimes play along by asking, "Suppose we give you the grant. What exactly would you do with it?" And sometimes the grantseekers will reply, "If you give us the money, we'll find the answer." Yorke Allen derisively called such proposals "blank check" requests, and few foundations find them attractive (1965, p. 97).

Many grant projects begin as ideas that require very little personnel or equipment—that take more work than money. But many grantseekers are reluctant to ask for small grants, having heard that foundations prefer to fund large programs with equally large budgets. (Some joke that it is easier to get $500,000 from a foundation than $5,000.) They therefore sometimes expand their projects with layer upon layer of advisory committees, policy analysts, field interviewers, data entry teams, and network managers until they bear little resemblance to the original ideas. William Whyte saw a colleague work on a grant proposal for a year, and each time he rewrote it he got farther away from his original idea and closer to what Whyte considered to be "plain merchandising" (1956, pp. 234–235). A college in the mid-Atlantic states developed a program in much the same way when it discovered that many of its students wanted to learn to use computers. The institution did not have the money to buy enough machines to create a computer lab, so the college's development officer tried to interest a few foundations in the idea, but with no success. However, a faculty member who had worked for a large foundation offered to write a proposal for an experimental program in which computers would be used not only for instructional purposes but to maintain school finances, student records, and class schedules. The principal of a local high school expressed interest in sharing the computers to manage his school's records. In the proposal, the college pledged to develop a course on computers for the faculty, train administrators to use the machines, and hire two new employees to run the whole program. The professor also stipulated consulting fees in the proposal for himself, the principal, and the high school's business manager. When the application was finished, what had begun as a simple request had mushroomed into a project calling for $3.5 million over three years, which a major foundation funded six weeks later. The professor who created the program and wrote the proposal received a $2,000 raise (in addition to his consulting fees from the project) and was awarded tenure a year ahead of schedule (Goulden, 1971).

Other Deceptive Practices

Another violation of partnership by grantseekers is sending the same proposal to several foundations at the same time, hoping that one will show interest. This practice, called *shopping a proposal, spray and pray,* or the *shotgun approach,* sometimes backfires; Manning M. Pattillo (1965, p. 92) knew of a university that submitted the same proposal to two foundations simultaneously and received grants from both. Embarrassed, the university president had to apologize awkwardly and decline one of the grants.

Another deceitful tactic is doing an end run around foundation staff by appealing directly to trustees or using other personal contacts to try to acquire an advantage over other applicants. Many such cases involve new, small, or donor-controlled foundations that have not yet established procedures for reviewing proposals or principles to guide their grant decisions, and whose grantmaking, therefore, still largely follows the often impulsive patterns of personal giving. John M. Russell, an officer of the John and Mary R. Markle Foundation, received a call from a friend who was a bank president, saying that one of his old college friends was sitting in his office and wanted to see Russell. When the visitor arrived at Russell's office, it was evident he was a fund-raiser. He immediately began making a pitch for his university's medical school, presenting a proposal in a fake leather binder embossed with the foundation's name in gold letters. Apparently he had never seen a Markle Foundation annual report because he had no idea what the foundation did. Nor did he realize that the dean of his university's medical school was a friend of Russell's, as were many of the school's professors, several of whom had received grants from the foundation. Russell suspected that *he* knew more about the medical school than the fund-raiser did, which was not saying much. Perhaps as a result of this experience, Russell recommended that fund-raisers be required to open a foundation's mail for a week to appreciate the multitude of requests received—and to learn to spot deceptive proposals (Russell, 1977). In the same vein, Alan Pifer suggested that foundation officers spend time raising money from foundations to appreciate the challenges of dealing with them (Pifer, 1984d).

Some deceptions amount to outright fraud. In the 1930s, for example, the General Education Board gave a grant of $10,000 to an organization after negotiations conducted entirely by mail. No one at the foundation thought any more of it until the post office returned a piece of correspondence stamped "Addressee Unknown." The grantee was never identified and no one knows what happened to the money (Goulden, 1971). A company-sponsored foundation that matched employee contributions to schools and colleges suddenly received a huge list of contributions to a local church-related school, all duly certified and ready to be matched. On investigation, the foundation discovered that members of the church that operated the school had been instructed to make contributions to the school, which would then rebate them to the church and collect the matching gifts from the foundation. An official of the foundation who objected to the scheme told the pastor of the church that although the gifts may have been legal, they were certainly deceitful: "not illegal; just immoral" is how he put it (Andrews, 1973, pp. 243–244). Many other cases have been cited, but in general, one foundation officer summarized the situation nicely: "I could tell you half a dozen ways you could slip a phony application through our office and have a fair chance of receiving some money," admitting that he would not be surprised if a million dollars of foundation money each year was spent on "motorcycles and blondes" (Goulden, 1971, pp. 106–107).

"Fawning Sycophants"

Deference toward foundations is another way that grantseekers violate their partnership with them. Ingratiating, even groveling deference is common among applicants. Kiger called those who engage in it "fawning sycophants" because they show foundations a degree of reverence usually reserved for royalty (1954, p. 107).

Deference often has more to do with the size of a foundation's assets—and the likelihood of getting a grant—than with actual respect for foundation staff. Even the worst jokes of program officers are received with hilarity and their most inane comments are taken as pearls of wisdom by some deferential grantseekers. Many foundation staffers succumb to such adulation, contrived as it is, just as grantseekers often take the remarks of foundation officers far too seriously, interpreting even passing suggestions as orders to be followed religiously (Andrews, 1956). When a foundation officer visits a college, as Harold Laski observed in 1930, he is like an important customer in a department store: "Deferential salesmen surround him on every hand, anticipating his every wish, alive to the importance of his good opinion, fearful lest he be dissatisfied and go to their rival across the way . . ." (p. 150). John Sawyer (1989) saw the situation from both sides; he was president of both the Andrew W. Mellon Foundation and Williams College. As a college president, Sawyer said that he was challenged on almost every issue even when he was correct, but as a foundation officer he was seldom even interrupted even when he was wrong. The most humble and self-deprecating foundation officers cannot escape the adulation of grantseekers; the aura of power that surrounds them, which George Bernard Shaw described as "the unconscious arrogance of conscious opulence," induces quick responses to their telephone calls and allows them to believe, if they so choose, that the compliments paid to them are justified (Branch, 1971, p. 15).

Program officers who enjoy toying with people often toss out suggestions for changes in grantseekers' boards, staff, or programs, to say nothing of their proposals. There once was a Scottish foundation official with a glass eye who delighted in taunting grantseekers, and he had as a visitor one day an Irish college president. The Irishman spoke long, earnestly, and persuasively of his college and its need for aid. The Scot listened and said, "I don't like your plan very much, but it has its good points, so here's what I'll do. One of my eyes is a glass eye—a perfect match, I think, for the other eye. If you can tell me which eye is the glass eye, I'll give you the money." "Fair enough," said the Irishman. "I have watched your eyes carefully and I think I can tell which eye is the glass one." "Which?" asked the Scot. "The left one," said the Irishman. "Correct you are," said the Scot, "but how did you know that my left eye is the glass eye?" "Well," said the Irishman, "I thought I saw a gleam of sympathy in it" (Lester, 1935, p. 10).

Some grantseekers try to anticipate hurdles such as this and adopt the appropriate facade for the foundations they face. To appeal to British foundations, Whitaker (1974) suggested facetiously, applicants should be able to engage in small talk and not be too serious, too clever, too articulate, or too successful with the opposite sex. To appeal to German foundations, grantseekers should be hard-working, keen on private initiative, technically oriented, and capable of making a complex philosophical argument in concise terms. To appeal to American foundations, applicants should be frank, professional, unpompous, and good at facts and figures.

Violations of Partnership by Foundations

Arrogance is the greatest violation by foundations of their partnership with grantseekers. There is in foundations a pervasive haughtiness, often seen in everyone from the switchboard operator to the president, and it is the least attractive attribute of the philanthropic profession and rightly causes considerable hostility toward foundations by grantseekers, government officials, researchers, and journalists.

The most common form of arrogance in foundations is simple discourtesy, which regrettably seems to be increasing in all organizations to the point that "I'll get back to you" more often means "I'll *never* get back to you" and "Let's have lunch" means "I don't ever want to see you again." Almost all grantseekers can attest to substantial discourtesy in foundations, including unreturned telephone calls, breaking appointments without explanation or apology, letting months go by before replying to inquiries or proposals, or, worse, not responding at all. After a lifetime as a foundation officer, John M. Russell (1977) said he often wished Emily Post had written a book of etiquette for foundation people. Particularly inexcusable is program officers acting as if the foundation's money is coming out of their own pockets, behavior they have in common with some unemployment office bureaucrats. The longer people work in foundations, one program officer conceded, the more they think it is *their* money: "You want more and more discretion. You want more and more authority. You begin to think you know everything about everything" (Odendahl, Boris, and Daniels, 1985, p. 3).

One grantseeker reported that a foundation had expressed interest in his proposal and had met with him regularly for eighteen months before it suddenly balked. The program officer promised to have an answer, one way or the other, within a week. Said the applicant: "I never heard from him again. He had been jerking us along for a year" (Bailey, 1992, pp. 13, 15). An official of a mid-western university sent a proposal to approximately a hundred foundations using the dreaded shotgun approach, but only about twenty-five had the courtesy to reply. A few foundations agreed to see him and gave him a routine meeting after which he was ushered out the door. He soon realized that none of the foundation people he had met had read the proposal, and, if a foundation did not reject the application at a meeting, he received a letter to this effect shortly after his visits (Zurcher and Dustan, 1972).

Such stories are commonplace (see, for example, Healey, 1987; *Chronicle of Higher Education*, 1988b). Alan Pifer had to acknowledge the existence of arrogance in his own foundation when a friend complained to him of the "well-known Carnegie hauteur." When charged with arrogant behavior, however, foundation people are often shocked, not so much because they admit their egotism but because they sincerely believe that as members of a worthy profession such as philanthropy they are automatically honorable too (Pifer, 1984d, pp. 13, 18). Many foundation staff members find it difficult to be humble when they believe that they are smarter than either the trustees or the grantseekers; giving money away is intoxicating, and the job is undeniably good for the ego and helpful in getting people to do what you want them to do. Money—and all the psychological baggage that comes with it—sits next to the foundation officer, and it is tempting to jingle the money bag a little, telling the grantseeker, "Now, if you were interested in . . . ." And if the applicant misses the signal, it is tempting to jingle harder and ask a leading question such as "Don't you think . . . ?" Those three words, Warren Weaver said, should never be used by a foundation officer to start a sentence (Goulden, 1971, p. 93).

The Power of Advice

Another form of arrogance by foundations is what Colburn S. Wilbur called "the power of advice." It occurs when program officers insist on giving unwanted and probably unneeded advice to grantseekers, saying, "Let me tell you how to do it. . . ." Nothing is as repugnant as the arrogance of people who try to impose their norms on society based on no other rationale than their pecuniary success or their connections to people with money. This kind of conceit, which Pantin called *cultural arrogance*, is the belief of some foundation officers that because they attended certain universities or are members of a certain class or ethnic group they are superior to others, especially those who come asking for money (Lindeman, 1936; Pantin, 1990).

Working in a foundation involves a curious mix of altruism and arrogance. As one foundation president explained, "You're not trying to make a profit. You're not trying to win a championship. You're not trying to do anything but make a difference on the right side . . . [and] that can be a very comforting circumstance, provided that you don't get smug and complacent." Foundation staff are particularly susceptible to treating people with condescension, if not derision, especially if they are not members of a favored circle of grantees. Unassuming young people who become program officers are perhaps most susceptible; the incessant red-carpet treatment, the ready acceptance into the power structure of the community, and the ceaseless deference from applicants can cause a quick slide from idealism to egotism (Zurcher and Dustan, 1972). More than one veteran foundation officer has questioned whether foundation work is appropriate for young people because its obvious seductions can be disorienting for those who lack wide experience in the ways of the world.

Most people seem willing to tolerate a certain amount of arrogance in artists, athletes, and entrepreneurs who must prove themselves in highly competitive fields, but not in foundation staff; grantmaking is not competitive and receives almost no evaluation. "It's a great job," one grantmaker confessed. "You're guaranteed 100 percent success, because no grantee will ever tell you it was a lousy grant, and certainly you're not going to tell your board that it was" (O'Neill, 1989, p. 152; 1990, p. 28).

Using foundations for nonphilanthropic purposes is another form of arrogance. Some foundations are so poorly staffed, so managed by personal whim, and so lacking a sense of public service that they are little more than quackeries masquerading as foundations, toys for rich adults whose philanthropy is, at best, dubious. The Julius S. Eaton Education Foundation was supposedly created to make interest-free loans to needy students at the University of Miami, but the actual purpose was to recruit players for the football team. The elderly millionaire founder of the St. Genevieve Foundation supported twin sisters through several years of partying, spending an estimated $100,000 on them, some of which came from his foundation. One of the twins was domiciled in a posh duplex, the other in a five-bedroom mansion on Lake Oswego in Oregon; the latter was paid $36,000 as the house's "caretaker." The donor claimed he needed companionship and knew no other way to find it. A jury convicted him of tax evasion (Goulden, 1971). The son of the donor of a foundation "sold" more than $2 million—at his valuation—of stock in a family corporation to the foundation. In the year of record, however, the foundation realized only about $500 in dividends from its $2 million purchase, indicating that the stock was probably grossly overvalued, significantly underperforming, or both. Another foundation awarded some $4,000 in scholarships to whom it described as "worthy college students," all of whom were later identified as sons or daughters of trustees of the foundation (Andrews, 1973, pp. 243–244).

Rejecting Grant Proposals

Another way foundations violate their partnership with grantseekers is by rejecting grant proposals in inappropriate ways. Rejections are a fact of life in foundations and, as H. Thomas James said (1973), to fund one program out of ten is to make nine enemies and one ingrate. Eugene Wilson, former president of the ARCO Foundation, rejected grant proposals from his brother-in-law, the best man at his wedding, and the man who gave him his first job, employed his father, and offered to name a building for him if the grant came through (Johnston, 1988).

No institutions in America are so experienced at performing rejection as foundations; the most selective academies, colleges, and universities do not have to turn down the proportion of applicants for admission that most foundations have to decline for grants. But though most proposals must be rejected, *how* it is done is important because it is one way of judging a foundation. An important question is whether applicants should get detailed explanations of why their proposals were rejected. Most foundations believe it unwise; it is next to impossible to explain all the subtle considerations, and even if it could be done few rejected applicants would accept the criticism constructively.

John May said that of twenty proposals considered, as many as eighteen may be good but the foundation has only enough money to fund a couple. This means that applicants whose proposals were rejected should not think of them as no good. Choices always involve issues besides the applications themselves—for example, the foundation's experience with similar projects, or a shift in program interests known by its officers but not yet communicated to grantseekers. If a foundation can explain at least some of its reasoning for rejecting a proposal ("and you usually can't," says May), the relationship with the applicant can at least be partially salvaged (Kennedy, 1977, p. 44). To avoid confrontations, Charles Dollard suggested facetiously that every foundation should hire a refugee of distinguished appearance who speaks no English and assign him the job of listening sympathetically to applicants whose proposals are about to be rejected. Give him an impressive title and a large office, and teach him just two English sentences for use during conversations with applicants: "That is very interesting" and "I will take it up with my associates" (Macdonald, 1956, p. 112).

Grantseekers whose proposals have been rejected almost always take the rebuff personally, despite their salutary attempts to maintain their objectivity and professionalism, often biting their lips to keep from telling foundations what they really think. Some respond by comparing their rejected project to similar ones that the foundation did fund: "You rejected our proposal, but funded *theirs!*" Others accuse foundations of favoritism, of making grants only to people with connections to their staff or trustees. Charles Dollard admitted that foundations are often characterized as the country of the blind by unsuccessful applicants (Andrews, 1956), so it is not surprising that some grantseekers rail against the foundation community as a whole or plot revenge against a single foundation, its program officers, or trustees. That is usually counterproductive, though; "If you do that," says Andy Robinson, a fund-raising consultant, "you're not going to be considered in the future by that funder, and what more than likely will happen is the word will get out in the funding world that you're a jerk, and that will make it much harder for you" (Dundjerski, 1996b, p. 26).

Wise foundations will expect some response from rejected grantseekers, whether it be felicitous accommodation or resentful aggression. Whatever the reaction, it is difficult to explain the reasons for rejecting proposals because few applicants are really listening, especially immediately after they receive the news of a rejection. Chester Barnard said there is little if anything foundations can do because "you cannot tell people why you do not give them money." If an unqualified individual asks for money, he said, you cannot tell him that in your judgment he is not competent. "You couldn't say it publicly because it hurts the institution. So you have to let them say, 'You must be playing favorites with Harvard or Yale or the University of Chicago,' and so forth, and let it go at that. To publish the truth about these things is not publicly acceptable" (Andrews, 1956, pp. 185–186).

Nor is the case necessarily closed even after a proposal is rejected; the applicant may resubmit it with new supporting arguments, especially if the foundation thoroughly explains why it was rejected. Weaver (1965, p. 70) therefore recommended that rejections be cast in "perfectly spherical, polished form" so that nothing can be "grabbed hold of to be thrown back" at a foundation for reconsideration. If a foundation points out a flaw in a proposal, the applicant will quickly write back with the good news that the shortcoming has been corrected, asking the foundation to "please send the check by return mail." Or the applicant may use the foundation's criticism as the basis for giving criticism in return. To avoid starting a debate, Robert M. Johnson (1976, p. 5) suggested the following two sentences for nonjudgmental rejection letters:

1. There is a real conflict of interest between the intent of your application and some economic or social conditions in the lives of those who run this foundation.

2. Your proposal is for work that really makes us feel uncomfortable. We don't know much about it, but we just don't feel we want to have anything to do with it.

Several philanthropoids, among them F. Emerson Andrews, Harry J. Carman, and John M. Russell, considered Frederick P. Keppel's rejection letters to be perfect, possibly because he reportedly suffered personally when he wrote them. Keppel allowed that good news such as notices of grant awards could be sent by anyone at the Carnegie Corporation, but rejections had to be written and signed by him. Nothing made Keppel's heart bleed more than to have to say no. "Constitutionally," said Carman, "he was not built to run a foundation." When the final decision on a proposal could not be made immediately, Keppel tried to give applicants what Carman called "a prophetic estimate of probabilities," an informed judgment of what probably would be recommended to the trustees because foundation executives usually have a good idea of what the final answer will be, however reluctant they may be to admit it or to share their predictions with applicants (Carman and others, 1951, pp. 52, 78–79). Like other philanthropists, Henry Ford did not enjoy face-to-face encounters with people who asked him for money and he often gave notes to underlings on how he wanted such requests handled. If a note said, "Please *s-e-e* this man," it meant to grant the request, but if a note read, "Please *s-e-a* this man," it meant to deny it (Marquis, 1923, pp. 70-71).

The usual commentary on a rejected proposal, therefore, is evasive, philanthropic doubletalk that avoids the real reasons for the rejection: "We have nothing but praise for your proposal" or "We shall waste no time in reading it" (Brim, 1973, p. 246), a tactic that novelist Umberto Eco described in *Foucault's Pendulum*: "The visitor was dismissed hastily, with expansive promises. The usual committee of advisors would carefully weigh the proposal" (1989, p. 259). John Sawyer (1989) decided that the next best thing to a grant from a foundation is early candor, but precisely what to say in rejecting a proposal is another matter. Although most people in foundations believe that the less said the better, some argue that explaining the reasons for rejection will strengthen the relationship of foundations and grantseekers. The Council on Foundations (1984) has not commented on that issue, but does recommend prompt acknowledgment of serious applications and immediate notification if a proposal is out-of-program. Applicants whose proposals are under consideration should be informed of the steps and timing that will be taken in reaching the final decision. According to Orville Brim, applicants who are not as competent as others for the work they propose should be told so. One of Brim's friends who used to judge music competitions said that he wished that he had a big rubber stamp that said, "Give up!" "This may be too rough," says Brim, "but it moves in the right direction" (1973, p. 246).

It is possible to turn down proposals in a courteous and considerate way, and some foundation officers are good at it. But many do not seem to care about grantseekers' feelings, which is not particularly smart; over time, the applicants rejected by foundations number in the thousands and could represent a formidable body of hostile opinion toward them (Pifer, 1984d). Explaining the weaknesses in proposals, however, can enable grantseekers to improve future applications. The process of preparing and submitting a grant proposal is itself instructive and can help applicants learn to write more compelling proposals and understand better the intricacies of foundation grantmaking and the dynamics of giving and getting money.

Implications for Grantseekers of Foundations as Partners

The relationship of foundations and grantseekers, often portrayed as a partnership, better resembles a calculative transaction in which neither party is completely honest with the other. Funds may change hands, but a full emotional exchange rarely occurs because of the gamesmanship and contrived dynamics involved. People who seek grants do not often confide in foundations lest their candor expose the cracks in their operations, and foundations rarely confide in them lest their openness imply favoritism and forthcoming grants. Collaboration between foundations is low, and substantive communication between foundations and grantseekers is just as poor.

Foundations need grantseekers to conduct projects and thereby help fulfill their charters, and grantseekers need foundations for money to do their work. Foundations award responsibility to grantees in addition to money, and grantees contribute action to foundations in addition to a reason for being. Money can distort their relationship no differently than it can impair that between husbands and wives, preachers and parishioners, merchants and customers, and politicians and voters. For foundations, every grant buys something: power, respectability, participation, or a sense of self-righteousness. For grantees, every grant also buys something: recognition, approbation, and the confidence that they have achieved an alliance with foundations that others have not.

Recommendations to Foundations as Partners

The metaphor of foundations as partners speaks to the need for trust between foundations and grantseekers, on which every other principle in their relationship depends. Without trust, their alliance can quickly become a sham, a manipulative exchange inconsistent with the spirit of philanthropy.

Trust is an essential element in enduring human relationships, and violating it disrupts not only social relations but those between the parties in philanthropy as well. Foundation officers need to remember that applicants are personally involved in their proposals and convinced, rightly or wrongly, that their projects are important, original, and worth funding. Treating grantseekers rudely or arrogantly is inexcusable. Foundations should acknowledge that applicants are essential and should establish a code of conduct with them based on honesty and respect. Honesty is asking questions about projects directly, being clear about how proposals are reviewed, and making evaluations that are forthright, not vague or evasive. Honesty is telling applicants up front that proposals do not have much chance to be funded and giving them a clearer idea why proposals were rejected. Respect is approaching grantseekers as partners, not as supplicants who must come on bended knee. Respect is responding to them promptly and making an effort to describe the rationale used in grant decisions, even if it subjects foundation logic to scrutiny by those not truly qualified to judge.

Foundations should promptly acknowledge receipt of every application and give an indication of when a decision is expected, particularly if it will be delayed, as often happens when foundation boards meet infrequently. If a grant request is urgent but does not match a foundation's program interests, the applicant should be told immediately so it can submit the proposal elsewhere.

If grantseekers are to be partners with foundations, they should have a voice in determining how charitable dollars are used; they are closest to the problems foundations seek to correct. If surplus wealth is to be used by foundations to advance the culture, the investment of funds should involve those directly involved in developing the culture—scholars, artists, writers, and composers, for example, who cannot be subservient if they are to retain their integrity.

Foundations and grantseekers may indeed become partners, but today they cannot be considered very good partners. Fawning deference, pressure tactics, and manipulation by grantseekers are just as common as arrogance, rudeness, and lack of candor by foundations. A genuine alliance is needed between the two, and that requires both parties to reject attitudes and behavior that threaten to further damage their partnership.

Chapter Eight

Conclusion
Faces of Foundations in the Future

Judges. Editors. Citizens. Activists. Entrepreneurs. Partners. These metaphors offer new portraits of foundations and invite us to examine the accuracy of our perceptions of them. Many of our ideas about foundations are based on images that enable us to see them only in certain ways, but this book examines the truth and falsehood of these ideas and suggests new ways for managers, fund-raisers, and researchers to understand foundations.

By no means do the metaphors represent all perspectives; no single metaphor or set of metaphors can do that because foundations are many things at once. Each of the faces of foundations, no different than human faces, has two sides, a light side symbolizing exemplary conduct such as action and vision and a dark side representing offensive behavior such as secrecy and arrogance. An assessment of the performance of foundations as judges, editors, citizens, activists, entrepreneurs, and partners, therefore, depends on which side of their faces they show.

Foundations are judges because their fundamental task is to determine the merits of grantseekers and the projects they propose, to decide that one applicant shall be funded and another shall not. On one side of their face as judges, some foundations demonstrate exceptional discretion and develop grantmaking principles that honor the intent of their donors, reflect the wisdom of their trustees, and serve the needs of their communities. They use both the head and the heart in their grantmaking decisions and resist the temptation to rely on inflexible and mechanistic measures to evaluate applicants. But on the other side of their face as judges, some foundations function with a complete absence of mission and are little more than vehicles to satisfy the whims of their founders or trustees. Some satisfice in their grantmaking decisions by funding only the safest projects; others fail to assess their missions and refuse to evaluate their operations, insisting nonetheless that evaluation be a part of every grant proposal and that all their grantees evaluate themselves.

Foundations are editors because they associate the quality of applicants with the caliber of their writing, linking the ability to describe a project cogently with the capacity to administer it efficiently. On one side of their face as editors, some foundations know that great ideas are sometimes hidden in poorly phrased proposals and that bad writing does not necessarily mean inferior people. Some foundations recognize that grantseekers use Proposalese because they think foundations expect it, having seen ample Foundationese in the publications of foundations. Others know that some talented people do not write well but can do the work they propose, just as some people write well but perform the work they describe poorly. But on the other side of their face as editors, some foundations blindly reject any proposal that contains jargon and are unwilling to look below the surface of a poorly written application. Thus they abdicate their responsibility to find promising ideas and people, no matter how difficult it may be to uncover them—as it certainly is in proposals riddled with Proposalese.

Foundations are citizens because, like people in a democracy, they have responsibilities to their fellow citizens: grantseekers, other foundations, and associations in philanthropy, as well as Congress, the federal government, and the American people. On one side of their face as citizens, some foundations endorse the principle of full disclosure and acknowledge their accountability to the public. They comply fully with their legislated accountability obligations, conduct exemplary communication programs, and cooperate with regulatory agencies, reporters, and researchers who seek information from them. Some foundations recognize that they themselves—not rogue politicians or disgruntled applicants—instigated Congressional investigations of them because of their obstinate opposition to the concept of public accountability. But on the other side of their face as citizens, some foundations disavow any responsibility to the public and reject the role of the federal government in overseeing them. They are secretive, refuse to publish annual reports, and hide behind unlisted telephone numbers and post office boxes for addresses. Some respond to inquiries into their operations in a reactionary way, threatening to disband when even the mildest review of them is suggested.

Foundations are activists because they support people and organizations that seek to formulate public policy or lead movements advocating for issues such as peace, justice, or the environment or on behalf of people such as the poor, the elderly, or the handicapped. On one side of their face as activists, some foundations make important, even landmark, contributions to public policy, finance social movements to rectify injustice, inform people of policy issues, and expose corruption or incompetence in organizations. Others fight for the rights of children or minorities and provide technical assistance in management, governance, and fund-raising to organizations at the forefront of activism. But on the other side of their face as activists, some foundations are guilty of political extremism and blind partisanship and look the other way when they encounter scandal, especially in their own ranks. They ignore social issues and public policy questions, denigrate those who advocate on behalf of the disenfranchised, and prefer the safety of the rear echelon to the danger of the front lines of activism.

Foundations are entrepreneurs because they are the venture capitalists of philanthropy, able to support people, projects, and organizations unlikely to receive funds from conventional donors such as corporations or government. On one side of their face as entrepreneurs, foundations are in a unique position to take risks because they are generally free from external controls and need not answer to customers or constituents, positioning them to attack any problem or challenge any assumption in the interest of the public good. Some foundations support maverick people, innovative organizations, and unpopular causes when less daring funding sources turn their backs on these grantseekers. But on the other side of their face as entrepreneurs, some foundations are terrified of risk and abandon their responsibility to be the venture capitalists of philanthropy. They are led by cowardly trustees who are quite comfortable with the status quo and whose propensity for risk taking is rhetorical as opposed to actual. Others profess a philosophy of risk taking in their publications and testimony, but practice a philanthropy of fear and timidity.

Foundations are partners because they fulfill their missions through the work of other people and organizations, without whom they would have little or no constructive purpose. On one side of their face as partners, some foundations work tirelessly to achieve and maintain relationships of respect, honesty, and candor with grantseekers. They recognize that their treatment of applicants—and their treatment by grantseekers—can violate the trust between them and they encourage nonprofits and other foundations to acknowledge and correct this problem. But on the other side of their face as partners, some foundations practice gamesmanship that strains their partnership with grantseekers through petulance and arrogance and by refusing to respond to inquiries, not answering their mail, or treating applicants as though the money was coming out of their own pockets.

In the movie *Dances with Wolves,* Lieutenant John Dunbar, the character played by Kevin Costner, keeps a journal of his experiences on the Great Plains with Sioux Indians who adopt him into their tribe. Struck by the beauty of their culture and the complete fallacy of the white man's negative perceptions of them, he observes that "nothing I have been told about these people is correct." As a person who has lived with foundations, as it were, these past few years and is likewise moved by the complexity of their culture, I believe that much the same could be said about them.

One purpose of this book has been to assess the conduct of foundations in their first hundred years, a process that naturally leads us to ask about them in the future. In the coming years, foundations as citizens are not likely to acknowledge their accountability to the public and accept the principle of full disclosure because many equate the word *account* with the word *report* and are unwilling to place themselves in a subordinate position to the federal government. Communication between foundations and people and other organizations is poor, despite the encouragement of the Council on Foundations and many respected trustees and staff members. Some foundations consider themselves the nation's last truly free organizations and refuse to acknowledge any obligation to bureaucrats, legislators, the media, or the public.

Nor are they likely to become the activists they often claim to be by assuming a proactive role in the formation of public policy. To many foundations, involvement with lobbyists, demonstrations, lawsuits, and the political process—even indirectly through other organizations—is anathema, and few are likely to reverse their long-standing fear of the government and become players on the public stage. Neither are foundations inclined to increase their risk taking because it is inconsistent with the conservatism of foundation trustees and the prudent allocation of the limited assets of foundations. Risky people and organizations contradict the preference of foundations for subsidizing benign organizations such as museums, symphonies, galleries, and private colleges, which preserve and advance the culture of wealthy people. Most foundations abhor the idea of wasting money, and their trustees feel a distinct responsibility to protect the assets under their auspices, consistently choosing to invest them in quiet and established organizations whose possibility of failure is negligible.

For all their wealth and power, foundations are organizations whose reach has not exceeded their grasp, whose promise is yet unfulfilled. Their secrecy, condescension, arbitrariness, gamesmanship, aversion to risk, and lack of public accountability are arguably as prevalent today as they were a hundred years ago, for as Willa Cather suggested in one of the opening epigraphs of this book, a handful of stories, in foundations and elsewhere, go on repeating themselves as though they had never happened before. As foundations end their first century, they are engaged in a major reassessment of their missions and program interests and they function in an environment of unprecedented selectivity and competition for their grants. The reduction or elimination of federal funding for many programs, the intractability of problems such as drug addiction, and the increase in the number of nonprofit organizations have contributed to the pervasive introspection and palpable anxiety in foundations frustrated with the insolubility of problems. Forces such as these have reduced the time that foundations can spend explaining their priorities to grantseekers or discussing the reasons that proposals were rejected. Curtness among foundation staff, never a virtue, is unlikely to decrease, and, given the competitive climate for their grants, the estimate that foundations fund only 5 percent of their applications does not bode well for grantseekers in general, particularly for those inexperienced with foundations.

In their first 100 years, foundations have shown both the light and the dark sides of their faces as judges, editors, citizens, activists, entrepreneurs, and partners. The question for the next century is which side of their faces we shall see.

References

Adams, G. *Age of Industrial Violence: The Activities and Findings of the United States Commission on Industrial Relations.* New York: Columbia University Press, 1966, p. xi.

Allen, W. H. *Rockefeller: Giant, Dwarf, Symbol.* New York: Institute for Public Service, 1930.

Allen, Y. "How Foundations Evaluate Requests." In F. E. Andrews (ed.), *Foundations: Twenty Viewpoints.* New York: Russell Sage Foundation, 1965, p. 96.

Anderson, A. "Aristotle and the Ethics of Philanthropy." In D. F. Burlingame (ed.), *The Responsibilities of Wealth.* Bloomington: Indiana University Press, 1992, p. 51.

Andrews, F. E. *Philanthropic Foundations.* New York: Russell Sage Foundation, 1956, pp. 18–19, 184–185, 195, 221–222, 228.

Andrews, F. E. "Foundation Funds—Whose Money?" *Foundation News,* Jan. 1963, pp. 5–7.

Andrews, F. E. *Foundation Watcher.* Princeton, N.J.: Princeton University Press, 1973, pp. 82, 151, 243–244, 259.

Archabal, J. "Inspecting the Damage." *Foundation News,* Mar.-Apr. 1984, pp. 58–59.

Arenson, K. W. "Woeful '95 Leads U.S. Charities to Introspection." *New York Times,* Dec. 10, 1995, p. 38.

Aristotle. *The Rhetoric of Aristotle: An Expanded Translation with Supplementary Examples for Students of Composition and Public Speaking by Lane Cooper.* New York: Appleton-Century Company, 1932.

Arnove, R. F. "Introduction." In R. F. Arnove (ed.), *Philanthropy and Cultural Imperialism: The Foundations at Home and Abroad.* Boston: G. K. Hall, 1980.

Bailey, A. L. "More Scholars, Colleges Taking an Interest in the Study of Philanthropy and Non-Profit Organizations." *Chronicle of Higher Education,* Sept. 21, 1988, p. A34.

Bailey, A. L. "Why Do the Wealthy Give to Charity?" *Chronicle of Philanthropy,* Apr. 17, 1990, pp. 4, 12.

Bailey, A. L. "A Tough Balancing Act at MacArthur." *Chronicle of Philanthropy,* Oct. 6, 1992, pp. 6–16.

Bailey, A. L. "A New Leader for the Ford Foundation." *Chronicle of Philanthropy,* Jan. 12, 1995, p. 6.

Baldridge, J. V., D. V. Curtis, G. P. Ecker, and G. L. Riley. "Alternative Models of Governance in Higher Education." In R. Birnbaum (ed.), *ASHE Reader in Organization and Governance in Higher Education.* Lexington, Mass.: Ginn, 1984, p. 12.

Barnard, C. I. *The Functions of the Executive.* Cambridge, Mass.: Harvard University Press, 1938, p. 32.

Barzun, J. *Teacher in America.* Boston: Little, Brown, 1945.

Barzun, J. *The House of Intellect.* New York: Harper, 1959, pp. 191–192.

Bennett, J. Letter to the Editor. *Chronicle of Philanthropy,* Sept. 18, 1990, p. 34.

Boris, E. "Increasing What We Know." *Foundation News,* May-June 1985, p. 60.

Boris, E., and T. Odendahl. "Ethical Issues in Fund Raising and Philanthropy." In J. Van Til and Associates (eds.), *Critical Issues in American Philanthropy.* San Francisco: Jossey-Bass, 1990, p. 190.

Bothwell, R. O. *Testimony Before the Subcommittee on Taxation and Debt Management of the Senate Committee on Finance.* Washington, D.C.: U.S. Senate, Feb. 24, 1984, pp. 1–4, 7, 11–12.

Bothwell, R. O., and T. Saasta. "Now More Than Ever." *Grantsmanship Center News,* May-June 1981, p. 93.

Bothwell, R. O., and T. Saasta. "The Foundations of Change." *Grantsmanship Center News,* Jan.–Feb. 1982, p. 71.

Boulding, K. E. "Towards a Pure Theory of Foundations." Paper presented at Conference on Foundations, at Dayton, Ohio. Nov. 11–13, 1970, p. 7.

Boulding, K. E. *The Economy of Love and Fear: A Preface to Grants Economics.* Belmont, Calif.: Wadsworth, 1973, p. 2.

Branch, T. "The Case Against Foundations." *Washington Monthly,* July 1971, pp. 14–16.

Brewster, K. "Foreword." In R. Magat (ed.), *Philanthropic Giving: Studies in Varieties and Goals.* New York: Oxford University Press, 1989, p. A34.

Brim, O. "Do We Know What We Are Doing?" In F. Heimann (ed.), *The Future of Foundations.* Englewood Cliffs, N.J.: Prentice-Hall, 1973, pp. 229, 246.

Broce, T. *Fund Raising.* Norman: University of Oklahoma Press, 1979, pp. 103, 116.

Brown, D. "Ford and Other Foundations in Public Affairs." In F. E. Andrews (ed.), *Foundations: Twenty Viewpoints.* New York: Russell Sage Foundation, 1965.

Bruce, E., J. Moe, T. P. Saasta, J. W. Abernathy, and R. Bothwell. *Foundations and Public Information: Sunshine or Shadow?* Washington, D.C.: National Committee for Responsive Philanthropy, 1980, p. 1.

Cannon, C. J. "Philanthropic Doubts." *Atlantic Monthly,* Sept. 1921, p. 294.

Carman, H. J., R. Hayes, L. Galantiere, H. James, J. M. Russell, F.D.G. Ribble, T. W. McCurdy, and R. C. Leffingwell. *Appreciations of Frederick Paul Keppel by Some of His Friends.* New York: Columbia University Press, 1951.

Carnegie, A. Letter to the Editor. *The Independent,* 1913.

Carnegie, A. "The Gospel of Wealth." In B. O'Connell (ed.), *America's Voluntary Spirit: A Book of Readings.* New York: Foundation Center, 1983.

Carnegie Corporation. *Carnegie Corporation of New York: Annual Report.* New York: Carnegie Corporation, 1994, p. 156.

Carroll, L. *Through the Looking Glass.* In E. Guiliano (ed.), *The Complete Illustrated Works of Lewis Carroll.* New York: Avenel Books/Crown Publishers, 1982.

Cather, W. *O Pioneers!* Boston and New York: Houghton-Mifflin, 1913.

Chambers, M. M. *Charters of Philanthropies.* New York: Carnegie Foundation for the Advancement of Teaching, 1948.

Chapper, F. M. "Disclosure and Reporting: Present Requirements and Forms." Paper presented at the Eighth Biennial Conference on Charitable Foundations at New York, 1967, p. 192.

Cheit, E. F., and T. E. Lobman. *Foundations and Higher Education.* Berkeley, Calif.: Carnegie Council on Policy Studies in Higher Education, 1979, pp. 4, 8.

Chronicle of Higher Education. "Philanthropy Highlight: Acceptance Rates of Grant Proposals." Oct. 12, 1988a, p. 2.

Chronicle of Higher Education. "Hampshire College President Picked as Head of MacArthur Foundation." November 2, 1988b, p. 29.

Chronicle of Philanthropy. "Foundations' Impact is Undercut by Timid Grantmaking, Failure of Trustees to Fulfill Public Duties, a Book Charges." Mar. 7, 1989, p. 17.

Chronicle of Philanthropy. "Challenges for the 1990s." Jan. 9, 1990a, pp. 1, 12–19.

Chronicle of Philanthropy. "The Non-Profit World: A Statistical Portrait." Jan. 9, 1990b, p. 8.

Chronicle of Philanthropy. "9 Award-Winning Annual Reports." Mar. 6, 1990c, p. 21.

Chronicle of Philanthropy. "Book Buying at Gannett Prompts Criticism." Sept. 18, 1990d, p. 6.

Chronicle of Philanthropy. "3 Foundations Form New Fund to Focus on Energy Issues." Jan. 15, 1991a, p. 21.

Chronicle of Philanthropy. "Tax-Exempt Organizations Registered with the IRS." Sept. 10, 1991b, p. 43.

Chronicle of Philanthropy. "The Non-Profit World: A Statistical Portrait." Jan. 28, 1992a, p. 24.

Chronicle of Philanthropy. "Few Funds Made It Difficult To See Tax Forms." Sept. 8, 1992b, pp. 31–32.

Chronicle of Philanthropy. "Foundation Award-Winners." May 3, 1994, p. 40.

Chronicle of Philanthropy. "Non-Profit Groups Tell Congress They Cannot 'Do It All.'" Feb. 23, 1995a, p. 47.

Chronicle of Philanthropy. "Managing Institutional Advancement: A Certificate Program for the Development Leader." July 13, 1995b, p. 45.

Chronicle of Philanthropy. "$10 Million Pledged for Charity Leaders." Oct. 19, 1995c, p. 12.

Chronicle of Philanthropy. "Kellogg Supports Adult Education." June 13, 1996, p. 12.

Clark, B. R. "The Organizational Saga in Higher Education." In R. Birnbaum (ed.), *ASHE Reader in Organization and Governance.* Lexington, Mass.: Ginn, 1984.

Coffman, H. *American Foundations: A Study of Their Role in the Child Welfare Movement.* New York: Young Men's Christian Association, 1936, pp. 7, 66.

Cohen, M. D., and J. G. March. *Leadership and Ambiguity: The American College President.* New York: McGraw-Hill, 1974, pp. 33–34, 81.

Cohen, M. D., and J. G. March. "Leadership in an Organized Anarchy." In M. W. Peterson, E. E. Chaffee, and T. H. White (eds.), *ASHE Reader: Organization and Governance in Higher Education.* Needham, Mass.: Ginn, 1991, pp. 399, 408–409.

College of Saint Mary. Advertisement for president. *Chronicle of Higher Education,* Oct. 27, 1995, p. B66.

Colvard, R. "Risk Capital Philanthropy: The Ideological Defense of Innovation." In G. K. Zollschan and W. Hirsch (eds.), *Explorations in Social Change.* Boston: Houghton-Mifflin, 1964, pp. 729, 730, 741.

Colwell, M.A.C. *Private Foundations and Public Policy.* New York: Garland, 1993, pp. 11, 36.

Commerce Clearing House. *Internal Revenue Code.* Chicago: Commerce Clearing House, 1994.

Commission on Foundations and Private Philanthropy. *Foundations, Private Giving, and Public Policy.* Chicago: University of Chicago Press, 1970, pp. 77–78.

Commission on Private Philanthropy and Public Needs. *Giving in America: Toward a Stronger Voluntary Sector.* Washington: United States Treasury Department, 1975.

Coon, H. *Money to Burn: What the Great American Philanthropic Foundations Do with Their Money.* London: Longmans, Green, 1938, pp. 323, 334–335.

Coser, L. A. *Men of Ideas: A Sociologist's Views.* New York: The Free Press, 1965, p. 338.

Council on Foundations. *Some General Principles and Guidelines for Grantmaking Foundations.* New York: Council on Foundations, 1973, p. 4.

Council on Foundations. *Principles and Practices for Effective Grantmaking.* New York: Council on Foundations, 1980, p. 2, 9.

Council on Foundations. "Highlights of the Council's Legislation and Regulation Survey." *Foundation News,* July-Aug. 1981, p. 6.

Council on Foundations. *Principles and Practices for Effective Grantmaking.* New York: Council on Foundations, 1984, p. 3.

Covington, S., and L. Parachini. *Foundations in the Newt Era.* Washington, D.C.: National Committee for Responsive Philanthropy, 1995, pp. 2, 17, 26–27.

Crawshaw, R., and J. Bruce. "Reflections on the Art of Giving." *Foundation News,* Jan.-Feb. 1978, p. 27.

Crossland, F., and S. Trachtenberg. "Fifteen Pleas to Fund Raisers and Foundations." *Educational Record,* Summer 1982, pp. 18–19, 20.

Cuninggim, M. *Private Money and Public Service: The Role of Foundations in American Society.* New York: McGraw-Hill, 1972, pp. 7, 19, 107.

Curti, M., and R. Nash. *Philanthropy in the Shaping of American Higher Education.* New Brunswick, N.J.: Rutgers University Press, 1965, p. 230.

Curtis, J. "Annual Reports: Why Bother?" *Foundation News,* July-Aug. 1987, p. 38.

Curtis, J. "In Their Own Style." *Foundation News,* Mar.-Apr. 1988, p. 42.

Curtis, J. "Welcome to 1996: The Midpoint of the 'Re' Decade." *Foundation News and Commentary,* Jan.-Feb. 1996, p. 5.

DeBakey, L. "The Persuasive Proposal." *Foundation News,* July-Aug. 1977, pp. 20, 21, 23, 27.

Desruisseaux, P. "Reporting to the Public: Some Foundations Do, Most Don't." *Chronicle of Higher Education,* Jan. 22, 1986a, pp. 18, 37.

Desruisseaux, P. "30–Year-Old Foundation Center Keeps Track of Where the Money—$4.3 Billion of It—Goes." *Chronicle of Higher Education,* Oct. 8, 1986b, pp. 37–38.

Desruisseaux, P. "Conservative Foundations to Turn Attention to Philanthropy Itself." *Chronicle of Higher Education,* Sept. 2, 1987a, pp. A72, A74–A75.

Desruisseaux, P. "Rising Demand for Private Philanthropy Seen Putting Foundations in a 'Fishbowl.'" *Chronicle of Higher Education,* Apr. 15, 1987b, pp. 31, 34.

Dollard, C. *Testimony Before the Select Committee to Investigate Tax-Exempt Foundations and Comparable Organizations.* Washington, D.C.: U.S. House of Representatives, 1953, pp. 339–340, 350.

Donee Group. *Private Philanthropy: Vital and Innovative or Passive and Irrelevant?* Washington: National Committee for Responsive Philanthropy, 1976.

Dowd, M. "The Language Thing." *New York Times Magazine,* July 29, 1990, p. 48.

Duca, D. "How Foundations Undergo the Grantmaking Process." *Fund Raising Management,* Aug. 1981, p. 51.

Dundjerski, M. "Pew Cracks Down on Grants for Arts Organizations." *Chronicle of Philanthropy,* Apr. 4, 1996a, p. 12.

Dundjerski, M. "Foundation Leaders Urge Grant Seekers to Do More Homework." *Chronicle of Philanthropy,* Apr. 4, 1996b, p. 26.

Dundjerski, M. "As Congressional Scrutiny Grows, Foundations Are Urged to Spread the Word About Their Work." *Chronicle of Philanthropy,* May 2, 1996c, p. 12.

Eco, U. *Foucault's Pendulum.* New York: Ballantine, 1989.

Edie, J. A. "Congress and Foundations: Historical Summary." In T. Odendahl (ed.), *America's Wealthy and the Future of Foundations.* New York: Foundation Center, 1987a, pp. 3, 50.

Edie, J. A. *Congress and Private Foundations: An Historical Analysis.* Washington, D.C.: Council on Foundations, 1987b, pp. 11–12, 17–18.

Edie, J. A. "A Lift for Lobbying." *Foundation News,* Mar.-Apr. 1991, p. 40.

Eisenberg, P. "Philanthropic Ethics from a Donee Perspective." *Foundation News,* Sept.-Oct. 1983, p. 50.

Eisenberg, P. "Still Needed: Reform Movement in Philanthropy." *Chronicle of Philanthropy,* Oct. 8, 1991a, pp. 41–42.

Eisenberg, P. "Why We Know So Little About Philanthropy." *Chronicle of Philanthropy,* Dec. 17, 1991b, p. 37.

Eisenberg, P. "Foundations Should React to GOP Policies." *Chronicle of Philanthropy,* Nov. 30, 1995, pp. 37–38.

Elliott, E. "On Being a Trustee." *Foundation News,* May-June 1984, p. 40.

Embree, E. R. "The Business of Giving Away Money." *Harper's Monthly,* Aug. 1930, p. 329.

Embree, E. R. "Timid Billions: Are the Foundations Doing Their Job?" *Harper's Magazine,* Mar. 1949, p. 30.

Eskenazi, G. "On Language: Wordgame Champs." *New York Times Magazine,* June 16, 1985, p. 12.

Famiglietti, A. "Carnegie's Proposed Proposal Guidelines." *Foundation News and Commentary,* May-June 1996, p. 37.

Field, M. Testimony Before the Select Committee to Investigate Foundations and Other Organizations. Washington D.C., 1954.

Fisher, J. L. "Editor's Notes." In J. L. Fisher (ed.), *New Directions for Institutional Advancement: Presidential Leadership in Advancement Activities.* San Francisco: Jossey-Bass, 1980.

Fix, J. L. "Wealth in New Hands." *Foundation News,* Jan.-Feb. 1994, pp. 18–23.

Flexner, A. *Funds and Foundations.* New York: Harper, 1952.

Foote, J. "Small Sums from Big Givers." *Foundation News,* May-June 1990, p. 68.

Fosdick, R. B. *The Story of the Rockefeller Foundation: 1913 to 1950.* New York: Harper, 1952, pp. 2, 3, 100, 296.

Fosdick, R. B. *A Philosophy for a Foundation.* New York: Rockefeller Foundation, 1963, pp. 14–17.

Foundation Center. *Foundation Directory.* New York: Foundation Center, 1964.

Foundation Center. *Foundation Directory: Part 2.* New York: Foundation Center, 1995, pp. v, xi.

Freud, A. *The Ego and the Mechanism of Defence.* London: Hogarth, 1948, pp. 140, 146.

Friedman, R. E. "Private Foundation-Government Relationships." In F. Heimann (ed.), *The Future of Foundations.* Englewood Cliffs, N.J.: Prentice-Hall, 1973, pp. 173, 186.

Friedrich, O. "Of Words That Ravage, Pillage, Spoil." *Time,* Jan. 9, 1984, p. 76.

Gates, F. T. *Chapters in My Life.* New York: Free Press, 1977, pp. 163–164.

General Accounting Office. *Statistical Analysis of the Operations and Activities of Private Foundations.* Washington, D.C.: General Accounting Office, 1984, p. 24.

Glenn, J. M., L. Brandt, and F. E. Andrews. *Russell Sage Foundation.* New York: Russell Sage Foundation, 1947.

Goodwin, W. M. "Thirty Financial Questions to Cut Funding Risks." *Foundation News,* Mar.–Apr. 1976, p. 32.

Gorey, H. "The Big Senate Battlegrounds." *Time,* Oct. 24, 1988, p. 31.

Gorman, J. "A Congressional Call for More Accountability." *Foundation News,* May-June 1983, pp. 25–26.

Gorman, J. "Adding the Human Dimension." *Foundation News,* May-June 1987, p. 32.

Gorman, J. P. "Class Distinctions." *Foundation News,* Nov.-Dec. 1988, pp. 30, 33–34.

Goss, K. A. "Some Foundations Try New Solutions for an Old Problem: Whether to Help Non-Profit Groups Meet Operating Costs." *Chronicle of Philanthropy,* June 27, 1989, pp. 4–6.

Goss, K. A. "Conservatives Dominate Major Foundation Boards, but Policy Grants Tilt to the Left, Researchers Say." *Chronicle of Philanthropy*, Jan. 25, 1994, pp. 8–10.

Goulden, J. C. *The Money Givers*. New York: Random House, 1971, pp. 72, 74–75, 102, 106–107, 130, 178–179.

Gray, S. "Foundations Urged to Give More Aid to Immigrants." *Chronicle of Philanthropy*, Oct. 5, 1995, p. 16.

Greene, E. "Some Young Philanthropists Shun Gifts to Alma Maters in Favor of Support for Direct Social-Action Projects." *Chronicle of Higher Education*, May 24, 1989, p. A27.

Greene, E. "Drug and Alcohol Abuse: Foundations Grope for Ways to Deal with the Issue, But Solutions Are Hard to Find." *Chronicle of Philanthropy*, Apr. 3, 1990, p. 1.

Greene, E. "A Gadfly Challenges Philanthropy—Again." *Chronicle of Philanthropy*, Nov. 5, 1991, p. 7.

Greene, E. "The Keeper of Creativity's 'Safety Net.'" *Chronicle of Philanthropy*, June 29, 1995, pp. 8, 12.

Greene, J. D. "A Memorandum on Principles and Policies of Giving." New York: Rockefeller Foundation, 1913.

Greene, S. G. "Should More Grants Fail?" *Chronicle of Philanthropy*, Aug. 7, 1990, pp. 2, 10, 11.

Greene, S. G. "Philanthropy's Population Explosion." *Chronicle of Philanthropy*, May 31, 1994, pp. 6–8.

Greene, S. G., and B. Millar. "Non-Profits in a Shaky Economy." *Chronicle of Philanthropy*, Sept. 18, 1990, pp. 1, 13.

Greene, S. G., and J. Moore. "Conservative Foundations on the Move." *Chronicle of Philanthropy*, Feb. 23, 1995, pp. 1, 3, 13–16.

Hall, H. "The Great Game of Grantsmanship." *Chronicle of Philanthropy*, June 13, 1989, p. 18.

Hall, H. "Giving Money To Raise Money." *Chronicle of Philanthropy*, Apr. 21, 1992, p. 19.

Hall, H. "Fund Raising Goes to College." *Chronicle of Philanthropy*, Oct. 5, 1995a, pp. 30, 39–41.

Hall, H. "Master's Programs Are Said to Slight Fund Raising." *Chronicle of Philanthropy*, Oct. 5, 1995b, pp. 41–42.

Hall, H., and J. Murawski. "Fund Raising: Hot Career or Hot Seat?" *Chronicle of Philanthropy*, June 29, 1995, p. 21.

Hall, L. V. (ed.). *Foundation Grants to Individuals*. New York: Foundation Center, 1995, pp. v–vi, xii–xiii.

Harrison, G. B. (ed.). *Shakespeare: The Complete Works*. New York: Harcourt, Brace, 1968.

Harrison, S. M., and F. E. Andrews. *American Foundations for Social Welfare*. New York: Russell Sage Foundation, 1946, pp. 48, 51, 103.

Hart, J. "Foundations and Social Activism: A Critical View." In F. Heimann (ed.), *The Future of Foundations.* Englewood Cliffs, N.J.: Prentice-Hall, 1973.

Harwood, R. "The Power Ignored by the Press." *Washington Post,* Feb. 24, 1997, p. A19.

Healey, J. K. "Not Yet a Profession." *Foundation News,* July-Aug. 1987, pp. 26–27.

Henry, W. A. "An Open and Shut Case." *Foundation News,* Mar.-Apr. 1987, pp. 46–47.

Hettleman, R. Letter to the author. Washington, D.C.: Council on Foundations, June 18, 1992.

His Majesty's Commissioners for Inquiring into the Administration and Practical Operation of the Poor Laws. *Report from His Majesty's Commissioners for Inquiring into the Administration and Practical Operation of the Poor Laws.* London, 1834, p. 361.

Hollis, E. *Philanthropic Foundations and Higher Education.* New York: Columbia University Press, 1938, pp. 8, 9-10, 81.

Hollis, E. *Hearings Before the Select Committee to Investigate Tax-Exempt Foundations and Comparable Organizations.* Washington, D.C.: U.S. House of Representatives, 1953, p. 17.

Hutchins, R. M. *Freedom, Education, and the Fund: Essays and Addresses, 1946–1956.* New York: Meridian, 1956.

Illinois Benedictine College. Advertisement for Vice President of Development. *Chronicle of Higher Education,* Sept. 23, 1992, p. B37.

Jacquette, F. L., and B. Jacquette. "What Makes a Good Proposal?" *Foundation News,* Jan.-Feb. 1973, pp. 18, 20.

James, H. T. "Perspectives on Internal Functioning of Foundations." In F. Heimann (ed.), *The Future of Foundations.* Englewood Cliffs, N.J.: Prentice-Hall, 1973, pp. 197–198, 202, 204, 205, 209–210, 211, 212, 222.

Jenkins, C. J. "Nonprofit Organizations and Policy Advocacy." In W. W. Powell (ed.), *The Nonprofit Sector: A Research Handbook.* New Haven, Conn.: Yale University Press, 1987, p. 313.

Jenkins, C. J. "Social Movement Philanthropy and American Democracy." In R. Magat (ed.), *Philanthropic Giving: Studies in Varieties and Goals.* New York: Oxford University Press, 1989, pp. 294, 295–298, 299, 303–304, 305–306.

Johnson, R. "On Foundations." Paper presented at the Annual Conference of the Council for the Advancement and Support of Education at New York, Jan. 28, 1985.

Johnson, R. M. "Notice." *Foundation News,* Jan.-Feb. 1975a, p. 14.

Johnson, R. M. "We Turned You Down Because . . ." *Foundation News,* Nov.-Dec. 1975b, p. 6.

Johnson, R. M. "Four Parting Pearls of Wisdom and Truth." *Foundation News*, Mar.-Apr. 1976, p. 5.

Johnston, D. "Looking for an Honest Answer." *Foundation News*, Jan.-Feb. 1988, p. 55.

Joseph, J. A. "Six Trends Shaping Philanthropy's Future." *Foundation News*, May-June 1983, p. 24.

Joseph, J. A. *Private Philanthropy and the Making of Public Policy.* Washington, D.C.: Council on Foundations, 1985, pp. 3–4, 10.

Joseph, J. A. "Trusteeship in Transition: Challenges to Governance." *Foundation News*, Jan.-Feb. 1986a, pp. 53, 54.

Joseph, J. A. "The Other Side of Professionalism." *Foundation News*, May-June 1986b, p. 51.

Joseph, J. A. "Reaffirming Our Public Accountability." *Foundation News*, July-Aug. 1992, p. 44.

Kanfer, S. "The State of the Language, 1977." *Time*, Jan. 2, 1978, p. 36.

Kanfer, S. "80s Babble: Untidy Treasure." *Time*, Jan. 28, 1980, p. 90.

Karl, B. D. "The Moral Basis of Capitalist Philanthropy." In Independent Sector (ed.), *Working Papers for the Spring Research Forum: Philanthropy, Voluntary Action, and the Public Good.* Washington, D.C.: Independent Sector, 1986, p. 109.

Katz, M. *The Modern Foundation: Its Dual Character, Public and Private.* New York: Foundation Center, 1968, p. 10.

Kennedy, P. "An Interview with John May." *Foundation News*, Sept.-Oct. 1977, p. 44.

Keppel, F. P. *The Foundation: Its Place in American Life.* New York: Macmillan, 1930, pp. 56, 94, 97, 107.

Keppel, F. P. *Annual Report of the Carnegie Corporation.* New York: Carnegie Corporation, 1933, p. 12.

Keppel, F. P. *Annual Report of the Carnegie Corporation.* New York: Carnegie Corporation, 1939, p. 39.

Kiger, J. *Operating Principles of the Larger Foundations.* New York: Russell Sage Foundation, 1954, pp. 18, 49.

Kimball, L. F. "Patterns of Financial Support." In H. Sellin (ed.), *Proceedings of the New York University Fourth Biennial Conference on Charitable Foundations.* New York: Matthew Bender, 1959, p. 122.

Kimball, L. F. "Guidelines on Grantmaking." *Foundation News*, Mar.-Apr. 1974, pp. 43, 44.

Kirkman, L. "A Conversation with Sara Engelhardt." *Foundation News*, July-Aug. 1995, pp. 19–22.

Kitzi, J. "Easier Said Than Done." *Foundation News and Commentary*, Mar.-Apr. 1997, pp. 39–41.

Kohler, R. E. *Partners in Science: Foundations and Natural Scientists, 1900–1945.* Chicago: University of Chicago Press, 1991, p. 47.

Kostelanetz, R. "Foundations That Constantly Reject Worthy Projects Deserve to Be Sharply Criticized by the Public." *Chronicle of Philanthropy,* June 13, 1989.

Lacayo, R. "Heading for the Hills." *Time,* Mar. 26, 1990, p. 20.

Landau, R. "Do's and Don'ts for Development Officers." *Foundation News,* Nov.-Dec. 1975, p. 25.

Laski, H. J. *The Dangers of Obedience.* New York: Harper, 1930, p. 163.

Lefferts, R. *Getting a Grant.* Englewood Cliffs, N.J.: Prentice-Hall, 1978, p. 6.

Lefferts, R. *Getting a Grant in the 1980s.* Englewood Cliffs, N.J.: Prentice-Hall, 1982, p. 7.

Lefferts, R. *Getting a Grant in the 1990s: How to Write Successful Grant Proposals.* New York: Prentice-Hall, 1990, pp. 26, 69.

Lenkowsky, L. "Does Philanthropy Need a New Gospel of Wealth or Should It Heed the Old One More Faithfully?" *The Chronicle of Philanthropy,* Dec. 12, 1989, p. 36.

Leonard, J. "Grants for Growth." *Foundation News,* May-June 1989a, pp. 38–42.

Leonard, J. "Best Supporting Role." *Foundation News,* Sept.-Oct. 1989b, pp. 42–43, 46.

Lester, R. M. "The Philanthropic Endowment in Modern Life." *South Atlantic Quarterly,* Jan. 1935, pp. 4, 7, 10, 13.

Lindeman, E. *Wealth and Culture: A Study of One Hundred Foundations and Community Trusts and Their Operations During the Decade 1921–1930.* New York: Harcourt, Brace, 1936, pp. 5–6, 25, 59.

Lindeman, E. C. *Wealth and Culture: A Study of One Hundred Foundations and Community Trusts and Their Operations During the Decade 1921–1930.* New Brunswick, N.J.: Transaction Books, 1988, pp. viii, 12.

Louis, M. R. "Organizations as Culture-Bearing Milieux." In J. M. Shafritz and J. S. Ott (eds.), *Classics of Organizational Theory.* Belmont, Calif.: Wadsworth, 1992.

Macdonald, D. *The Ford Foundation: The Men and the Millions.* New York: Reynal, 1956, pp. 5, 110, 119, 148, 159, 170–171.

Magat, R. "Decisions! Decisions!" *Foundation News,* Mar.-Apr. 1983a, p. 24.

Magat, R. "Agreeing to Disagree." *Foundation News,* July-Aug. 1983b, p. 26.

Magat, R. "Out of the Shadows." *Foundation News,* July-Aug. 1984, pp. 25, 26, 29.

Magat, R. "Introduction." In R. Magat (ed.), *Philanthropic Giving: Studies in Varieties and Goals.* New York: Oxford University Press, 1989.

Magat, R. *Publishing About Philanthropy: Essays on Philanthropy.* Indianapolis: Indiana University Center on Philanthropy, 1990, pp. 1–4.

March, J. G., and H. A. Simon. "Administrative Decision Making." In L. E. Boone and D. D. Bowen (eds.), *The Great Writings in Management and Organizational Behavior.* New York: Random House, 1987, pp. 159–164.

Marquis, S. S. *Henry Ford: An Interpretation.* Boston: Little, Brown, 1923, pp. 70–71.

Marts, A. C. *The Generosity of Americans.* Englewood Cliffs, N.J.: Prentice-Hall, 1966.

Mathews, D. "The Civil Opportunities of Foundations." *Foundation News,* Mar.-Apr. 1991, pp. 30–33.

Mayer, R. A. "What Will a Foundation Look for When You Submit a Grant Proposal?" *Foundation Center Information Quarterly,* Oct. 1972, pp. 1, 3, 4.

McGuire, B. E. "Plain English: The Language of Foundations." In J. D. Ross (ed.), *New Directions for Institutional Advancement: Understanding and Increasing Foundation Support.* San Francisco: Jossey-Bass, 1981.

McMillen, L. "Questions on Influence of 'Left' and 'Right' Come Up in Debate on Political Character of Philanthropy." *Chronicle of Higher Education,* Sept. 30, 1987, pp. A27–A28.

McMillen, L. "Pew Trusts Conclude Sweeping Reorganization of Grant-Making Programs and Leadership." *Chronicle of Higher Education,* May 2, 1990a, p. A27.

McMillen, L. "Several Big Foundations Revise Their Grant Making to Focus on Elementary and Secondary Education." *Chronicle of Higher Education,* Dec. 19, 1990b, pp. A23–A24.

Menninger, R. *Foundation Work May Be Hazardous to Your Health.* New York: Council on Foundations, 1981, pp. 5–6, 7.

Mercer, J. "Private Giving to Colleges Increased 11.8% in 1996, Reaching $14.2 Billion." *Chronicle of Higher Education,* May 30, 1997, p. A41.

Millar, B. "Business Booms at the Foundation Center." *Chronicle of Philanthropy,* Feb. 25, 1992, pp. 20–24.

Miller, J. I. "Time to Listen." *Foundation News,* May-June 1984, p. 19.

Montague, W. "A Conservative Study Center Stirs Heated Controversy by Attacking Corporate Grant Makers' 'Liberal Bias.'" *Chronicle of Philanthropy,* May 15, 1990, pp. 1, 12–13.

Moore, J. "Group of Progressive Funds." *Chronicle of Philanthropy,* Oct. 30, 1990, p. 9.

Moore, R. Letter to the Author. July 28, 1995.

Morgan, G. *Imagination: The Art of Creative Management.* Newbury Park, California: Sage, 1993.

Morrow, L. "The Hazards of Homemade Vows." *Time,* June 27, 1983, p. 78.

Murrah, J. "Foundation's Firm Hand from the Very Beginning." *Foundation News,* Sept.-Oct. 1990, p. 64.

Nason, J. *Trustees and the Future of Foundations.* New York: Council on Foundations, 1977, pp. 91, 92.

Nason, J. W. *Foundation Trusteeship: Service in the Public Interest.* New York: Foundation Center, 1989, pp. 31, 35, 82–83, 108, 109.

National Committee for Responsive Philanthropy. "Serious Implications for Charities of FY 1996–2002 Budget Resolutions." *Responsive Philanthropy,* Spring 1995, p. 14.

Newman, E. *Strictly Speaking.* New York: Bobbs-Merrill, 1974.

Newman, E. *A Civil Tongue.* New York: Bobbs-Merrill, 1975a.

Newman, E. "Viable Solutions." *Esquire,* Dec. 1975b, p. 138.

Newman, E. "Language on the Skids." *Reader's Digest,* Nov. 1979, pp. 41, 42–43.

Nicklin, J. L. "Public Colleges Scoring Big in Private Fund Raising." *Chronicle of Higher Education,* Jan. 29, 1992, pp. A31–A32.

Nielsen, W. A. *The Big Foundations.* New York: Columbia University Press, 1972, pp. 305, 307.

Nielsen, W. A. *The Golden Donors.* New York: Dutton, 1985, pp. 29, 416, 431, 433–434.

Nielsen, W. A. "What Foundations Must Do to Tackle Society's Problems." *Chronicle of Philanthropy,* Feb. 11, 1992, pp. 33–35.

Nietzsche, F. *Thus Spoke Zarathustra.* (M. Cowan, trans.) Chicago: Regnery, 1957.

Odendahl, T. "Foundations and the Nonprofit Sector." In T. Odendahl (ed.), *America's Wealthy and the Future of Foundations.* New York: Foundation Center, 1987, p. 28.

Odendahl, T. *Charity Begins at Home: Generosity and Self-Interest Among the Philanthropic Elite.* New York: Basic Books, 1990, p. 241.

Odendahl, T., and E. Boris. "The Grantmaking Process." *Foundation News,* Sept.-Oct. 1983, pp. 21, 23, 31.

Odendahl, T., E. Boris, and A. K. Daniels. *Working in Foundations: Career Patterns of Women and Men.* New York: Foundation Center, 1985.

O'Neill, M. *The Third America: The Emergence of the Nonprofit Sector in the United States.* San Francisco: Jossey-Bass, 1989, pp. 6, 151–152.

O'Neill, M. "The Grant-Making Process Would Be Improved if Foundations Were Reviewed by Outsiders." *Chronicle of Philanthropy,* Feb. 20, 1990, p. 28.

Ostrander, S. A. "Diversity and Democracy in Philanthropic Organizations: The Case of Haymarket People's Fund." In D. R. Young and Associates (eds.), *Governing, Leading, and Managing Nonprofit Organizations.* San Francisco: Jossey-Bass, 1993, p. 196.

Ostrander, S. A. "Charitable Foundations, Social Movements, and Social Justice Funding." In John H. Stanfield II (ed.), *The Non-Profit Sector and Social Justice.* Indianapolis: Indiana University Press, 1994, p. 7.

Ostrander, S. A., and P. G. Schervish. "Giving and Getting: Philanthropy as a Social Relation." In J. Van Til and Associates (eds.), *Critical Issues in American Philanthropy: Strengthening Theory and Practice.* San Francisco: Jossey-Bass, 1990, pp. 67–75, 93.

Ostrower, F. *Why the Wealthy Give: The Culture of Elite Philanthropy.* Princeton, N.J.: Princeton University Press, 1995.

Pantin, G. "To Be Truly Effective, We Must Show Respect for the People We Help." *Chronicle of Philanthropy,* Feb. 6, 1990, p. 29.

Patman, W. 1969. *Report of the Subcommittee on Foundations.* Senate Finance Committee. Washington, D.C.: Government Printing Office.

Pattillo, M. M. "Address to the American College Public Relations Association." Paper presented at American College Public Relations Association, at New York. November 2 and 3, 1962.

Pattillo, M. M. "Preparing the Foundation Proposal." In F. E. Andrews (ed.), *Foundations: Twenty Viewpoints.* New York: Russell Sage Foundation, 1965.

Payton, R. "Major Challenges to Philanthropy." Washington, D.C.: Independent Sector, Aug. 1984, pp. 52–53.

Payton, R. "Philanthropy as Moral Discourse." In L. Berlowitz and Associates (eds.), *America in Theory: Theory in America.* New York: Oxford University Press, 1989, p. 189.

Payton, R. L. *Philanthropy: Voluntary Action for the Public Good.* New York: Macmillan, 1988, p. 123.

Peabody Education Fund. *Proceedings of the Trustees of the Peabody Education Fund from Their Original Organization on the 8th of February, 1867.* Boston: John Wilson and Son, 1875.

Penfield, W. *The Difficult Art of Giving: The Epic of Alan Gregg.* Boston: Little, Brown, 1967, pp. 143, 390–391, 393.

Perry, S. "Getting a Foundation Grant Takes More than a Good Idea, Program Officers Say." *Chronicle of Higher Education,* Oct. 20, 1982, pp. 25, 26.

Phillips, E. H. *Fund Raising Techniques and Case Histories.* London: Business Books, 1969.

Pifer, A. "Foundations at the Service of the Public." In A. Pifer (ed.), *Philanthropy in an Age of Transition.* New York: Foundation Center, 1984a, p. 33.

Pifer, A. "Twenty Years in Retrospect: A Personal View." In A. Pifer (ed.), *Philanthropy in an Age of Transition.* New York: Foundation Center, 1984b, pp. 99, 100.

Pifer, A. "Foundations and Public Policy Formation." In A. Pifer (ed.), *Philanthropy in an Age of Transition.* New York: Foundation Center, 1984c, pp. 106, 107–108, 111, 115.

Pifer, A. *Speaking Out: Reflections on Thirty Years of Foundation Work.* Washington, D.C.: Council on Foundations, 1984d, pp. 9–10, 13, 14–15, 18, 19–20, 25, 28–29, 37–38.

Powell, W. W. *Getting into Print: The Decision-Making Process in Scholarly Publishing.* Chicago: University of Chicago Press, 1985.

Prince, R. A., and K. M. File. *The Seven Faces of Philanthropy.* San Francisco: Jossey-Bass, 1994, pp. 45–46, 49.

Pritchett, H. S. "A Science of Giving." *Carnegie Corporation Annual Report.* New York: Carnegie Corporation, 1922.

Pritchett, H. S. "The Use and Abuse of Endowments." *Atlantic Monthly,* Oct. 1929, p. 517.

Quay, J. K. "Experiences in Approaching Foundations." Paper presented at the Conference on Wills, Annuities, and Special Gifts at New York, 1952, p. 85.

Reeves, T. C. *Foundations Under Fire.* Ithaca, N.Y.: Cornell University Press, 1970, pp. vii, 10, 16.

Regelbrugge, L. "Access Is Not Inherently Restricted." *Foundation News,* July-Aug. 1995, p. 16.

Renz, L. (ed.). *The Foundation Directory.* New York: Foundation Center, 1985, p. v.

Renz, L., S. Lawrence, and R. R. Treiber. *Foundation Giving.* New York: Foundation Center, 1995, pp. 2, 72–73, 74, 77, 93–94, 103–104.

Rich, W. S. "Memorandum to Members of the National Council on Community Foundations." Washington, D.C.: National Council on Community Foundations, 1962, pp. 3–4.

Richman, S. "Update on Annual Reports: Coming Out of the Stone Age." *Foundation News,* Nov.-Dec. 1975, p. 47.

Ridings, D. S. "Looking Upstream." *Foundation News and Commentary,* May-June 1997, p. 16, 18.

Robinson, A. "Brevity, Clarity, Honesty." *Foundation News and Commentary,* May-June 1996, pp. 38–39.

Rockefeller, D. "Foundation Fireside: Dusting the Mantel or Stirring the Ashes?" *Foundation News,* Mar.-Apr. 1973, pp. 24, 25.

Rockefeller Foundation. *Annual Report: 1913–14.* New York: Rockefeller Foundation, 1914.

Rockefeller, J. D. *Random Reminiscences of Men and Events.* New York: Doubleday, Doran, 1933.

Rockefeller, J. D. "The Difficult Art of Giving." In B. O'Connell (ed.), *America's Voluntary Spirit: A Book of Readings.* New York: Foundation Center, 1983.

Rockefeller III, J. D. "Self-Renewal for Foundations." *Foundation News,* Nov.-Dec. 1971, p. 237.

Roelofs, J. "Foundations and the Supreme Court." *Telos,* Winter 1984–1985, p. 75.

Rosenman, M. "Non-Profit Leaders Must Publicly Condemn Corruption in Philanthropy and Society." *Chronicle of Philanthropy,* Apr. 3, 1990, p. 28.

Rosenwald, J. "The Burden of Wealth." *Saturday Evening Post,* Jan. 5, 1929, pp. 12–13, 136, 138.

Rudy, W. H. *The Foundations: Their Use and Abuse.* Washington, DC: Public Affairs Press, 1970.

Rusk, D. *The Role of the Foundation in American Life.* Claremont, Calif.: Claremont University College, 1961.

Russell, J. M. *Giving and Taking: Across the Foundation Desk.* New York: Columbia University Press, 1977, pp. 36, 38, 69–70.

Russell Sage Foundation. "Confidential Bulletin." New York, 1907.

Safire, W. *On Language.* New York: Avon, 1981.

Safire, W. "On Language." *New York Times Magazine,* Apr. 17, 1983, p. 14.

Safire, W. "Dam That Tinker." *New York Times Magazine,* Jan. 10, 1988, p. 12.

San Francisco Art Institute. Ad for dean. *Chronicle of Higher Education,* Aug. 4, 1982, p. 43.

Sawyer, J. "In Making Grants It's Usually Better to Be Approximately Right Than Precisely Wrong." *Chronicle of Philanthropy,* Apr. 4, 1989, p. 36.

Schon, D. A. *The Reflective Practitioner: How Professionals Think in Action.* New York: Basic Books, 1983.

Simon, H. A. *The New Science of Management Decision.* New York: Harper, 1960, pp. 5–6.

Simon, J. "Foundations and Public Controversy: An Affirmative View." In F. Heimann (ed.), *The Future of Foundations.* Englewood Cliffs, N.J.: Prentice-Hall, 1973, pp. 59, 60–61, 80, 83.

Southern Education Foundation. "Letter of Gift of John F. Slater." *Biennial Report for 1950–51 and 1951–52.* Southern Education Foundation, 1952.

Sports Illustrated. "They Said It." Dec. 8, 1986, p. 18.

Stamp, T. "Searching for Excellence." *Foundation News,* July-Aug. 1987, p. 39.

Stehle, V. "Federal Cuts 'Terrifying' for Charities." *Chronicle of Philanthropy,* June 29, 1995a, p. 25.

Stehle, V. "Honored for Doing What Others Won't." *Chronicle of Philanthropy,* July 13, 1995b, p. 9.

Stephens, W. W. *The Life and Writings of Turgot.* New York: London, Longmans, Green, 1895, p. 220.

Sykes, C. J. *Profscam: Professors and the Demise of Higher Education.* New York: St. Martin's Press, 1988.

Taylor, E. K. *Public Accountability of Foundations and Charitable Trusts.* New York: Russell Sage Foundation, 1953, pp. 6, 115, 118.

Teltsch, K. "Foundations Criticized on Hispanic Aid." *New York Times,* May 11, 1981, p. 39.

Thoreau, H. D. "Philanthropy." In B. O'Connell (ed.), *America's Voluntary Spirit: A Book of Readings.* New York: Foundation Center, 1983.

Time. "Killing Laughter." Aug. 2, 1976, p. 58.

Time. "Negotiating a Build-Down." Oct. 17, 1983, p. 16.

Time. "Now . . . Words from a Sponsor." Mar. 15, 1983, p. 92.

Tirman, J. "U.S. Grant Makers Are Missing Opportunities to Promote Democracy in Eastern Europe." *Chronicle of Philanthropy,* July 10, 1990, p. 34.

Todd, A. J. "Mainsprings of Philanthropy." In E. Faris (ed.), *Intelligent Philanthropy.* Chicago: University of Chicago Press, 1930, p. 1.

Townsend, T. H. "Criteria Grantors Use in Assessing Proposals." *Foundation News,* Mar.-Apr. 1974, pp. 1, 31, 33–36.

United States Treasury Department. *Treasury Department Report on Private Foundations.* Washington, D.C.: U.S. Treasury Department, 1965, p. 5.

Viscusi, M. "Annual Reports: Making a Good Idea Better." *Foundation News,* Jan.-Feb. 1985, pp. 30, 32.

Wall, J. F. *Andrew Carnegie.* New York: Oxford University Press, 1970.

Weaver, W. *U.S. Philanthropic Foundations.* New York: Harper and Row, 1967.

Weick, K. E. "Educational Organizations as Loosely-Coupled Systems." In R. Birnbaum (ed.), *ASHE Reader in Organization and Governance in Higher Education.* Lexington, Mass.: Ginn, 1984, pp. 68–69.

Whitaker, B. *The Foundations.* Birkenhead, England: Eyre Methuen, 1974, pp. 26, 62, 81, 132, 133, 191, 197, 200, 263.

White, J. E. "The Limits of Black Power." *Time,* May 11, 1992, pp. 38–39.

Whyte, W. H. *The Organization Man.* New York: Simon and Shuster, 1956.

Wilbur, C. S. "Sacred Cows II." *Foundation News,* Sept.-Oct. 1993, pp. 26–30.

Williams, G. "Charities Must Prepare to Confront Greater Scrutiny of Their Affairs, Leaders Say." *Chronicle of Philanthropy,* Nov. 3, 1992, p. 8.

Williams, R. M. "An Interview with William E. Simon." *Foundation News,* Sept.-Oct. 1983, p. 21.

Williams, R. M. "The Readiest Reference." *Foundation News,* Nov.-Dec. 1984, p. 31.

Williams, R. M. "To Each His Own." *Foundation News,* May-June 1989, pp. 27–28.

Winkler, M., and D. E. Mason. "Letter to Members of the Association for Research on Nonprofit Organizations and Voluntary Action." Washington, D.C.: Association for Research on Nonprofit Organizations and Voluntary Action, 1996, p. 1.

Ylvisaker, P. "Foundations and Nonprofit Organizations." In W. W. Powell (ed.), *The Nonprofit Sector: A Research Handbook.* New Haven, Conn.: Yale University Press, 1987a, pp. 63, 363–364.

Ylvisaker, P. "Foundations and Faith Keeping." *Foundation News and Commentary,* Jan.-Feb. 1996, pp. 22–24.

Ylvisaker, P. "Is Philanthropy Losing Its Soul." *Foundation News,* May-June 1987b, p. 63.

Young, D., and W. Moore. *Trusteeship and the Management of Foundations.* New York: Russell Sage Foundation, 1969, pp. 67, 147.

Zurcher, A. J. *The Management of American Foundations: Administration, Policies, and Social Role.* New York: New York University Press, 1972, pp. 53, 67–68, 150.

Name Index

Subject Index

Credits